Questions About Language

Questions About Language sets out to answer, in a readable yet insightful format, a series of vital questions about language, some of which language specialists are regularly asked, and some of which are so surprising that only the specialists think about them.

In this handy guide, sixteen language experts answer challenging questions about language, from *What makes a language a language?* to *Do people swear because they don't know enough words?* Illustrating the complexity of human language, and the way in which we use it, the twelve chapters each end with a section on further reading for anyone interested in following up on the topic.

Covering core questions about language, this is essential reading for both students new to language and linguistics and the interested general reader.

Laurie Bauer FRSNZ is Emeritus Professor of Linguistics at Victoria University of Wellington, New Zealand. He is the author of over twenty books including *The Oxford Reference Guide to English Morphology* (2013), which won the LSA's Leonard Bloomfield Prize. In 2017 he was awarded the Royal Society of New Zealand's Humanities Medal.

Andreea S. Calude is a Senior Lecturer in Linguistics at the University of Waikato, New Zealand. She has a background in mathematics and linguistics and researches (spoken) grammar, language evolution, loanwords and just about any quantitative language-related question she can get data on. She has authored the TED ED Lesson "Does Grammar Matter?".

Questions About Language
What Everyone Should Know About
Language in the 21st Century

**Edited by Laurie Bauer and
Andreea S. Calude**

LONDON AND NEW YORK

First published 2020
by Routledge
2 Park Square, Milton Park, Abingdon, Oxon OX14 4RN

and by Routledge
52 Vanderbilt Avenue, New York, NY 10017

Routledge is an imprint of the Taylor & Francis Group, an informa business

© 2020 selection and editorial matter, Laurie Bauer and Andreea S. Calude; individual chapters, the contributors

The right of Laurie Bauer and Andreea S. Calude to be identified as the authors of the editorial material, and of the authors for their individual chapters, has been asserted in accordance with sections 77 and 78 of the Copyright, Designs and Patents Act 1988.

All rights reserved. No part of this book may be reprinted or reproduced or utilised in any form or by any electronic, mechanical, or other means, now known or hereafter invented, including photocopying and recording, or in any information storage or retrieval system, without permission in writing from the publishers.

Trademark notice: Product or corporate names may be trademarks or registered trademarks, and are used only for identification and explanation without intent to infringe.

British Library Cataloguing-in-Publication Data
A catalogue record for this book is available from the British Library

Library of Congress Cataloging-in-Publication Data
Names: Bauer, Laurie, 1949- editor. | Calude, Andreea S., editor.
Title: Questions about language: what everyone should know about language in the 21st century / edited by Laurie Bauer and Andreea S. Calude.
Description: 1. | New York: Taylor and Francis, 2020. |
Includes bibliographical references and index.
Identifiers: LCCN 2019052684 | ISBN 9780367175009 (hardcover) | ISBN 9780367175016 (paperback) | ISBN 9780367175023 (ebook)
Subjects: LCSH: Language and languages. | Language and languages–Miscellanea.
Classification: LCC P112 .Q84 2020 | DDC 415–dc23
LC record available at https://lccn.loc.gov/2019052684

ISBN: 978-0-367-17500-9 (hbk)
ISBN: 978-0-367-17501-6 (pbk)
ISBN: 978-0-367-17502-3 (ebk)

Typeset in Times New Roman
by Deanta Global Publishing Services, Chennai, India

In memory of James E. (Jim) Miller (1942–2019)
Mentor extraordinaire
From the first and the last of his supervisees

Contents

List of illustrations ix
About the contributors x

Introduction 1
LAURIE BAUER AND ANDREEA S. CALUDE

1 Do animals communicate using a language? 4
STEPHEN R. ANDERSON

2 Is talking work doing work? 18
JO ANGOURI AND IFIGENEIA MACHILI

3 What makes a language a language? 36
LAURIE BAUER

4 Do people swear because they don't know enough words? 47
KATE BURRIDGE

5 Is written grammar better than spoken grammar? 65
ANDREEA S. CALUDE

6 Is language change good or bad? 80
LYLE CAMPBELL AND RUSSELL BARLOW

7 Are the sounds of languages influenced by climate, environment and biology? 91
DAN DEDIU AND SCOTT R. MOISIK

8	Can you tell someone's sexuality from the way they speak? EVAN HAZENBERG	108
9	Is learning a signed language easier than learning a spoken language? SARA PIVAC ALEXANDER AND GEORGE MAJOR	123
10	Can you forget your native language? MONIKA S. SCHMID	137
11	Can people really disguise themselves when writing or speaking? CORINNE A. SEALS AND NATALIE SCHILLING	151
12	What is universal about intonation? PAUL WARREN	167
	Index	183

Illustrations

Figures

2.1	Example of an email chain	23
9.1	TABLE in many sign languages. All images are from the NZSL Online Dictionary (https://nzsl.nz) by Deaf Studies Research Unit, Victoria University of Wellington, and are licensed under Creative Commons BY-NC-SA 3.0	126
9.2	SISTER in NZSL	127
9.3	UNUSUAL in NZSL	129

Table

11.1	A sample Q-Doc, K-Doc analysis	159

About the contributors

Stephen R. Anderson is the Dorothy R. Diebold Professor of Linguistics, Emeritus, at Yale University, Connecticut. His work includes phonetics, phonology, morphology, syntax, semantics, historical linguistics and the history of the field, as well as the descriptive study of languages in several families. He has focused on morphological theory and the cognitive science of language, especially the relation between human language and animal communication.

Jo Angouri is Professor and Director of Undergraduate Studies at the University of Warwick, UK and a Visiting Distinguished Professor at Aalto University, Business School. Her research is in sociolinguistics, pragmatics and discourse analysis. Angouri has published extensively on language and identity and teamwork and leadership in medical settings.

Russell Barlow is a researcher at the Max Planck Institute for the Science of Human History, Jena, Germany. His research includes documenting endangered languages in Papua New Guinea and Indonesia. Among other interests, he studies the syntax and morphology of languages of the Pacific, as well as how languages change over time.

Laurie Bauer FRSNZ is Emeritus Professor of Linguistics at Victoria University of Wellington, New Zealand. He is the author of over twenty books including *The Oxford reference guide to English morphology* (2013), which won the LSA's Leonard Bloomfield Prize. In 2017 he was awarded the Royal Society of New Zealand's Humanities Medal.

Kate Burridge is Professor of Linguistics at Monash University, Melbourne, Australia and a fellow of the Australian Academy of the Humanities. She has authored/edited more than 20 books on different aspects of language, is a regular presenter of language segments on radio and has given a TED Talk on euphemism and taboo.

Andreea S. Calude is a Senior Lecturer in Linguistics at the University of Waikato, New Zealand. She has a background in mathematics and linguistics and researches (spoken) grammar, language evolution, loanwords and just about any quantitative language-related question she can get data on. She has authored the TED ED lesson "Does Grammar Matter?".

Lyle Campbell is Professor (Emeritus) at University of Hawai'i Mānoa. His specializations are: historical linguistics, American Indian languages, language documentation and typology. He has published 23 books and c. 200 articles, held appointments in Linguistics, Anthropology and Spanish, and taught in nine different countries. He won LSA's Leonard Bloomfield Book Award twice.

Dan Dediu is a computer scientist turned linguist, particularly interested in human evolution, genetics and the origins, evolution and diversity of language. He applies statistics/data science and computer modelling to almost anything he can get his hands on.

Evan Hazenberg is a Lecturer in World Englishes at the University of Sussex, Brighton, UK. He works on language variation and sociophonetics, with a particular interest in gender, sexuality and identity. He has worked with English spoken in Canada, New Zealand and the United Kingdom.

Ifigeneia Machili is an EAP instructor in the Department of Economics at the University of Macedonia, Greece. Her research interests lie in workplace discourse, identity construction and qualitative methodologies in discourse analysis. She has published work on multilingualism at work, business emails and formality in the corporate setting.

George Major is a Senior Lecturer at Auckland University of Technology, New Zealand. She is a non-native signer who once enrolled in a university paper to learn sign language, and later went on to become an interpreter. She now teaches NZSL interpreting and does sociolinguistics research.

Scott R. Moisik is an articulatory phonetician with a passion for the "meat" of speech: he is interested in the anatomy and physiology of speech and is fascinated by how sometimes seemingly insignificant physical details of the vocal tract can have profound effects on speech sound systems. He is an Assistant Professor at Nanyang Technological University, Singapore.

xii *About the contributors*

Sara Pivac Alexander is a Deaf linguist and New Zealand Sign Language (NZSL) lecturer. She also trains Deaf people to teach NZSL to second language learners. Alexander is a native signer from a Deaf family.

Natalie Schilling is a Professor of Linguistics at Georgetown University in Washington, DC. She has served as an expert forensic linguist in cases involving authorship attribution and speaker profiling, and frequently presents training sessions to law enforcement professionals. Her publications include books and articles on language variation and American English.

Corinne A. Seals is a Senior Lecturer of Applied Linguistics at Victoria University of Wellington and a practising forensic linguist in New Zealand. She is particularly interested in authorship attribution and the reliability of earwitness testimony. She has also published extensively in the areas of heritage language education, translanguaging and linguistic landscapes.

Monika S. Schmid received her PhD from the University of Düsseldorf, Germany in 2000 and has since held positions at the Vrije Universiteit Amsterdam, the Rijksuniversiteit Groningen and currently at the University of Essex, UK. She has worked and published widely on the topic of first language attrition and is considered an international leading expert in this field.

Paul Warren is Professor of Linguistics in the School of Linguistics and Applied Language Studies at Victoria University of Wellington, New Zealand. He is the author of *Introducing psycholinguistics* (2012) and *Uptalk: the phenomenon of rising intonation* (2016), both published by Cambridge University Press.

Introduction

Laurie Bauer and Andreea S. Calude

In this book, internationally recognized language professionals respond to questions that they have considered in their professional capacity. As the chapter titles indicate (e.g. *Can you tell someone's sexuality by the way they speak? What makes a language a language?*), each chapter is phrased as a question and its content as an answer.

Being language professionals, we know that people of all kinds are interested in the phenomenon of language. It is not really surprising. Language is a powerful tool that helps us think and make sense of the world, that we use to transmit our cultural histories, that we use to entertain, convince, seduce, inform and mislead. Except in pathological cases, we start using language before the time of which we have reliable memories, and we cannot imagine not being able to use our language (see the chapter by Schmid).

But even if we know how to use language for many purposes, in general terms we know little about the language system per se or the details of the ways in which it is used. We can use language but we don't understand its inner workings. Our educational system spends a lot of time teaching us to read and to write, yet remarkably little time teaching us how to use language to convince and explain, and, these days, extremely little time teaching us about language. Often, we know so little that we cannot even ask the questions that we would like to have answered, because we cannot formulate those questions. We don't know what it is we want to know. In setting up the chapters of this book we have attempted to provide challenging, interesting and relevant questions, based on the assumption that language is part of our lives and that what language professionals are concerned with is of relevance to the wider public. Put simply, language is everyone's business.

Access to knowledge of the appropriate kind is often restricted because people who investigate language most closely (called "linguists", though the term is unfortunately ambiguous) are trained to write for other linguists and not for the curious and dissatisfied. Part of the result is that the questions non-linguists tend to ask (and there are far more of them than there are linguists), are questions which linguists find trivial or irrelevant, or tend to be phrased in ways which linguists do not find answerable. For example, linguists find questions such as "Does text language ruin English spelling?" trivial because spelling is always changing anyway, yet the question "Is – and if so, in what ways – text language affecting the kinds of language we produce?" is so deep that, in the present state of our knowledge, we are only beginning to develop ways to answer it. This book addresses the gap by bringing in experts working in various areas of language analysis to write for a wide audience on topics which they find exciting and challenging, but which are also relevant for our everyday experience as language users.

So in this book, we provide answers to a series of questions about language that illustrate just how much language influences all sorts of aspects of everyday life, and just how difficult it is to pin down the nature of language and the way we exploit it (see for example the chapters by Angouri and Machili, by Burridge and by Hazenberg).

One of the themes that emerges from the chapters in this book is how much the study of language involves the study of other areas of knowledge as well; and the influence goes in both directions. In these pages, you will find references not only to the work of psychologists (which might not seem particularly surprising), but also to the work of anthropologists, biologists, ecologists, educationalists, geneticists, literary scholars, lawyers, palaeontologists and philosophers. This is really another reminder of the centrality of language to human behaviour.

Some of the ideas presented here are right at the cutting edge of what linguists are concerned with at the beginning of the 21st century. Some of the other questions included here address issues that linguists may have been asking for centuries but where modern research has led to a better appreciation of the multiple factors involved, and often has led to more subtle answers (see Anderson, Dediu and Moisik, Warren and others in this volume).

Just over 20 years ago, *Language myths* (Bauer and Trudgill 1998) brought together a set of societal beliefs about language that were, if not clearly wrong, then at least not straightforwardly true. The authors in that book were asked to explain why something that many people thought was a fact was more fiction than fact. This volume has some of the same aims as the *Language myths* book: it aims to inform a wide range of people about a number of issues concerned with language; it aims to have experts in the field address questions about language that we are aware non-experts want to know about; and more generally, it aims to shine a little light onto the way language works and is used by humans. This volume is different from its predecessor in that the questions dealt with here are not necessarily ones about which non-linguists have strong views for us to engage with. In many cases, perhaps most, readers may not have considered the questions that are raised in this book at all. But we hope you will agree that they are all interesting questions that make you think about the complexities of human language in new ways.

Communication is very complex, whether we are dealing with the way in which traffic lights communicate their "meaning" to control vehicular traffic or something far more nuanced. Human language is probably the most complex of all methods of communication, and we see in many of the chapters just how complex human language is. Whether we consider the way in which human language differs from the communication system of songbirds and chimpanzees (Anderson), the way in which language functions differently when we speak it or when we write it (Calude), the ways in which we manage to forget our language (Schmid), and how difficult it is to copy someone else's language use (Seals and Schilling), we are reminded of how much we achieve every time we speak, and just how much five-year olds have attained in so few years, while they have also been learning to walk, run, jump, perceive depth of vision and the hundreds of other things that take up their waking hours. When we think about the ways in which language can vary – from user to user, within the speech of the same user, in one language over time or from one language to another (chapters by Bauer, Campbell and Barlow, Dediu and Moisik, Hazenberg, Pivac Alexander and Major) – and how some of that variation is available for us to exploit for social purposes, we glimpse a different view of the complexities that lie behind one of our greatest intellectual achievements.

We hope that readers will be as fascinated by the answers to these questions as we have been and come away with a new appreciation of the intricacies of language.

Reference

Bauer, Laurie and Peter Trudgill (eds.). (1998). *Language myths*. London: Penguin.

1 Do animals communicate using a language?

Stephen R. Anderson

Introduction

How we take this question clearly depends on how we define its terms. If communication is a matter of one organism emitting some indicator (behavioural or otherwise) from which another organism derives information, then it is evident that animals do this, even bacteria, some of which are sensitive to chemical signals produced by others, and whose activity is regulated in part by this (Miller and Bassler 2001). Everything from there on up "communicates" in this general sense.

Indeed, genes themselves communicate with one another: the inappropriately described "Language gene" *FOXP2* codes for a protein that does not build structure but is rather a transcription factor that regulates the expression of a variety of other genes (Fisher and Vernes 2015). Everything turns on what we want to think of as a "language".

The word is sometimes used in a way that includes essentially any collection of indicators with reasonably consistent interpretations in some context: thus, one finds mention of the "language" of traffic lights, the "language of the cinema", etc. If that is what we mean by a language, there is no question that animals of all sorts do indeed "communicate using a language", and the question becomes essentially trivial. If, on the other hand, we mean by language "the method of human communication, either spoken or written, consisting of the use of words in a structured and conventional way", as my online dictionary (https://lexico.com/en/definition/language) puts it, the question becomes an interesting one: do the communication systems of animals have the essential properties of human language or not?

Hugh Lofting's Doctor Dolittle (Lofting 1920 *et seq.*) certainly believed animal communication systems have the same character and expressive capacity as human languages, though perhaps sometimes conveyed in different modalities. That made for a series of good stories, but the scientific issue of the relation between animal and human "languages" remains (see

Anderson [2004] for discussion). The current chapter, then, approaches the matter by attempting to outline the central properties of specifically human language, asking how known animal communication systems line up in this regard.

Some essential properties of human language

Over the years, numerous efforts have been made to characterize human language in its relation to the communication systems of other organisms, and to identify important differences. Undoubtedly, the best known in this regard is the effort of Charles Hockett to identify the "Design Features" of human language, a framework that evolved somewhat over time and whose last formulation is in Hockett (1960). This effort, however, like many that preceded it, suffers somewhat from its purely external and descriptive nature: that is, Hockett tries to identify the character of communicative systems (including language) in terms of their communicative function. In contrast, the focus of the present chapter is on the cognitive capacities that underlie the possibilities of communication, a perspective that provides a somewhat more categorical delineation of human language as opposed to other systems, while also drawing out some previously under-emphasized parallels.

We can take as a starting point a widely noted feature of human language that seems to provide a unique strength, its richness and flexibility of expression: the essentially unbounded range of things that sentences in a language can express, including the ability to refer to things and situations arbitrarily distant from the speech situation in time and space, to things and situations that may not or do not exist, to logical relations between states of affairs as well as to those states themselves, etc. Descriptively, this aspect of human languages is inescapable, but we must ask what sort of capacity supports it, and how this capacity is grounded in the nature of our species. We approach this in terms of the organization of linguistic knowledge as this is characterized in modern theories of language.

Syntax and semantics

Glossing over a great many matters of detail, it is fair to say that students of language agree that our knowledge of a language includes several distinguishable components. Among these, obviously, is our knowledge of a range of lexical items, the words of the language. Each of these is a direct association between an externalizable expression and the meaning of that expression.

While some of these meanings are tied to a specific situation – pronouns, such as *I, we, you, they* and demonstratives such as *this, that, there, then* – most are independent of a particular context. The word *cat* designates a particular kind of animal, regardless of whether we are talking about the one on the mat, one that we used to have or might plan to look for at the animal shelter, or the fact that some object looks like a small bear and not like a cat. The meanings of words include not only objects, actions and properties, but also relations (*on, around, if ... then*) and logical operators such as *not, all, any*. The properties of the lexical items of our language, the diversity and range of the meanings they can convey directly, obviously begins to account for the richness of human linguistic expression referred to above.

The notion of a *word* is a notoriously difficult one and may differ somewhat from one language to another. Some of the lexical elements of a language, in the sense of expressions that have a direct relation to meaning, may consist of more than one "word" in another sense: thus, when something does not *cut the mustard* we mean it does not meet our expectations, where no part of *cut the mustard* corresponds to some part of 'meet expectations', but rather the whole expression has this sense irreducibly. Idioms of this sort are part of our lexical knowledge along with simple words.

If you ask the proverbial person on the street what is involved in learning another language, the answer might often be the need to learn the words of that language, but obviously there is more involved than that. In particular, our knowledge of a language also includes knowledge of a system of syntax, principles by which the words of the language are combined with one another to form larger structural units: phrases, clauses, sentences. Languages differ from one another in the ways in which these units are constructed: in Turkish, the verb in a simple declarative sentence comes at the end, while in Irish it comes at the beginning and in English after the subject but before the object. The extent to which these apparent differences actually follow in some way from some more general principles is a matter of dispute among theories, but our point here is that there is always some system to syntactic combination. In no language are words simply strung together at random, although some languages allow considerable freedom of word order, in association with ways of marking individual words to allow their structural relations to be recovered.

By itself, the richness of lexical meaning does not adequately account for the fact that humans have an unbounded range of things that can be expressed in language. Syntactic combination expands the possibilities of lexical expression by means of what Steven Pinker (1994) has called a "discrete combinatorial system": new messages are formed as new combinations of members of a set of basic elements, rather than as novel signals or as modulations of intensity or some other continuous variable in an existing message. This system is based on recursive, hierarchical combination, where "recursion" refers to the fact that structural units can include other instances of the same sort as components. As a result, there is no limit to the number of different structures that can be accommodated by a small, fixed number of structural regularities.

Given the principles for constructing a few basic phrase types, these can be re-used to produce and understand an unbounded range of novel expressions. For instance, a sentence like (1) below is built up from a comparatively small vocabulary, together with a few principles governing the structure of prepositional phrases, noun phrases and verb phrases. Since a prepositional phrase, for example, can contain a noun phase as a constituent, and a noun phrase in its turn can contain a prepositional phrase, it is easy to see that this small set of structures can be used to construct novel messages of arbitrary length.

(1) [s [np [np The cat] [pp in [np [np the picture] [pp on [np my phone]]]]] [vp resembles [np the one [s that you [vp lost]]]]]
(In this representation, the subscripted labels identify the category of the phrase composed of the material enclosed in the corresponding brackets, where S = 'Sentence', NP = 'Noun Phrase', VP = 'Verb Phrase' and PP = 'Prepositional Phrase'.)

Our lexical knowledge, then, together with the principles of the syntax, underlies our knowledge of a potentially unlimited collection of distinct (and distinguishable) symbolic expressions. This knowledge, in turn, is completed by our knowledge of the ways in which these expressions have their meaning, as a function of the meanings of their parts and the manner of their combination. We know that (in informal if traditional terms) when the verb phrase *feed the cat* is formed from the verb *feed* and the noun phrase *the cat* (itself formed from the determiner *the* and the noun *cat*), *the cat* is to be interpreted as the direct object of *feed*. The resultant combined meaning can then be further combined with the meaning of another noun phrase, interpreted as its subject, to yield the overall interpretation of a sentence like *The cat-sitter will feed the cat* (incorporating also the future sense contributed by *will*). This kind of knowledge of the semantics of linguistic expressions is another component of our overall knowledge of our language.

Phonology and morphology

Discussion of the cognitive underpinnings of the rich expressivity of human language often stop at a discussion of words, their syntax and recursivity, but these are not the only structural dimensions that deserve discussion in this regard. One of Hockett's (1960) "design features" for language was what he called "duality of patterning". Languages are built on the basis of not just one combinatory system, the syntax, but also rely on another: phonology. The syntactic system combines meaningful words into larger meaningful units (phrases, clauses, etc.) while the phonological system combines individually meaningless elements (sounds, or in their linguistic function phonemes) into meaningful words. A relatively small number of sound units (44 in English, according to one widespread account, with a few more or less in any particular dialect) combine according to strict rules to form all of the thousands and thousands of words in the language.

It is tempting to see the presence of phonology as simply an ornament, an inessential elaboration of the way basic meaningful units are formed. This would be a mistake, however: it is phonology that makes it possible for speakers of a language to expand its vocabulary at will and without effective limit. If every new word had to be constructed in such a way as to make it holistically distinct from all others, our capacity to remember, deploy and recognize an inventory of such signs would be severely limited, probably to something like a few hundred. As it is, however, a new word is constructed simply as a new combination of the inventory of familiar basic sound types, built up according to the regularities of the language's phonology. This is what enables us to extend the language's lexicon freely as new concepts and conditions require.

It is necessary to note in this regard that speech is not the only possible medium for a human language. In particular, as research over the past half century or so has demonstrated, the visually transmitted signed languages that emerge and become current in communities with large numbers of deaf members develop all of the richness of expression and all of the basic structural characteristics of spoken languages, apart from modality (see Chapter 9 of the present volume for some discussion). And in that connection, it is important that the individual meaningful signs of such a language also have an internal organization based on the rule-governed combination of limited numbers of separately meaningless formative elements (handshape, location, movement, etc.). In signed as in spoken language, this combinatory system, quite separate from syntax, makes possible the arbitrary expansion of the language's lexicon to express many more ideas than if signs had to be separate but unanalysable wholes.

Knowledge of a language's phonology, then, is another aspect of a speaker's cognitive organization that allows for the communicative deployment of the language. In fact, there is arguably yet a third combinatory system, knowledge of which is essential to the functioning of language. This is morphology, the system by which meaningful indicators combine within a single lexical word. *Cat*, on the one hand, has no particular structure beyond the combination of the sounds [k], [æ] and [t], but *undescribable* is

Do animals communicate using a language?

a combination not only of sounds, but also of meaningful parts (*un-*, *-able* and *describe*, which may itself be seen as a combination of *de-* and a root *scribe*, according to yet another system of regularities).

Some linguists wish to see morphology as simply a special case of syntax, internal to whatever a given language may treat as its words, while others emphasize the ways in which the internal organization of words may be quite different from ways in which these are organized by the syntax. We can ignore this theoretical dispute here, however, and simply recognize that knowledge of the internal organization of words as well as that of larger structures constitutes a substantive part of what makes it possible for languages to be as expressive as they are. Indeed, in some languages the resources of word-internal organization may be much more important to this than is evident in the case of English. A well-known instance is provided by West Greenlandic "Eskimo", a language famous for much elaborate morphology and in which an example like (2) constitutes a single word, combinable with other words by the (distinct) principles of the syntax.

(2) tusaa -nngit -su   -usaar -tuaannar -sinnaa -nngi -vip -putit
    hear not   INTR-PART pretend all.the.time can   not really 2S.INDIC
    'You simply cannot pretend not to be hearing all the time'
    (Fortescue 1984: 315)

When we look at the richness of expression provided by human languages (and thus by our species' capacity for language), we see that there are a number of rather essential aspects of our cognitive organization that make this possible: in particular, knowledge of the particular sorts exemplified by the phonological, morphological, syntactic, lexical and semantic systems of natural languages. If we want to address the question of whether non-human animals make use (or indeed, are capable of making use) of a "language" in the human sense, we can do so by asking whether there is reason to attribute to them the cognitive capacities necessary to support such systems.

Characteristics of animal communication systems

For a great many animals, a major form of communication is through some form of visual display. This may range from the passively produced signals of the stickleback (Shettleworth 2009: 508), a classic model of communication in the literature of behavioural biology, to the elaborate strutting behaviour of the greater sage grouse (*Centrocercus urophasianus*) and the complex mating dance of the western grebe (*Aechmophorus occidentalis*). Importantly, most of these convey essentially the same rather simple message: advertising the availability of the individual for mating. This is of course by no means the only message an animal can communicate, but it is typical in its directness and its relation to the immediate context in which the signal is presented.

Apart from visual displays, there are a number of other channels through which animals inform one another. Chemicals including pheromones and other olfactory signals (in ants, bees, moths, mice, lemurs and many others), ultrasound (in bats, dolphins and the courtship songs of mice, among others), infrasound (in elephants) and the production and perception of characteristic electric fields (in certain fish) all provide efficient signalling channels under ecologically appropriate conditions.

Of course, many non-human species communicate in sound as humans do. This includes frogs, birds (who produce a variety of calls, in addition to the specialized class of vocalizations represented by true song in most of the nearly 4,000 species belonging to the order Passeriformes), as well as virtually all mammals to at least some extent. Birdsong is a particularly interesting and complex form of vocal signalling, of which more will be said below. However, despite a number of distinctive characteristics, the songs of birds are in the end no different in their essential character from other animal signals. The song is an assertion of the bird's possession of a territory, for the purpose of defending it against competitors and attracting potential mates. No matter how internally complex, that complexity is never linked to a more complex message.

Compared with the lexicon of a human language, the inventories of available signals in animal systems are several orders of magnitude smaller. Abstracting away from varying degrees of the intensity with which a communicative display is produced, the characteristic repertoire of any given species is quite limited. A sensitive observer will generally find a number of distinguishable signals, but that number is still typically quite limited: fewer than 40 in any species that has been seriously studied.

Each message in these systems is limited to the here and now, driven by the immediate circumstances of production. The messages typically reflect the immediate internal state of the organism, and their production is often triggered by measurable internal factors such as hormone levels. For example, in most temperate species of oscine birds (song birds), it is the male that defends territory, and thus only male birds sing. When injected with appropriate levels of testosterone, however, female birds of such species can be induced to sing as well, as do normal females in other species where they defend territories.

The interpretation of an animal's signal is dependent on the immediate spatial and temporal context in which it is produced, in contrast to the words of a human language that have meanings not bound to the immediate context. Thus, we can describe objects or events that are in the past or future, hypotheticals, negatives, and other concepts that are outside the immediate factual horizon. None of the ideas formulated in the sentences in (3) are expressible in any non-human communication system, however useful that might be in a particular situation.

(3) a Far away in the middle of that forest, there lives a dangerous leopard.
    b Last week there was a leopard around here, but it's gone now.
    c If I had seen a leopard, I would have climbed a tree.
    d Any bird that is not an eagle is not dangerous.

As described above, the expressive capacity of a human language rests largely on the existence of a system of hierarchical, recursive syntactic combination. No such system has ever been found in the communicative signals of any non-human species, and attempts to teach such systems to animals in the laboratory have been quite unsuccessful. A review of the relevant literature in support of this assertion would take us far beyond the scope of the present chapter; some discussion will be found in Anderson (2004). Of course, in the absence of generalized syntactic combination, there is no need (or evidence) for a system of semantic interpretation.

As a result of the limitations just discussed, all non-human animals have limited, fixed sets of discrete messages that they can convey. These messages constitute a fixed list, and one that cannot be expanded by combining elements to form new and different messages to respond to new and different communicative needs.

The bounded nature of non-human animal communication systems can be related to the absence of systems for elaborating the inventory of signals by employing something like the phonology (and morphology) of human languages. To the extent that every signal in an inventory is produced and recognized as a whole, completely distinct from all the others, the number that can be independently controlled and deployed is subject to significant cognitive limitations. The duality of patterning found in human languages allows us to circumvent that limitation, by constructing arbitrary numbers of new words out of a limited set of meaningless elements of sound (or gesture, in the case of signed languages). This capacity is not present in animal signalling systems, and such efforts as have been made to elicit something similar in the laboratory have not produced results.

There are some limited exceptions to the generalization that phonology is not present in animal communication, but these do not affect the general point. Most notably, song in many oscine bird species is constructed out of a set of basic formative elements. Individual members of a given species may have a repertoire of a few, or even hundreds of different songs all built from the same basic components, combined according to species-specific regularities. What is significant about this, however, is the fact that no matter how many various songs a bird may sing, they all have the same content: fundamentally, an assertion of territorial possession and/or an advertisement for mating. While humans combine sounds in different ways to convey different meanings, birds do something analogous while maintaining the same message. The reasons for the repertorial diversity of birds are to some extent disputed, though in some cases it seems that this serves to advertise high levels of fitness.

Something similar seems to be the case in some cetacean species, especially in the well-known songs of some whales. These can be shown to be composed of recurrent motifs, variously combined and used to identify individuals, to maintain contact over long distances, and to warn others of dangers. Once again, however, there is no reason to believe that the difference between one combination of groans, moans, roars, sighs and high-pitched squeals, and another, is used to distinguish meanings.

Apart from the sorts of knowledge underpinning the use of human language, there are other aspects of cognitive organization that can be explored in comparing human and non-human communicative behaviour. One of these is the path by which the communicative system emerges in the development of the individual.

In humans, knowledge of the language(s) of the surrounding speech community arises on the basis of experience in the early years of life. Many if not most linguists believe this is made possible by a rather rich set of cognitive principles (the "Language Acquisition Device") that is structured by the nature of human language and able to take advantage of relatively weak and impoverished cues in the environment to arrive at a particular system as evidenced by observed utterances. Although the richness of assumptions in this regard is a matter of dispute, there is no question about the most basic point: a human language is acquired fairly rapidly on the basis of somewhat limited early experience.

This path to communicative knowledge is quite distinctive. In nearly all non-human species, the communication system emerges without need for relevant experience, although in some instances there may be some "fine tuning" possible concerning the precise conditions of use of some signal in the system. As in the case of phonological organization, the outstanding exceptions to this generalization are provided by birds: oscine songbirds (and probably also hummingbirds, although the evidence here is more fragmentary) are apparently the only animals apart from us that acquire a significant communicative signal on the basis of experience, rather than having it emerge innately without a role for conspecific models. The shaping effect of a species-specific acquisition system can be quite strong: experiments with zebra finches have shown that even in the absence of any other adult models from which to learn, the song patterns that emerge converge on species-typical song within a few generations (Fehér et al. 2009). For a communication system in the vocal-auditory modality, of course, any possibility of experience based learning rests on a prerequisite that the animal be capable of imitating a model. In this connection, it is significant that the capacity for vocal imitation is extremely limited in nature. Apart from oscine songbirds and hummingbirds, this capacity is obviously present in even more general form in members of the order Psittaciformes (parrots), who can imitate a wide range of sounds although unlike oscines, they do not learn a song in this way. Outside of birds, some limited vocal imitative abilities have been shown in a few mammals, including elephants. Importantly this capacity is not present in non-human primates apart from the possibility of minor shaping effects on innately present vocalizations: some convergence of pant-hoots within a troop of chimpanzees, for example, is apparently useful in coordinating hunting behaviour.

Another important property of human language is that its use is voluntary, controlled mainly by cortical centres, while other animals produce communicative signals under various sorts of non-voluntary control mediated by other parts of the brain. Animal vocalizations (and other signals) are apparently always under the control of involuntary sub-cortical structures, particularly the limbic system (Jürgens 1992, 2009). This kind of vocalization can be suppressed under some circumstances, but not produced voluntarily. Some human vocalizations are similar, such as laughter, cries of pain, moans of pleasure or of pain, etc. Of course, humans also have a system of voluntary sound production, and we can imitate the involuntary sounds of our own (or other animals') vocalizations, but this is not the same. Human vocalizations like speech, singing and intentional imitation are under the control of a completely separate system that other animals lack, based on cerebral motor cortex and related pathways.

The distinct neural underpinnings of communicative vocalization in humans and non-humans are an instance of the general fact that animal communication systems of all sorts can typically be shown to be deeply embedded in the species-specific biology of the animals that employ them. In many cases, specialized organs of production and perception are involved, something that is obvious in the use of ultrasound by (Microchiroptera) bats and dolphins or the use of electric fields by fish. The mouse, for whom olfactory signals associated with pheromones are extremely significant, has a specialized sensory organ, the vomeronasal organ, that is sensitive specifically to a range of substances including most pheromones. This organ (shared with a great many other animals, including humans, in which its function is somewhat controversial) is distinct from the more general olfactory sensory system (the olfactory epithelium) and projects to different regions in the mouse's brain.

Somewhat similarly, the sensory membranes in the auditory systems of frogs tend to be most sensitive in exactly those frequency regions that predominate in the calls of their species. The brains of birds that learn their songs contain specialized nuclei that support the song learning system, structures that are absent in other species. In general, when we examine the ecologically significant communicative signals of any animal species, we find that evolution has shaped the animal's biology so as to be particularly effective in the relevant domain.

Given the otherwise highly distinctive character of human linguistic communication, it would be surprising indeed if the same were not true in this instance. We expect that our linguistic abilities are grounded in evolved biological characteristics of our species. In that case, there is no reason to anticipate that the communicative behaviour of any different species would be based on something like a human language, and as we have seen, there are excellent reasons to doubt this.

The other side of "communication"

If we deny that the systems of communicative signals employed by non-human animals have the essential characteristics of a human language, how then are we to account for the fact that animals do indeed manage to communicate a great deal of ecologically relevant information with one another, enough to manage sometimes quite complex social lives, coordinate hunting parties, etc.? The answer to this apparent contradiction lies in the fact that the information humans convey through their utterances is by no means limited to the literal content of the linguistic forms themselves. While words, phrases and sentences have a semantic interpretation provided by their individual meanings and the manner of their combination, the information conveyed by an utterance can be much richer, given the context in which it is produced and understood. Understanding the role of context, pre-existing knowledge concerning the individuals involved and their relationships to one another, the inferred intent of the speaker, and other factors is the business of *pragmatics*, which studies the way language conveys meaning in use, as opposed to semantics, which studies the meanings of linguistic expressions independent of the circumstances in which they are used.

In important ways, animal signals do not have a "meaning" that is independent of the context in which they occur. There are apparent exceptions to this, including the famous alarm calls of vervet monkeys (Cheney and Seyfarth 1990), which appear to refer to specific types of predatory threat (eagles, leopards and snakes), but the point to note here is that these calls are only produced in rather restricted contexts, and so there is virtually no effort of interpretation required to understand the information they convey to conspecifics. Indeed, when we look at alarm calling behaviour more generally, we can see that the specificity of the vervet example is rather exceptional, closely connected with the world in which the vervets live and the threats they encounter, and that the interpretation of alarm signals elsewhere in the animal kingdom is generally somewhat more reliant on contextual conditions. For some discussion of these and related matters, see Anderson (2017).

Animals, including primates, are quite skilled at interpreting their environment, and that includes the behaviour of other animals, including (but not limited to) their conspecifics. Some of that behaviour, including visual, auditory, olfactory and other signals, is likely to be characteristic of somewhat restricted circumstances, and thus to convey substantial information (in the sense of reducing uncertainty about what may be going on in the world) without much elaboration. Other behaviour is rather less informative in itself, requiring more interpretation.

Animals are also sensitive to the contexts in which they produce their signals. Thus, female primates engaged in copulation with a male other than the dominant one in their group can suppress their characteristic vocalizations when the dominant male is within earshot. While the system of vervet alarm calls emerges in the infant without need for experience, the developing baby vervet observes that some of the observations that might trigger an "eagle" call – for instance, a falling leaf, or a bird other than the two species of eagle that are dangerous – do not elicit such a call from others in the vicinity, and so learns to attune the system so as to produce this call only in the context of a narrower class of events.

The fact that the particular signals that animals produce do not have the structural characteristics (and thus the intrinsic richness) of expressions in a human language does not mean that they are uninformative. In real-world situations, a rich capacity for pragmatic interpretation can derive a great deal of information from otherwise sparsely informative events.

Conclusion

It appears, then, that while the answer to the question in the title of this chapter is "no" if we interpret *language* in terms of the essential properties of human language, that does not mean that animal communication does not share important properties with the language based communication of humans. In particular, both human and non-human animals derive a great deal of the information they actually obtain from pragmatic interpretation of the signals observed in relation to the situational context, what they already know about the world and the individuals involved, and other factors. As a result, animal communication systems can often be quite rich, subtle and closely attuned to the ecological circumstances of the animals involved without making use of a signal system comparable to ours. Animals communicate quite accurately about the circumstances in their worlds that matter to them, on the basis of fine abilities to interpret their observations in relation to the contexts in which they are made; it's just that the sets of signals they employ in this way do not have the properties of a "language" in the human sense. Every species has a range of species-specific properties: "language" is one of ours.

Acknowledgements

The discussion and descriptions in this chapter are drawn from many past lectures and publications, and would require acknowledgement of a large number of students, colleagues and commentators, too many to be enumerated here. Some of the specific points made here are also presented in Anderson (2017).

Further reading

For Hockett's design features of language, see Hockett (1960), and for a critique, Wacewicz and Żywiczyński (2015). On animal communication more generally, see Bradbury and Vehrencamp (2011). And on the specific relationships between human and animal communication systems, see Anderson (2004).

References

Anderson, Stephen R. (2004). *Doctor Dolittle's delusion: Animals and the uniqueness of human language*. New Haven: Yale University Press.
Anderson, Stephen R. (2017). The place of human language in the animal world. In Joanna Blochowiak, Cristina Grisot, Stephanie Durrleman and Christopher Laenzlinger (eds.), *Formal models in the study of language*, 339–351. Dordrecht: Springer.
Bradbury, Jack W. and Sandra L. Vehrencamp. (2011). *Principles of animal communication*. 2nd edition. Oxford: Oxford University Press.
Cheney, Dorothy L. and Robert M. Seyfarth. (1990). *How monkeys see the world*. Chicago: University of Chicago Press.
Fehér, Olga, Haibin Wang, Sigal Saar, Partha P. Mitra and Ofer Tchernichovski. (2009). *De novo* establishment of wild-type song culture in the zebra finch establishment of wild-type song culture in the zebra finch. *Nature*, 459(7246), 564–568. DOI:10.1038/nature07994

Fisher, Simon E. and Sonja C. Vernes. (2015). Genetics and the language sciences. *Annual Review of Linguistics*, 1(1), 289–310. DOI:10.1146/annurev-linguist-0 30514-125024

Fortescue, Michael. (1984). *West Greenlandic*. London: Croom Helm.

Hockett, Charles F. (1960). Logical considerations in the study of animal communication. In W. E. Lanyon and W. N. Tavolga (eds.), *Animal sounds and animal communication*, 392–430. Washington, DC: American Institute of Biological Sciences.

Jürgens, Uwe. (1992). On the neurobiology of vocal communication. In H. Papoušek, U. Jürgens and M. Papoušek (eds.), *Nonverbal vocal communication: Comparative and developmental approaches*, 31–42. Cambridge: Cambridge University Press.

Jürgens, Uwe. (2009). The neural control of vocalization in mammals: A review. *Journal of Voice*, 23(1), 1–10. DOI:10.1016/j.jvoice.2007.07.005

Lofting, Hugh. (1920). *The story of Doctor Dolittle*. New York: Frederick A. Stokes.

Miller, Melissa B. and Bonnie L. Bassler. (2001). Quorum sensing in bacteria. *Annual Review of Microbiology*, 55, 165–199. DOI:10.1146/annurev.micro.55.1.165

Pinker, Steven. (1994). *The language instinct*. New York: William Morrow.

Shettleworth, Sara J. (2009). *Cognition, evolution, and behavior*. Oxford: Oxford University Press.

Wacewicz, Sławomir and Przemysław Żywiczyński. (2015). Language evolution: Why Hockett's design features are a non-starter. *Biosemiotics*, 8, 29–46. DOI:10.1007/s12304-014-9203-2

2 Is talking work doing work?

Jo Angouri and Ifigeneia Machili

Introduction

The importance of communication in the workplace is now considered a truism. In scholarly and lay business literature it is normatively associated with profitability, productivity, team building and client relationships (e.g. McQuerrey 2017). A detailed treatment of what this actually means and how we can better understand the way we interact in the world of work did not preoccupy researchers until about the '70s. Linguists, and particularly Sociolinguists, turned a firm eye on the workplace, initially as a domain of human activity, and the new field, under Workplace Sociolinguistics, grew exponentially in the '80s and the '90s. At the same time, scholars in other fields, and particularly in International Business, also started raising questions about language in multilingual workplace settings. The two fields, however, did not interact and there is, still, little synergy between them in the present day (Angouri and Piekkari 2018). This chapter is firmly within the Sociolinguistics discipline, although we hope the issues raised will bear relevance to a wide range of readers.

Workplace Sociolinguists have argued that *talking work is doing work* and interpersonal or relational interaction is not only prevalent but inseparable from transactional or task-based talk. In the fluid business world, organizations compete for global talent and employees operate in a multilingual, diverse and highly competitive environment, and are called to work in and across linguistic, national, professional and geographical boundaries. People in different positions, with varying backgrounds, expertise and years of experience, carry out their professional roles by negotiating "norms" which are different to their own and their own ways of doing things. Further to this, any workspace is a political setting where power relationships are at play. In this context, the management of mundane daily events requires a handling of complexity which is often unacknowledged. We discuss here one of the most common tasks in the workplace, the reaching of decisions, and we draw on data from business emails. We pay special attention to the way interactants negotiate formality and use of global and local languages as they project, claim and resist group membership.

The field of Workplace Sociolinguistics at a glance

Sociolinguists turned to the workplace as a place which could be used to test some claims from current theories analysing how language is used to express politeness (Brown and Levinson 1987) and theories of Conversational Analysis. Similar to Conversational Analysts, Sociolinguists also became preoccupied with detailed analysis of interactions, and the Interactional Sociolinguistics approach provided the theoretical framework and methodological tools for studying interactions within their immediate and wider sociocultural context. Unlike Conversational Analysts, however, who primarily focused on the sequential organization of conversation in professional encounters, Interactional Sociolinguists sought to interpret the situation through the participants' eyes as well as on the researcher's understanding of the context. Interactional Sociolinguistics became a dominant model in Workplace Sociolinguistics.

Rather than working with a priori assumptions about how things work, Workplace Sociolinguists look at interactions as an ongoing process of negotiation, where participants infer what their interlocutors intend to convey and re/align their uptake; in doing so they perpetuate or challenge existing social structures and power hierarchies. As the workplace is a site of conflict where power relationships are continually challenged and changing (Wodak 2012), Sociolinguists explore the situated nature of meaning in interpersonal relations as they are formed and negotiated in situ. One of the first systematic attempts to discuss power and politeness in the workplace was Holmes (1995), as part of the New Zealand Language in the Workplace project. Others looked into the way formality is used to negotiate decisions at work (e.g. Erickson 1999). More recent discourse analyses of business emails and meetings still reveal that language is a tool employed strategically by employees and acquires meaning within the interpersonal and organizational context of their interactions (e.g. Bremner 2012; Gimenez 2002; Skovholt, Grønning and Kankaanranta 2014).

Over the years, the field has moved from looking at the workplace as a site for data collection to broader phenomena around commodification and marketization of society and human capital. Currently the field is preoccupied with questions around workplace integration and global centres and peripheries that are prominent in the negotiation of power structures and resources. Particularly, in the current political context "work" becomes a site separating those who are a "resource" from those who are a "burden". This highlights the need for further research into the practices of teams in different professional settings and the implications of training, particularly for work-related language use. We return to these issues in the conclusions of the chapter. Let us now turn to the business email.

The ever-dominant business email

Since their uniform adoption in the world of business around the 1990s, emails have become the dominant means of communication. Popular literature suggests that on average employees receive 120 emails every day and the daily number of business emails received and sent is 124.5 billion (Lyncova 2019).

Their high frequency is unquestionable and they have penetrated all levels and functions of any organization using computer-based information systems. Their ease of use and access, and multiple addressability to geographically dispersed teams, enable all parties to share information or participate in the resolution of complex issues. The information flow becomes regularized and procedures are standardized. Collective decisions are made faster, the cost is reduced and organizational productivity is enhanced. Further, through their CCing function, messages to employees at various hierarchical levels, with different expertise and agendas, can be stored and retrieved establishing accountability in both vertical and horizontal communication. Emails are used to carry out everyday procedural tasks and more complex issues for various purposes and agendas. Although they have attracted some attention in Sociolinguistic research in relation to their variable linguistic features (Gains 1999; Crystal 2006), emails are still under-studied, particularly given their frequency and significance. In a recent paper, we argued that their primary function largely relies on the organizational community where they are employed (Machili 2014a).

In addition to their technical traits, emails also afford important social characteristics, which have spawned a heated debate about the depersonalizing nature of email in informational and communication technology circles (Lucas 1998). On the one hand, email fosters an, allegedly, egalitarian environment by filtering out social status cues. On the other, email has its own mechanisms to enable maintenance and negotiation of power asymmetries at work. In recent work (Machili et al. 2019), we have shown how users manage the system to index and negotiate power asymmetries. Although the CCing facility, for example, enables participants from various hierarchical levels and professions to participate in Decision Making equally, it is strategically used by participants to include and/or exclude others from the chain and shift between active and passive positions. The structural elements of emails (e.g. absence or presence of greetings), variability of linguistic features (e.g. formality, politeness) and purposes (formal-informal, transactional-relational, personal-professional) and CCing facility are used differently by people in and across different organizations, departments and levels to mark status differences and/or build rapport, thus fostering an egalitarian or non-egalitarian environment depending on the local context (Bremner 2006; Machili 2014a).

Emails are also ideal for studying the construction and negotiation of interpersonal relationships as employees engage in Decision Making. In addition to the more stable power asymmetries in relation to hierarchy, established roles and years of experience, situated forms of power are formed and negotiated in discourse. This can, and at times does, create space for a renegotiation of power balance at work; junior members can, in principle, check on their senior colleagues when copied in, outsiders can claim membership by virtue of whom they know, newcomers can *do* power over old-timers because of their expertise.

Evidently this negotiation is reflected and strategically enacted linguistically through variations in style and choice of global and local languages according to what is considered appropriate within the interactants' immediate interpersonal and wider organizational context. Thus, workplace discourse becomes a set of resources drawn upon for the enactment of professional roles and identities in daily transactional interactions. Task oriented interaction becomes inseparable from relational talk as employees make decisions on organizational matters and this talk in turn "makes" the organization. "The organization emerges in and through the discourse of the interactants" (Angouri and Locher 2017: 221). We now turn to the core activity we will be discussing through the data, Decision Making.

Decision Making (DM) at work

Addressing (complex) problems and reaching decisions is daily practice for professionals. DM has been extensively studied over the years and organizational DM and behavioural DM models have been suggested in relevant literature (e.g. Panagiotou 2008; Yeh and Chang 2009).

It is not until recently however that Sociolinguistic research has turned its eye to the complex architecture of decisions and shown the importance of interaction. As Huisman (2001: 84) aptly puts it, "there appears to be a wall between theories of decision making and the features of the actual interactional procedures through which organizations shape their future".

This work has shown that DM is far from linear; it is a complex process where it is not often possible to identify what comprises a decision and the moment it is taken (Boden 1994; Halvorsen 2013; Sarangi and Roberts

1999), and it is generally viewed as the process where participants jointly construct the formulation of a state of affairs and through further assessment and formulation commit to future states of affairs (Huisman 2001: 75). Therefore, what "counts" as a decision is difficult to define (Marra 2003; Kim and Angouri 2019). It is equally difficult to identify the moment when a decision is reached. Although analytically decisions and problems can be studied separately, we consider them here and in earlier work to be interrelated (Angouri 2012; Machili 2014a). Looking into DM from a sociolinguistic perspective involves exploring the context where a negotiation of issues that are ratified as problems in an organization trigger commitment to a set of "future actions". Although DM has been studied in meetings (Holmes and Marra 2004), one of the core events where organizations (re) define their priorities for the future, there is little Sociolinguistic research on the role of business email for DM. Emails, however, also provide a prime space for making and negotiating decisions, particularly given their versatility in terms of time and speed.

DM is the product of interactional processes, engaging people from different disciplines and areas of expertise, from distinguishable hierarchical levels within and across different organizations. It is a linguistic and social process where the participants *position themselves in relation to competing agendas for future action*. DM is highly dependent on the norms of the particular organization, which means that practice cannot be easily extrapolated but patterns can be usefully compared across settings. We discuss this further in the light of a small dataset we analyse to illustrate the points made here. We focus on the way collective decisions are taken in an example email chain (Figure 2.1); the use of global and local languages and negotiation of formality constitute the primary considerations of the analysis.

Unpacking emails

In this section, we discuss how language is used strategically in DM. We posit that an examination of formal and informal linguistic features, and global and local languages, can shed light on the way employees negotiate their professional roles and relations. In practice, this results in ways to *do* power, to include and/or exclude access to DM as employees participate in collective problem solving. We base the discussion on our analysis of the data supplemented with the participants' views as these were expressed in discourse-based interviews (for a discussion of the methodology see Machili 2014a). We look at greetings, reference (use of *I* and *we*) and degree of explicitness in relation to formality, as well as use of German and Greek as local languages and English as the global Lingua Franca (the language understood by all members of the organization).

Is talking work doing work? 23

Specifically, the use of *we* is associated with formality as it is employed to represent an organization when *I* indexes more personalized style in business emails (see Machili 2014a). A high degree of explicitness has been linked to formality and implicitness (i.e. shared contextual implications mainly through the use of pronouns) with informality (Heylighen and

---

Context: The email chain provided here concerns the handling of a complaint, made by Maria, sales manager of a particular line of diagnostic equipment in PharmaMed (a pharmaceutical company based in Greece) about not being informed by BioMedical co (BM), their company-supplier in Germany, about the recall of ASTRA (equipment used in clinical diagnosis and treatment), a line of products she was being supplied with and selling to the Greek market. The complaint is addressed to Niklas, a BM high executive, responsible for the product sales in Europe. The chain is copied to all relevant parties – her two bosses (Andrew and Kolias) and Bert, the BM person she regularly communicates with on sales issues. The official language in external communication is English and all participants speak fluent English. Informant: Maria

---

(1)
From: Maria
Sent: Thursday, 20/1/2011 11:11
To: Niklas
Cc: Andrew; Kolias; Bert
Subject: ASTRA RECALL CANADA

Dear Niklas,

I was informed today by a prospect ASTRA customer about the recalls in Canada. I am sure she was informed about it by BM.

I would suggest in the future that you inform us about similar issues as it helps with customers and competition.

I goggled to find the link below.

[link]

Best regards

Maria
Signature

Figure 2.1 Example of an email chain.

(2)
From: Niklas
Sent: Thursday, 20/1/2011 12:48 PM
To: Maria
Cc: Andrew; Kolias; Bert
Subject: RE: ASTRA RECALL CANADA

Dear Maria,

Thanks for your message, I understand your concerns and agree that information like this comes as an unpleasant surprise. As Canada is not part of my area I am not automatically informed about regulatory issues in this geography, however will need to discuss if there is a possibility for better communication.

Best regards,

Signature

---

(3)
From: Maria
Sent: Thursday, 20/1/2011 15:26
To: Niklas
Cc: Andrew; Kolias; Bert
Subject: RE: ASTRA RECALL CANADA

Dear Niklas,

Thank you for your prompt reply. We do not really expect you to let us know within a few days after a problem reveals. I have noticed the recall is more than three months.

A similar issue received as IPCA-14399A letter last summer and may be arise from Canada installations.

In any case as we usually receive information on new products or even BM trouble from other sources we can also be informed about these serious issues which competitors can easily take advantage of resulting in loss of credibility to our customers.

Thank you for understanding

Regards
Maria

Figure 2.1 Continued.

(4)
From: Andrew
Sent: Thursday, 20/1/2011 16:00
To: Niklas
Subject: RE: ASTRA RECALL CANADA

Hi Niklas,

Wie geht es Deutschland wirklich? ich habe seit langem nichts von dir gehört. Wie es scheint, wie bekommen keine genügende Informationen, was die Widerrufung der Waren in Kanada betrifft. Bist du darüber informiert?

Machs gut!

Andrew

Hi Niklas,

How're things in Germany? Haven't heard from you for a while. We seem to be having some problems with being properly informed about product recalls in Canada. Do you happen to know what's going on?

Take care!
Andrew

---

(5)
From: Niklas
Sent: Thursday, 20/1/2011 5:31 PM
To: Maria
Cc: Andrew; Kolias; Bert
Subject: RE: ASTRA RECALL CANADA

Dear Maria,

Following the comments from yourself as well as Andrew I did a bit of research in order to get further clarification. I found that a service memo went out on Aug 17th, to which your service organization has access. Stating the issue as well as describing the resolution. If this issue results in a recall (which is a bit of a misleading term as no instruments are being physically moved) for the EU countries, I don't know. However, should this happen you always get the appropriate IPCA letter through our GC/QA department.

Best regards,
Signature

Figure 2.1 Continued.

(6)
From: Maria
Sent: Friday, 21/1/2011 10:09 AM
To: Niklas
Cc: Andrew; Kolias; Bert
Subject: RE: ASTRA RECALL CANADA

Dear Niklas,

Thank you for your answer but I am afraid we complain to BioMedical not because we have not received IPCA letters or have access to service memos. We are actually very pleased about these procedures and measures taken.

What we do not know and cannot evaluate is the impact of a problem in some countries which cause action such as IPCA letters. Canada is not a third world country and maybe has a very strict legislation therefore had ASTRA recalled.

What we imply is BioMedical policy to representatives. We would not like to endanger our sales because we are not informed on serious issues by BM and hear about these from competition. We can defend our sales better especially because we have procedures such as corrective actions.

I hope this clarify our views.

Have a nice weekend

Maria
Signature

---

(7)
From: Maria
Sent: Saturday, 22/1/2011 09:10 AM
To: Andrew
Subject: RE: ASTRA RECALL CANADA

Το κλείσαμε. Ελπίζω δηλαδή. Για το καλό όλων μας.
Αν τα κατάλαβα όλα καλά τα Γερμανικά μου θέλουν λίγο ξεσκόνισμα. Είχατε στο παρελθόν επικοινωνία στα Γερμανικά;

We settled it. That is I hope (we did). For all our sakes.
If I understood everything correctly my German is a little bit rusty. Did you communicate in German in the past?

Figure 2.1 Continued.

Dewale 1999). Greetings with last names and signatures index formal style while a lack of greetings and more personalized salutations like *hi, bye, take care* index informality (Rice 1997; Gains 1999; Crystal 2006).

All emails were written in English except (4), which was in German and (7) which was in Greek. The idiomatic translation in English is provided below. At the firm's request anything that could identify the firm, products or the participants themselves has been replaced by pseudonyms and participants have given their consent to the use of their emails and interview data.

The chain functions as a predominantly formal interaction between parties from two different companies as in emails 1, 2, 3, 5, 6 writers are representative of their respective companies and accountable to the internal senior managers who are copied in, and emails 4 and 7 are more personal and informal. Scholars have often associated email chains involving multiple participants with record keeping, accountability to superiors and company representativeness, and accord the chain official formal status (Stanton 2004; Machili et al. 2019). Yet through the CCing facility, participants' status may change from "active decision makers" to mere "observers" and others may be added or excluded from particular emails of the chain, with the status of emails alternating from formal to informal and public to private accordingly, as the chain evolves (Machili et al. 2019).

The analysis shows that with the exception of the first email, virtually all references Maria makes to the complainant are with *we* (e.g. *we complain, we are actually very pleased*, etc.) constructing herself as her company representative and adding a formal tone to the interaction. This representation is also evident in her copying in her senior managers in all steps of the complaint. Her consistent use of the more personalized *I* in place of *we* in the first email, therefore, stands out indexing a variation in the formality consistent with the rest of the chain. In this way, she projects her complaint as her own initiative in her role as a sales manager rather than in her capacity as a PharmaMed representative employee. As she explains,

> *it looks more personalized a little less formal but it's my duty as a senior sales manager to know about these and cannot possibly find out about it out in the street so I took the risk [.] a <u>calculated</u> risk*

Maria launches a complaint towards a superior, risking being perceived inappropriately informal, yet acknowledging the norms of the particular interaction, she perceives it as a safe risk. The (small) breach of norms is instigated by her feeling of being mistreated and her strong sense of responsibility as a sales manager, and it is these perceptions that place her in a stronger position than her addressee, who is by default higher in the hierarchy.

A bit further down the chain, Maria stands out once again but with respect to a different linguistic feature. In her response to Niklas' denial of responsibility for the oversight (email 2), Maria varies her greeting from the rest of her public emails by consciously omitting her signature (email 3). In all the public exchanges, openings and closures are typically formal (albeit not very formal) in the context of the two affiliate companies between two senior managers in different ranks who know each other; all emails start with *Dear* + first name and end with variants of *regards* (*best regards* is used three times, *regards* is used once) + first name +/signature (signature is used three times). Asked about her omission, Maria comments:

> here (in PharmaMed) [.] we can decide whether to add it or not [.] I don't like projecting my credentials every single time you talk to someone [.] especially in our internal communication [.] I used it in the beginning (email 1) and <u>yes</u> I should have used it again but [.] I got upset [.] you tell them something and they don't understand senior officers and all [.] so I [.] bent the rules a little (laughs)

As the quote reveals, Maria acknowledges the different practices between the two companies in the use of signature. The differences in communication practices between organizations, departments and work teams are ways for claiming membership and distinguishing one community from the other (Gimenez 2002; Angouri and Marra 2011; Incelli 2013). Employees belong, or claim to belong, to more than one community in their workplace, and variation in style is part of negotiating professional roles and identities. Accordingly, although Maria recognizes the appropriacy of the presence of her signature in this external upward directed interaction, she takes advantage of the freedom afforded in her company to vary her use of signature and risk sounding inappropriate to take her complaint further/to be heard. By "bending the rules a little", she constructs herself as a party who claims power by virtue of her rightfulness even in confrontation with a senior party. Sensitive issues such as complaints and grievances have been seen to cause a shift in formality (Gains 1999; Machili 2014a), but the appropriacy of the shift is subject to their organizational norms. A breach in those norms, therefore, tends to reflect an authoritarian move by either a party in a high hierarchical position or a low post holder *doing* power in the course of the interaction. Although here Niklas is higher in seniority, Maria's omission of signature indexes an authoritative style which risks appearing insulting in her perception. However, as the interaction unfolds, the move does not seem to be perceived as inappropriate, illustrating the significance of the local context for understanding the style of writing. The breach in formality is then balanced by Maria's shift from the informal *I* to the more formal *we*

Is talking work doing work? 29

and *our*, enabling herself to strategically pursue her claim further, but this time more as a complainant who has her company backing and support, than an isolated disgruntled employee. Clearly illustrated here is the invocation of different even contrasting identities to *do* power at work to achieve both relational and transactional goals.

The following email (email 4) is restricted communication between two higher rank holders. By being written in German, the addressee's local language, it indexes intention to build rapport and solidarity among equals. Other studies have similarly shown the use of local language in multinational workplaces to build collegiality and group alliance (Erickson 1999; Holmes 2000; Machili 2014b). The building of solidarity is further supported by the informality adopted in the interaction. The email opens informally with *Hi Niklas* and closes with the friendly *take care* + the writer's first name and omission of signature. The addition of social talk *How're things in Germany? Haven't heard from you for a while* is also consistent with the informal personal style. The use of German signals exclusion of all other parties from the interaction even when the email is later added to the chain. With this intervention, Andrew takes control of the DM while excluding Maria, the immediately affected and officially accountable party for its resolution. Maria's role is downplayed and her boss appears as a stronger decision maker.

In view of Niklas' second denial of responsibility (email 5) despite her boss' intervention, Maria claims the floor back to close the issue with a formal exposition of her views carefully constructing herself as company representative (email 6). This can be seen in her consistent use of *we* and additional explicit clarifications on the company views. The formality is slightly toned down with the social *Have a nice weekend* and picks up again in the formal addition of her signature. The issue appears to be publicly settled with Maria holding her ground this time in her double capacity as Senior Sales Manager and company representative.

The chain closes with the second private exchange in Greek this time, the local language of the interactants, Maria and Andrew, similar to other studies on use of global and local languages in multinational organizations (Ailon-Souday and Kunda 2003). The informality is indexed in the lack of opening and closing salutations and the high degree of implicitness. The latter is evident in the repeated use of *it* as reference to the issue discussed, *all our* as reference to the company and *everything* implying the email written in German. *For all our sakes* builds solidarity within the team and the closure of the issue is projected as a collective move/achievement. Strategically, though, this is followed by a comment about the use of a language incomprehensible to the remaining participants and unofficially employed by the highest rank holder. The hint is Maria's acknowledgement of her temporary exclusion from the discussion and the inappropriacy of that move. Her resentment for being superseded in the Decision Making process becomes clearer below:

> *I was set aside just like that [.] obviously I don't belong to the senior's world [.] but he should have known better [.] being dragged in like that (laughs) he probably meant to help but [.] German (?) [.] we've never used German before but then again he's been here much longer*

As the quote reveals, Maria feels excluded from what she perceived to be an issue falling within her own responsibility. She also feels justified, however, at her boss's failed attempt to keep this move private, and hits back by hinting that using German during the resolution of a problem that should take place in public is uncalled for and inappropriate. Filtering information to particular parties in email chains through the use of a local language is not a new practice and can be employed by higher and lower post holders alike who want to gain control of a collective resolution of an issue. By having the last word and taking control of the interaction again, Maria challenges Andrew's hierarchical authority but discretely minimizes the effect of her implications in *Did you communicate in German in the past?*, acknowledging his seniority by virtue of his years of experience in the same company. Although the informality and implications raised against her superior could be considered insulting, in the context of this company, they appear to be afforded. The chain also reflects the complexities in collective Decision Making. Although email 6 appears to signal the finalization of the issue, Maria's *I hope we did* in the private follow up implies there may be more to it. The fluidity of collective decisions and the difficulties in agreeing on when a decision is reached are illustrated in this example and have been well discussed in the relevant literature (e.g. Huisman 2001; Angouri and Bargiela-Chiappini 2011).

DM is a process and although agreement at certain points, such as the chain we read here, constitutes anchors for future actions, decisions feed into larger and more complex constellations of actions; this chain is also a succinct illustration of the use of multiple languages to in/exclude and manage social relationships. Professionals need to manage a sensitive equilibrium between their task-oriented activities and social relationships for which they deploy all the resources of meaning in their inventory.

To conclude, we see DM as an interactional and *ephemeral* process highly contingent on the identities the interactants project in situ, the way they linguistically formulate and reformulate these decisions, and the communicative norms of the organizations they are part of. What counts as a decision in one organization may not count as one in another.

As emails have been found to be more efficient than other means in reaching people from different organizations, departments and hierarchical

Is talking work doing work? 31

levels, and in different geographical and time zones and areas of expertise quickly and at no cost, they provide an ideal space for solving problems and making and negotiating "decisions" rapidly. And although as one employee from the company noted, "Whenever you have a problem, you can immediately reach a group of people who can help you", emails also provide the space for the participants to forward their own agendas by negotiating their professional roles and relations. Talking or rather emailing work in this context *is* doing work.

Conclusion and directions for future research

Workplace Sociolinguistics provides insights into the way employees employ linguistic resources strategically within and across workplace communities as they try to achieve relational and transactional goals. As the analysis of the data illustrates, formality and use of global and local languages are used as mechanisms for claiming and resisting group membership with the context of their group or organization. Far from blindly adopting the dominant organizational norms, employees negotiate and adapt them according to what is acceptable to their own groups and as they see fit to their own transactional and relational goals. Power at work is a dynamic concept dependent on employees *doing* control through core business activities, such as Decision Making processes. From this angle, language is not a static fixed national variety, but a set of resources employed skillfully in different contexts and for different purposes/agendas. Generalizations about the linguistic practices of managers versus post holders, old-timers versus newcomers, small versus large organizations etc. are seen as oversimplified and outdated and should be treated with caution.

To conclude, the modern world of work is changing. Employees change jobs, areas of expertise, and geographical and time zones more than in the past. They work in teams which cross disciplines, languages and organizations, and they need to be able to communicate their own work practices and to relate to those of others (Halvorsen 2013). Modern organizations have long become multinational and multilingual and the fast-developing technology accelerates the pace of their transformation. Employees from all types of workplaces immigrate, relocate or travel to other countries to do business. Accordingly, communication practices change to facilitate employees to work in teams across linguistic, departmental, organizational and national boundaries, time zones, and areas of expertise in their daily work schedule. This highly collaborative environment puts pressure on employees who must build rapport, learn from each other, solve problems and take decisions collectively. Emails have become the dominant means through which collective discussions and decisions on high stake company matters are held and recorded. Despite the suggested tendency of globalization to harmonize disparate professional cultures, the employees' daily work becomes highly variable, constantly demanding and highly competitive. As discrepancies between organizational policies and everyday practices have to be reconciled, and global and local demands met, daily routine often involves the need to communicate in a range of languages (e.g. global and local), genres (e.g. email, meetings, face to face interaction), and styles (e.g. formal and informal), and employees often adjust to a "what works best" solution rather than adhering to set official policies. Further, in the context of continuous financial crises, high pressure on human and financial resources leads to the commodification of employee skills, which acquire value according to their importance for the company's economy (Gee et al. 2018). Future research needs to unpack these dynamics and feed into the design of future work settings. In parallel, this work has immediate implications for those who offer/take language training for work purposes.

The 21st century work environment ultimately calls for a dynamic view of "workplace language" and of language needs for work purposes. Identifying and covering the language needs of people seeking work has been addressed by the language studies field for quite some time now, but it is still criticized for its prescriptive one-size-fits-all. Although some progress has been made, the gap still remains between what is actually taught and what actually happens at work. On the optimistic side, a lot has been and can be done to introduce students to the multivariate nature of workplace communication, such as, use of authentic materials and corpora. Cooperation between researchers, material developers and instructors across disciplines is equally promising. Generally, providing opportunities for practice of transferring their communication skills (e.g. writing and speaking) to different contexts and "learning how to learn" are steps in the right direction.

In the multilingual, diverse and highly competitive modern world of business, where people are called to cross a multitude of geographical, professional and linguistic boundaries, the need to better understand how we interact at work becomes more pertinent than ever.

A first step to managing this complexity is to acknowledge that the old static norms of the past are long gone and that talking work in the world of today can be nothing else but doing work.

Further reading

Angouri and Marra (2011) constitutes a dedicated piece of work on identity construction and negotiation in different professional settings. Through the discussion of a range of cases and contexts the reader gets an insight into professional practices as emerging in interaction.

Holmes and Stubbe (2003) is a seminal piece of work; it introduces the reader to core concepts and methodological approaches for unpacking workplace discourse. The volume constitutes one of the classics for novice and established researchers and is a good resource for designing projects in the field.

Sarangi and Roberts (1999) is a co-authored monograph, particularly useful for highlighting the complex relationship between power and workplace interaction. It provides the reader with a wealth of examples and detailed analysis.

References

Ailon-Souday, Galit and Gideon Kunda. (2003). The local selves of global workers: The social construction of national identity in the face of organizational globalization. *Organization Studies*, 24(7), 1073–1096. DOI:10.1177 %2F01708406030247004

Angouri, Jo. (2012). Managing disagreement in problem solving meeting talk. *Journal of Pragmatics*, 44(12), 1565–1579. DOI:10.1016/j.pragma.2012.06.010

Angouri, Jo and Francesca Bargiela-Chiappini. (2011). "So what problems bother you and you are not speeding up your work?" Problem solving talk at work. *Discourse and Communication*, 1–20. DOI:10.1177%2F1750481311405589

Angouri, Jo and Miriam Locher. (2017). Interpersonal pragmatics and workplace interaction. In Meredith Marra and Paul Warren (eds.), *Linguist at work: Festschrift for Janet Holmes*, 217–236. Wellington, New Zealand: Victoria University Press.

Angouri, Jo and Meredith Marra. (eds.). (2011). *Constructing identities at work*. New York: Palgrave Macmillan. DOI:10.1057/9780230360051

Angouri, Jo and Rebecca Piekkari. (2018). Organising multilingually: Setting an agenda for studying language at work. *European Journal of International Management*, 12(1–2), 8–27.

Boden, Deirdre. (1994). *The business of talk: Organizations in action*. Cambridge: Polity Press.

Bremner, Stephen. (2006). Politeness, power, and activity systems: Written requests and multiple audiences in an institutional setting. *Written Communication*, 23(4), 397–423. DOI:10.1177%2F0741088306293707

Bremner, Stephen. (2012). Socialization and the acquisition of professional discourse: A case study in the PR industry'. *Written Communication*, 29(1), 7–32. DOI:10.1177%2F0741088311424866

Brown, Penelope and Stephen Levinson. (1987). *Politeness: Some universals in language use*. Cambridge: Cambridge University Press.

Crystal, David. (2006). *Language and the internet*. 2nd edition. Cambridge: Cambridge University Press.

Erickson, Frederick. (1999). Appropriation of voice and presentation of self as a fellow physician: Aspects of a discourse of apprenticeship in medicine. In Srikant

Sarangi and Celia Roberts (eds.), *Talk, work and institutional order*, 109–143. New York: Mouton de Gruyter.

Gains, Jonathan. (1999). Electronic mail – A new style of communication or just a new medium? An investigation into the text features of E-mail. *English for Specific Purposes*, 18(1), 81–101. DOI:10.1016/S0889-4906(97)00051-3

Gee, James, Glynda Hull and Colin Lankshear. (2018). *The new work order: Behind the language of the new capitalism*. St. Leonards: Allen & Unwin. DOI:10.4324/9780429496127

Gimenez, Julio C. (2002). New media and conflicting realities in multinational corporate communication: A case study. *IRAL – International Review of Applied Linguistics in Language Teaching*, 40(4), 323–344. DOI:10.1515/iral.2002.016

Halvorsen, Kristin. (2013). Team decision making in the workplace: A systematic review of discourse analytic studies. *Journal of Applied Linguistics and Professional Practice*, 1(1). DOI:10.1558/japl.v1.i1.17289

Heylighen, Francis and Jean-Marc Dewaele. (1999). *Formality of language: Definition, measurement and behavioural determinants*. Internal Report. Brussels: Center "Leo Apostel", Free University of Brussels.

Holmes, Janet. (1995). *Women, men and politeness*. New York: Longman

Holmes, Janet. (2000). Doing collegiality and keeping control at work: Small talk in government departments. In Justine Coupland (ed.), *Small talk*, 32–61. London: Longman.

Holmes, Janet and Meredith Marra. (2004). Leadership and managing conflict in meetings. *Pragmatics: Quarterly Publication of the International Pragmatics Association (IPrA)*, 14(4), 439–462. DOI:10.1075/prag.14.4.02hol

Holmes, Janet and Maria Stubbe. (2003). *Power and politeness in the workplace*. London: Pearson Education.

Huisman, Marjan. (2001). Decision-making in meetings as talk-in-interaction. *International Studies of Management and Organization*, 31(3), 69–90. DOI:10.1 080/00208825.2001.11656821

Incelli, Ersilia. (2013). Managing discourse in intercultural business email interactions: A case study of a British and Italian business transaction. *Journal of Multilingual and Multicultural Development*, 34(6), 515–532. DOI:10.1080/ 01434632.2013.807270

Kim, Kyoungmi and Jo Angouri. (2019). "We don't need to abide by that!": Negotiating professional roles in problem-solving talk at work. *Discourse and Communication*, 13(2), 172–191. DOI:10.1177%2F1750481318817623

Lucas, William. (1998). Effects of e-mail on the organization. *European Management Journal*, 16(1), 18–30. DOI:10.1016/S0263-2373(97)00070-4

Lyncova, Darina. (2019). The surprising reality of how may emails are sent per day. Accessed 28/9/19 from https://techjury.net/stats-about/how-many-emails-are-sent-per-day/

Machili, Ifigeneia. (2014a). *Writing in the workplace: Variation in the writing practices and formality of eight multinational companies in Greece*. Unpublished doctoral dissertation. University of the West of England.

Machili, Ifigeneia. (2014b). "It's pretty simple and in Greek...": Global and local languages in the Greek corporate setting. *Multilingua*, 33(1–2), 117–146. DOI:10.1515/multi-2014-0006

Machili, Ifigeneia, Jo Angouri and Nigel Harwood. (2019). "The snowball of emails we deal with": CCing in multinational companies. *Business and Professional Communication Quarterly*, 82(1), 5–37. DOI:10.1177%2F2329490618815700

Marra, Meredith. (2003). *Decisions in New Zealand business meetings: A sociolinguistic analysis of power at work*. Unpublished doctoral dissertation. Victoria University of Wellington.

McQuerrey, Lisa. (2017). Why is effective communication important in management. Accessed 10/9/19 from https://careertrend.com/about-6514088-effective-communication-important-management-.html

Panagiotou, George. (2008). Conjoining prescriptive and descriptive approaches: Towards an integrative framework of decision making: A conceptual note. *Management Decision*, 46(4), 553–564. DOI:10.1108/00251740810865058

Rice, Rodney P. (1997). An analysis of stylistic variables in electronic mail. *Journal of Business and Technical Communication*, 11(1), 5–23. DOI:10.1177%2F1050651997011001001

Sarangi, Srikant and Celia Roberts. (1999). *Talk, work and institutional order: Discourse in medical, mediation and management settings*. Berlin: Mouton de Gruyter.

Skovholt, Karianne, Anette Grønning and Anna Kankaanranta. (2014). The communicative functions of emoticons in workplace e-mails. *Journal of Computer-Mediated Communication*, 19(4), 780–797. DOI:10.1111/jcc4.12063

Stanton, Nicky. (2004). *Mastering communication*. 4th edition. London: Palgrave Macmillan.

Wodak, Ruth. (2012). Language, power and identity. *Language Teaching*, 45(2), 215–233. DOI:10.1017/S0261444811000048

Yeh, Chung-Hsing and Yu-Hern Chang. (2009). Modeling subjective evaluation for fuzzy group multicriteria decision making. *European Journal of Operational Research*, 194(2), 464–473. DOI:10.1016/j.ejor.2007.12.029

3 What makes a language a language?

Laurie Bauer

There are at least two ways in which we might try to determine what it is that constitutes a language. The first one is to ask what makes a language different from any other communication system, such as mime or dogs barking or music or "the language of flowers". That question has been answered in Stephen Anderson's chapter (Chapter 1) and involves answers such as being able to negate a statement (as in *He's not in the office at the moment*) or being able to talk about the past or the future (as in *We'll have fish for dinner tomorrow*). We will have nothing further to say about such matters here. The second way to answer this question, the one that will be addressed here, is to ask how we know whether what is spoken in Washington DC and what is spoken in London are "the same language" or whether they are "different languages". It should be clear at the outset that this involves matters of definition, but providing the relevant definitions turns out to be harder than it may seem.

The first thing we have to consider is: if two things are the same language but are different from each other (as we might want to argue for what is spoken in Washington DC and in London), then what are they? Everyday usage provides us with a host of labels that we might want to apply, including *speech*, *tongue*, *parlance*, *jargon*, *dialect*, *argot*, *patois* and so on. The Slovak scholar Jozef Šafárik (after whom the university in Košice is named) created an even wider range of terms and categories, which have not been widely used except in relation to the Slavic languages like Slovak, Russian and Ukrainian. Some of the available terms might seem as though they mean just the same as *language*, others may seem as though they differ – slightly, or greatly. The term that most linguists prefer to use is *variety*. This is a scientific term in linguistics, and is defined quite specifically. Calling something a variety does not judge whether what is spoken (or written) is good or bad; it does not say what factors influence the difference between varieties (whether location, social status, age, sex, time at which the variety is observed, spoken versus written transmission, or whatever). Calling something a variety does not make it sound as though it is of high value or of low value; calling something a variety means that we are not committed to just what is different between one variety and another – that may be something we need to specify. We can say that what is spoken in Washington DC and what is spoken in London are different varieties, whether they are different languages or different varieties of the same language.

Part of the difficulty linguists face here is that a term like *dialect*, which might seem fairly neutral, is so often a disparaging term in English (and, indeed, as we shall see, in some other languages, too). Thomas Hardy, in *The mayor of Casterbridge* (1886: chapter 20) calls dialect words "those terrible marks of the beast to the truly genteel", and in French, Montaigne, in one of his essays (1582), says, "I have never known a man from our part of the world who did not obviously reek of dialect and who did not offend pure French ears". Some are even ruder, scarcely seeing dialect as being human language at all.

Another problem is that many consider a dialect to be completely separate from a language, and fail to recognize that everyone speaks some sort of dialect, even if it is a standard dialect. In fact, if it would help, we might define a language as a family of dialects, but that still would not allow us to draw a borderline.

Using the term *variety* helps us avoid both of these problems, although we still have to be able to interpret what people say and write about different varieties, and consider why their attitudes to some kinds of varieties are so negative.

If we look at the varieties that are regional dialects, we find that they tend to change gradually from village to village, from county to county. There are rarely sharp breaks between such varieties, unless people are prevented from talking to each other by, for instance, a large mountain range. So if we take, as an example, the difference between German and Dutch, what is spoken right on the border between Germany and the Netherlands is likely to be neither standard Dutch nor standard German, but something which is somewhere between the two. Despite that, a person who lives on the Dutch side of the border may fill out a tax declaration in Dutch, read a Dutch language newspaper, come home in the evening and watch television in Dutch, while a person who lives on the German side may carry out all these activities in German. The domains of the languages may have firmer lines between them than what is actually spoken on the ground. Similar borderlines are found between, for instance, Russian and Ukrainian, Slovak and Polish, Norwegian and Swedish.

One of the main criteria that are frequently offered for distinguishing between languages and varieties of those languages is that different languages are not mutually comprehensible whereas varieties of the same language (e.g. dialects) are. This can be shown to be false in both directions. There are languages whose speakers can understand each other and there are regional dialects whose speakers cannot understand each other. Moreover, what is comprehensible can change over time.

One point that must be made here, however, is that different varieties (whether we think of them as different dialects or different languages) are mutually comprehensible only if there is good will on both sides. Where there is no good will, mutual comprehension (or the report of it) can remain low. Danes who watch Swedish TV may nevertheless fail to understand Swedes when there is an international football match on between the two countries and Swedes are viewed as the opposition. The same people attending a professional conference may understand each other perfectly. In what follows, we shall assume that there is such good will applying.

Spaniards can understand the basic message when Italians talk Italian; Russian and Ukrainian can be understood by speakers of the other; Danish and Norwegian Bokmål can easily be read by people who speak the other language, although the spoken language may be harder to interpret; speakers of Hindi cannot read Urdu, because it is written in a different alphabet, but for everyday matters they can understand each others' speech; Spaniards can understand a fair amount of Portuguese. There is even a saying that *Good butter and good cheese is good English and good Fries*, which, although exaggerated, suggests some level of mutual understanding between speakers of English and Friesian. Mutual understanding is not an either/or state of affairs; some pairs of languages lend themselves to better understanding than others. But sometimes a degree of mutual understanding is possible between speakers of different languages.

At the same time, lack of understanding is possible between people who think they are talking the same language. Such a lack of understanding usually occurs between varieties which are quite distant from the standard varieties, but sometimes even varieties which are not very far apart can cause problems for speakers. Many people will have experience, if they have travelled in Britain, of having come across people that they have failed to understand. I couldn't understand some young farmers from rural Aberdeenshire I met on one trip. Most people from the south of England have difficulty in understanding Tyneside English, until they get used to it. There's a famous Tyneside song about a boy called George who loses something. Shorn of unnecessary repetitions and choruses, the song starts:

(1) Wor Geordie's lost his penker
    Doon the double raw
    It ralled into the coondy

Some of the unfamiliar words here are spellings designed to capture the Tyneside accent: *wor* means 'our', *doon* means 'down', *ralled* means 'rolled'. Such differences in pronunciation are sufficient for the uninitiated to fail to understand the spoken language. But very few people from south of Durham would understand *penker* 'a ball-bearing or stone sphere, used as a marble'. A *double raw* ('double row') is a set of back-to-back houses separated by a narrow lane in which there is a covered drain. And the *coondy* or *cundy* is the covered drain, a word unfamiliar to most people in central England, though it is found (or used to be found) in both the north and in Cornwall.

When the first talkies came from the US to Britain, people had great difficulty in understanding them, and when American servicemen arrived in Britain and in the Pacific in the Second World War, books were printed to help them understand the natives (and vice versa). Now, when we have been exposed to American English for so long through songs, films and television, this seems very strange, but it is the constant exposure that has made the difference. The traffic in the other direction is less intense, and some films set in places as diverse as Glasgow and New Zealand have had to be released with subtitles in the US.

Mutual comprehension, therefore, is not the answer to the division between dialect and language. And if we look at what speakers of a language share, the result is equally confusing.

It is generally acknowledged by phoneticians that if you say your own name three times in a row, no two of the repetitions will be identical. The differences may be tiny (a little extra length here, a slight difference in pitch there), but they indicate something of the ubiquity of variation. Tiny bits of variation within an individual can be magnified to quite large amounts of variability between individuals and even more between groups of individuals. So we could make a case for every single person speaking a different language. Linguists prefer the term *idiolect* here: the variety spoken by an individual. But there is variability even within an idiolect. I usually pronounce the word *neither* so that the first syllable rhymes with *sigh*, but in the expression *me neither*, the first syllable of *neither* rhymes with *see*. That is, I do not pronounce the word *neither* the same way on all occasions. If we look further afield, we find quite major differences between people who think they are speaking English. All of the things in (2) are usual from speakers who would claim to be speaking English.

(2) a I might could help you.
    b Kim is smoking a lot anymore.
    c These clothes need washed.
    d Don't talk while your mouth is empty.

(2a) is used by people on Tyneside, in the lowlands of Scotland and in parts of the eastern US to mean 'I might be able to help you'. (2b) means 'Kim is smoking a lot these days' for some speakers in the American mid-west. (2c) means 'These clothes need washing' for Scots and some Eastern US and Canadian speakers. And (2d) means 'Don't talk until your mouth is empty' for many speakers in Yorkshire (and the construction caused problems when notices went up on railway crossings which said *Don't cross while the light is flashing*). Yes, there is a lot that speakers of English have in common (for instance that *The cat bit the rat* is different from *The rat bit the cat*, with the first-mentioned animal doing the biting), but there is a huge amount that is not the same for speakers of what we might call "English".

One possible conclusion at this point might be that there is no such thing as "the English language". Instead there are millions of idiolects, some of which are similar enough to be mutually comprehensible, but all of which are distinct in some ways, and some of which are similar enough to a variety which is a standard variety for a large community to make that standard variety comprehensible. But this leaves out one very important factor in this debate, namely the political factor.

In 1945, the Yiddish scholar Max Weinreich famously stated that a language is a dialect with an army and a navy. He attributed the observation to an unnamed source. What this says is that for a variety to be recognized as a language, it has to have political and military power behind it. Since Weinreich's remarks were in Yiddish, the implication must have been that Yiddish was (and is) not a language – no doubt a deliberately provocative position. Burgess (1992: 146) later tried to capture the same insight by saying that "A language may be termed a dialect that waves a national flag". To support such a view, we have many situations where we can see that what is recognized as a language seems to be influenced by political factors, and the notion of a nation state. In the 1970s, Serbian and Croatian were seen as dialects of Serbo-Croat, but now that Serbia and Croatia are separate countries, Serbian and Croatian are seen as separate languages. It is probably true that individual Serbs and Croats always thought they were speaking different languages (just as some Americans and Britons are convinced that they are speaking different languages), but the picture presented to the world was one of linguistic unity. Similarly, Czech and Slovak became officially distinct languages with the break-up of the former Czechoslovakia in 1993. Mandarin and Cantonese are not mutually comprehensible. Different assessments put them as far apart as English and Swedish or English and French. A short example illustrating the difference is given in (3). Not only are the characters different, the individual elements are in many instances unrecognizable. Yet they are presented to the world as dialects of Chinese (the actual Chinese terms are not quite so definite). The attribution of a language to a state seems to take priority over any linguistic similarity or difference.

(3) 'He hasn't come back yet' in Mandarin and Cantonese. (The numbers under the Roman alphabet spellings indicate the tones (see Warren, Chapter 12 in this volume); *3sg* means 'he/she/it', *neg* means 'negative' or 'not')

Mandarin

他還沒回來。

Tʰa:	xai	mei	huei	lai.
44	25	31	25	25
3sg	yet	neg.	return	come

Cantonese

佢鍾未翻嚟。

Kʰœi	tsuŋ	mei	faan	lei.
12	22	21	55	21
3sg	yet	neg.	return	come

Similarly, Hindi in India and Urdu in Pakistan were once united under the name of Hindustani, but are given different labels in different nation states since the partition of India (in this case, they are also written in different writing systems). The political rule does not always apply, however. Norwegian Bokmål ('book language') and Nynorsk ('new Norwegian') are generally treated as distinct languages in Norway.

Counter-evidence to the political idea comes in the form of languages which are spoken across more than one country, sometimes being a national language in one, sometimes not being a national language at all. Basque is spoken in France and Spain, and is not a national language in either country. French is the national language of France, but is also spoken in Belgium and Switzerland. Warlpiri is spoken in Australia, but has no particular national standing. Yoruba is spoken in West Africa, including in Nigeria, Dahomey and Benin. Mari is spoken in Russia, but is not nationally important. Yiddish is spoken in, among other places, the US and Israel, without being a national language in either place. And there are, of course, many officially bilingual or multilingual countries, including Belgium, Canada, Finland, India, New Zealand, South Africa and Switzerland. Such examples imply that we might need to distinguish between languages spoken in many countries, languages spoken generally in one and languages which have minority status in just one country, and then, separate from that, languages which have official status as national languages and those that do not.

There are various assumptions built into the idea that a language and a state coexist, with the following implication that languages are defined politically. The first is the notion of the nation state – a single governed entity with a single culture and a single language – which is relatively modern. The ancient Greeks had city states. Italy and Germany were not united until the 19th century, Germany having had a series of principalities before then. To this day, the so-called United Kingdom contains several different cultures and, not necessarily matching those precisely, several different languages. Another assumption is that language and culture must match, yet there are many speakers who call their language English round the world but who live in very different cultural spaces, for instance, in Dublin, Edinburgh, London, Singapore and Sydney.

From all of this, the argument is that we cannot define the boundaries of "The English Language" (or many other languages) precisely, and that there is no solid definition to tell us whether something is or is not written or spoken in "the same language" as something else. What is spoken in Washington DC may be politically different from what is spoken in London, but they are largely mutually comprehensible (although given the large amount of variation in both cities, it would be foolish to assume that all London speakers of "English" can understand all Washington DC speakers of "English" and vice versa). Which criterion is given priority, and does it matter a great deal?

Linguists' definitions of a language provide little help. Language is variously defined as:

> It is a treasure buried by the practice of speech in people belonging to the same community ... ; language is not complete in any individual, but exists only in a collectivity.
>
> (de Saussure 1916)

> The totality of utterances that can be made in a speech community.
>
> (Bloomfield 1926)

> [A] language [is] a set (finite or infinite) of sentences, each finite in length, and constructed out of a finite set of elements.
>
> (Chomsky 1957: 13)

Yet what makes something a language is precisely the nature of the "community" which these definitions simply take for granted, and any set of sentences or utterances has to be a set which will be accepted by the community as part of the community's language. Even whether a language exists in the individual (as an idiolect) or only as part of a community is a controversial matter in linguistics, with people taking different points of view. The two need not be mutually incompatible.

Some of this is due to the very nature of a language. We can view a language as a series of structures, the structures built up of elements which we recognize as words (and their components). We can view a language as an entity in the brains of speakers. We can view a language as a social contract between speakers who agree (within limits, as we have seen) on what elements are words of the language and what structures in the language have which meanings. All of these are perfectly valid approaches to language, but none of them allows us to pin down the nature of "a language". If you think this is odd, consider the notion of "carpet". We could view a carpet as the transition from sheep to floor-covering, we could view it as an acoustic improvement, we could view it as interior design, and all of these things would be perfectly acceptable, but we might feel that none of them captures the essence of carpet-hood.

We also have "language" as distinct from "a language". Language is the facility which allows human beings to communicate by speech or by sign. It is the system which allows children to learn linguistic patterns from their parents and care-givers, and use those patterns creatively to make their own meanings and help make the world fit their desires. It is the cognitive ability which allows humans to create individual languages or dialects or idiolects or varieties and use them. The facility for language remains almost a total mystery, even when we understand some of the things it allows us to do. Various linguists have tried to define this sense of language, as well. Three definitions, from celebrated linguists, are quoted below. They indicate the difficulty of the task, the way linguists tend to focus on different aspects of language (and in the case of Hall's definition, sign language is surprisingly excluded), but they do not tell us what makes one language separate from another.

> Language is a purely human and non-instinctive method of communicating ideas, emotions, and desires by means of a system of voluntarily produced symbols.
>
> (Sapir 1921: 8)

> [T]he institution whereby humans communicate and interact with each other, conveying messages by means of systems of habitually used oral-auditory arbitrary symbols.
>
> (Hall 1966: 158)

[A] structure whose categorial elements can be exchanged with each other.

(Hjelmslev 1963: 98; my translation)

One way in which we might be able to start making inroads into all of this is to look at the notion of standard varieties. A standard variety is one that is codified, meaning that it is described in dictionaries and grammars. It is used in formal situations such as in government, in law courts, in the church, in higher education and in broadcasting. It tends to be relatively non-regional, and as a result may be spoken in a number of different accents (or pronunciations). This is unlike what happens with most regional varieties, which are pronounced only in the way that is normal in the relevant region. In England, the standard variety is what we might call Standard Southern British English, and although it can be spoken in accents from, for example, Yorkshire or Devon, is stereotypically pronounced in an accent which has various names, such as "Oxford English", "The Queen's English" and "Received Pronunciation". The labels are all slightly misleading. We might say that all the people who accept this as the standard form of their language are speaking "the same language".

There are various problems with such a position, or at least, things which might raise questions. American English and British English have their own dictionaries and grammars, and are used for the expected functions in their domains, although an American can function in higher education or the church on the European side of the Atlantic, and a Briton can function in such roles on the American side. Similarly, Australians have their own dictionaries and grammars, while New Zealanders have their own dictionaries, but not their own grammars. That is, we find clues pointing in both directions (the same language or different languages) with regard to these varieties. Scots may feel that they have competing standards: one based in Lowland Scotland, and another based in London. For some languages, there may not be a generally agreed standard variety at all: many speakers of New Zealand Māori try to avoid giving any variety the prestige of a standard, wanting to treat all varieties of Māori as equal.

To sum up, we have a situation where, in many cases, we cannot see firm boundaries between languages, we cannot explain why people think they are speaking the same language in some instances and different languages in other instances, where we know that mutual intelligibility does not provide a good definition of a language and where political considerations, although they are often a better guide to where we think of languages beginning and ending, do not always work, either. When linguists try to define languages, they often look at factors other than those which ordinary speakers use, and ignore the crucial question of what it is that makes a linguistic community (i.e. a group of people speaking the same language). The result is that we can only conclude that a label such as "the English language" denotes something which we cannot define – some kind of mythical entity in whose existence we all believe, despite the fact that none of us have ever seen it as an entirety. While we might be sure that a person speaking Basque and a person speaking English are speaking different languages, there are so many intermediate stages that all we might be able to say about a person from Washington DC and one from London is that they both think they are speaking English. And perhaps that is the best we can do in defining a language.

Acknowledgements

I should like to thank Catherine Churchman for the Mandarin and Cantonese examples, and Alexander Maxwell for the information on Šafárik.

Further reading

As an example of works explaining other varieties to Americans and American varieties to other people at the time of the Second World War, see Anon (1944), which can be found online at https://babel.hathitrust.org/cgi/pt?id=uiug.30112101024682&view=1up&seq=3

For the words *penker* and *cundy* see Wright (1898) under *panker* (and related usages under *pink*), and *cundy*.

For the examples in (2), see Trudgill (1983).

On Weinreich's definition of language, see Weinreich (1945).

On the Chinese terminology for languages and dialects, see Mair (1991).

The Danish original version of the definition from Hjelmslev (1963) is *en struktur, hvis kategorieled har indbyrdes udveksling.*

On Šafárik's classification of languages and dialects, see Maxwell (2018).

For previous attempts to define a language, see Simpson (1994) and Bauer (2007: chapter 1).

References

Anon. (1944). *A short guide to New Zealand*. Washington, DC: War and Navy Departments.
Bauer, Laurie. (2007). *The linguistics student's handbook*. Edinburgh: Edinburgh University Press.
Bloomfield, Leonard. (1926). A set of postulates for the science of language. *Language*, 2(3), 153–164.
Burgess, Anthony. (1992). *A mouthful of air*. London: Hutchinson.
Chomsky, Noam. (1957). *Syntactic structures*. The Hague and Paris: Mouton.

Hall, Robert A. Jr. (1966). *An essay on language*. Philadelphia and New York: Chilton.
Hardy, Thomas. (1886 [1995]). *The mayor of Casterbridge*. London: Everyman.
Hjelmslev, Louis. (1963). *Sproget*. København: Berlingske.
Mair, Victor. (1991). What is a Chinese "dialect/topolect'? Reflections on some key Sino-English linguistic terms. *Sino-Platonic Papers*, 29, 1–35.
Maxwell, Alexander. (2018). Effacing PanSlavism: Linguistic classification and historiographic misrepresentation. *Nationalities Papers*, 46(4), 633–653. DOI: 10.1080/00905992.2018.1448376
Montaigne, Michel de. (1582 [1991]). On presumption. In M.A. Screech (Tr.), *The essays of Michel de Montaigne*. London: Penguin.
Sapir, Edward. (1921). *Language*. London: Harvest.
Saussure, Ferdinand de. (1916). *Cours de linguistique générale*. Paris: Payot.
Simpson, J.M.Y. (1994). Language. In R.E. Asher and J.M.Y. Simpson (eds.), *The encyclopedia of language and linguistics, vol 4*, 1893–1897. Oxford: Pergamon.
Trudgill, Peter. (1983). *On dialect*. Oxford: Blackwell.
Weinreich, Max. (1945). Der YIVO un di problemen fun undzer tsayt. *YIVO Bletter*, 25(1), 3–18.
Wright, Joseph. (1898). *The English dialect dictionary, being the complete vocabulary of all dialect words still in use, or known to have been in use during the last two hundred years; founded on the publications of the English dialect society and on a large amount of material never before printed*. London: Frowde.

4 Do people swear because they don't know enough words?

Kate Burridge

Introduction

> In classrooms and hallways and on the playground, young people are using inappropriate language more frequently than ever, teachers and principals say. Not only is it coarsening the school climate and social discourse, they say, it is evidence of a decline in language skills.
>
> (Strauss 2005: A12)

One widely held view of swearing is that it is a sign of verbal deficiency. English teacher Dan Horwich, featured in Strauss's opinion piece, is clear on the matter – constant use of profanity reveals a poor vocabulary. James O'Connor, founder of the *Cuss Control Academy* (http://cusscontrol.com/remarks.html), is also quoted in this article:

> There are words virtually disappearing from our English language. When people are mad, what do they say? They say they are pissed off or [expletive] pissed off. No range. There is a big difference between being upset or livid. There is a big difference between irritated and infuriated.

A few years earlier, O'Connor had published his views on swearing in a best-selling self help book with the title *Cuss control: The complete book on how to curb your cursing.* In this book, he outlined four linguistic features of cuss words (under the heading "corruption of the language"):

- it's abrasive lazy language
- it doesn't communicate clearly
- it's the sign of a weak vocabulary
- it neglects more meaningful words

Judging by the media attention this book received, these criticisms struck a chord with many people – "[l]ess than two months on shelves, it was already into its third printing" (https://en.wikipedia.org/wiki/Cuss_Control). But is O'Connor correct here – are swearwords those "lazy" little words people reach for when they have no others at their disposal? And in a situation where we might find ourselves exclaiming that we are "pissed off", would alternatives like "upset" or "livid" really do the job? As with most aspects of language, it turns out swearwords are more complex and way more interesting than they appear in these popular accounts.

What is swearing?

> **Swear** *verb* **1.** To make a solemn declaration or statement with an appeal to God or a superhuman being, or to some sacred object, in confirmation of what is said; to take an oath. **2.** To promise or undertake something by an oath; to take an oath by way of a solemn promise or undertaking.
>
> (Oxford English Dictionary)

Modern English still has the original meaning of the verb *to swear*, as found in dictionary entries like the one given above; for example, *I swear by Almighty God to tell the truth, the whole truth, and nothing but the truth.* Such a formal act of swearing is described as *an oath.* At first profane oaths and profane swearing would have been statements made with disrespectful reference to the deity (the idea of taking of God's name in vain); these meanings have been around since at least the Middle Ages and probably much longer (there is a reference to them in the *First grammatical treatise* written around 1135; Haugen 1972). The idea then shifted from not respectful of religious practice (irreverent, blasphemous) to more generally coarse or indecent. The offensive senses of *swear* and *oath* have now come to dominate – if there is one regular feature of semantic change, it's that negative senses of words always take over from other senses! Profane swearing still includes religion-based profanity and blasphemy of course (i.e. irreligious language), but also encompasses the wealth of obscenities taken from the pool of "dirty words".

Hence, swearing these days is understood generally as the strongly emotional use of taboo terms to carry out such acts as abusing, offending, letting off steam, intensifying what is being said or simply signalling displeasure. Only taboo terms can really do the job; for instance, learned words for sexual organs and effluvia generally do not (**You faeces!*, **Urine off!*) and nor do certain mild obscenities and nursery terms (**You willie!* **Wee-wee on you!*) – the asterisk indicates that the following material is not natural English. Like slang, swearwords are more usually encountered in colloquial styles, though this is not to say they never occur in formal situations – indeed, since the 1990s "foul language" has been making regular appearances in the public arena, even in formal interviews on well-respected current affairs programmes (for example, ABC's *Lateline* and *Four Corners*; see Allan and Burridge 2010). This more public airing of swearwords is set against the backdrop of wide-ranging social changes. With growing egalitarianism and social democracy, we are now seeing all over the English-speaking world the solidarity function of language gaining over the status function, and with this comes the informalization of language, spoken and written – warts and all.

The reason swearwords attract so much attention is that they involve taboos, those aspects of our society that make us uncomfortable. These include the usual suspects – private parts, bodily functions, sex, anger, dishonesty, drunkenness, madness, disease, death, dangerous animals, fear, God and so on – what Adams and Newell (1994: 12) once described as "an infinite variety of things that go bump in the night". Taboo terms then provide the ready-made material for swearwords, and though there's remarkable agreement across languages, taboos do differ from society to society and they will also change over time. Many languages, for example, invoke disfiguring and, more especially, deadly diseases in maledictions (e.g. in some languages we find cholera invoked, as in the Polish expletive *Cholera!* and the Dutch curse *Krijg de klere!* 'get cholera'). Current English no longer does so, though *A pox on/of you!* (principally smallpox) was used in early modern English. More broadly, the English history of foul language has seen the sweeping transition from the religious to the secular (see Hughes 1998; 2006). When blasphemous and religiously profane language was no longer considered offensive (at least by a majority of speakers), what came in to fill the gap were the more physically and sexually based modes of expression (e.g. *bastard*, *bugger* and the so-called F and S words). More recently, it's the *-ist* taboos that have stepped up to the mark, making sexist, ageist, religionist and especially racist language not only contextually offensive, but legally so (e.g. *dago*, *kike*, *kaffir*, *nigger*, *mick*, *wog* and so on).

So why do we swear?

> As constructed in popular news media, swearing is superficially understood, masking its deeper and more complex communicative function.
> (Jay and Janschewitz 2008: 268)

Swearing has a number of uses that have been explored in recent publications such as Jay (2000), Pinker (2007), Stephens (2013) and Adams (2016). The following brief account has organized all the various uses into the four different (but overlapping) functions, as originally outlined in Allan and Burridge (2010). Each function is illustrated by examples drawn from actual conversations in the Australian and New Zealand contributions to the International Corpus of English (abbreviated ICE-AUS and ICE-NZ, respectively), and the Wellington Corpus of Spoken New Zealand English (abbreviated WSC).

The expletive function

Expletives are a kind of exclamatory interjection which, like other interjections, have a highly expressive function; cf. *Wow!*, *Ouch!*, *Shit!* They are uttered in intense emotional situations, as when a speaker is angry and frustrated, under pressure, in sudden pain, or confronted by something unexpected and usually, though not necessarily, undesirable (e.g. the 'onosecond', the horrible moment of realization that you've just made some terrible mistake). In the case of swearwords, it is the taboo quality that provides the catharsis required for the person to cope with the situation that provoked the expletive in the first place (e.g. an onosecond that involved pressing "reply all" and copying the embarrassing email to the entire organisation). It is the breaking of the taboo that triggers the release of energy.

(1) I ran off because it's something like you know eeh eeh eeh eh eh eeh eeh eeh eh suddenly this string just went Boom I don't know bang and I just went **Fuck** and ran off the stage. [ICE-AUS]
(2) Oh **shit** I'm getting lost. [ICE-NZ]

Sometimes the situation provoking the emotional outburst is pleasing; for example Britain's Bryony Shaw's outburst "I'm so fucking happy!" on winning a bronze medal at the 2008 Beijing Olympic Games.

(3) **SHIT** that's great. [WSC]

Expletives then are expressions of auto-catharsis, a release of extreme emotional energy. Clearly not everyone approves of this sort of auto-cathartic swearing, and society recognizes the dilemma by providing an out – people can choose between a swearword and one of the many conventionalized remodellings such as *Oh sugar!* or *Oh shucks!*

(4) Oh **sugar**. We've burnt it. [ICE-AUS]
(5) Oh **shucks** Tony could've made a gourmet. [ICE-AUS]

Euphemistic exclamations as illustrated in (4) and (5) are camouflaged cuss words – dubbed "linguistic fig leaves" by Rawson (2003), these words express the same emotions as full-blown obscenities. They nicely illustrate the sort of human doublethink that accompanies so much of our linguistic behaviour, especially in the area of euphemism and taboo.

The abusive function

Malediction can also "add insult to injury", and we do this by means of curses, name-calling or any sort of derogatory or contemptuous comments to intentionally slight, offend or wound a person in some way. Abusive language includes personal insults aimed at a second person (*You rotten bugger!*) or said of a third person (*The bastard stole my pen*); it also includes curses (*Bugger you!*) or directives (*Be buggered! Bugger off!*). Speakers may also resort to swearwords to talk about the things that irritate and annoy them, things that they disapprove of and wish to disparage, humiliate and degrade (*Writing grant applications is a bugger*).

(6) … show-off city **bitch** who thinks the sun shines out of her **arse**. [ICE-NZ]
(7) **Fuck** you NAME! [ICE-AUS]

Abusive swearing is also cathartic when it involves highly emotional language produced in anger or in frustration. However, while expletives are not generally addressed to anybody, in the case of the abusive language the release of extreme emotional energy can be directed at someone or even something, typically the source of the misfortune or the annoyance (e.g. the lid that has flown off the blender, causing soup to spray over the kitchen ceiling).

The social function

Across a range of different studies, social swearing has emerged as by far the most usual type (e.g. Ross 1960; Allan and Burridge 2010; Musgrave and Burridge 2014; Fägersten and Stapleton 2017). This is the use of swearwords to display in-group solidarity (especially when directed against outsiders), as a part of verbal cuddling or simply friendly banter.

(8) S1: pray to baby Jesus open up your heart let god's love come pouring in let god's love shine down on you like it has me and Miss Suzanne over here.
S2: oh **fuck off**. [ICE-AUS]
(9) Marketing strategies [for this uni project] are going to be interesting. Are you just choosing prostitution to be a **smart arse**? (WSC)

Examples (8) and (9) show the use of abusive terms with intended meanings that are the complete opposite of their primary meanings. It's a kind of mock impoliteness that is common between speakers who are close and who interact frequently. This usage is routine in Englishes around the world, and speakers often report that the more affectionate they feel towards someone, the more offensive the language can be towards that person.

Sometimes this banter becomes more like a ritual slanging match. In the following example (from urban Australia), you can see teenagers in front of an audience taunting each other with insults.

(10) **A:** If I had a pussy like yours I'd take it to the cat's home and have it put down ...
B: If I had brains like yours I'd ask for a refund ...
A: Well, if I had tits like yours I'd sell them off for basketballs ...
(Allen 1987: 66)

Ritual abuse of this nature is a competitive game, a kind of teasing. It uses precisely the same categories that you find in true insults, intended to wound, humiliate and belittle. However, they aren't an attack on an enemy or someone who is an outsider despised or disparaged, but an expression of group solidarity. These abusive address forms or epithets are uttered and reciprocated without animosity – and it all indicates strong bonds of friendship.

Ritual slanging matches are found in many communities, past and present. Late 19th-century American cowboys engaged in *cussing contests*, where a saddle would be awarded to the most abusive participant. *The dozens* is the term used to refer to the same behaviour among African Americans today. The dozens is also called *bagging, capping, chopping, cracking, cutting, dissing, hiking, joining, ranking, ribbing, serving, signifying, slipping, sounding* and *snapping*. An even earlier practice called *flyting* was around in Anglo-Saxon times and continued into the 15th and 16th centuries. Appropriately dubbed "the fine art of savage insult" (Hughes 2006: 141), it demonstrated considerable linguistic skill – the language could be sophisticated, passionate, poetic but also very vulgar. In true banter fashion (echoed these days by modern insult-trading rap battles), flyting contained imaginative abuse, including the sexual, religious and scatological (e.g. in a Scottish flyting match in 1585, *Kis þe cunt of ane kow* is how the poet Montgomerie begins his assault on rival poet Polward).

The stylistic function

The function of swearing can also relate to the manner of expression. For example, speakers might choose a taboo word (over a more benign synonym) and use it to display a particular attitude to what is being said; this might be exasperation, disapproval, surprise and so on. Consider the use of *bloody* in the following two examples:

(11) We're gonna **bloody** start doing that **bloody** extension to the house. (ICE-NZ)
(12) Oh yeah Essie Essie's There's no point in Eddie taking her out because she's **bloody** too stuffed you know. She's an old duck. She doesn't want to **bloody** stuff around town all day. […] Yeah she went down there and **bloody** went all over the place. (ICE-AUS)

In example (11) *bloody* expresses disapproval, but it's not aimed directly at the house extension (compare *that bloody extension* with *that beautiful extension*). It is the state of affairs that is lamentable (though of course the extension has something to do with it), and *bloody* smears the disapproval over the entire sentence. Words like *bloody* don't always convey an attitude of disapproval or exasperation, however, but may simply be markers of excitement or exuberance; in example (12) *bloody* serves more to colour or spice up what is being said.

The hidden benefits of swearing

> People need special words to convey emotion, which is, by nature, ineffable. For those who use them, swearwords are linked to emotion in a visceral way. People who speak more than one language report that they always curse in their native tongue; they can say swearwords in a second language but they don't feel them – the gut link to emotions just isn't there.
>
> (Tannen 2010)

Paradoxically, as Andersson and Trudgill (1990) point out, the line of reasoning given to argue the case against swearing is often the very same given in favour of swearing – people use swearwords when they have no others at their disposal. However, in the pro-swearing case, the taboo language is not perceived as a limitation or flaw in someone's character. "Instead, the argument says that there are certain situations in which no other words would be appropriate" (64). Indeed, all sorts of studies – linguistic, psychological, physiological and neurological – back up the story that swearwords are more arousing, more shocking, more memorable and more evocative than other language stimuli (see Allan and Burridge 2006: 244–50). So is it any wonder that people reach for them to vent spleen, hurl abuse, let off steam or simply colour their language? These words express a sentiment that ordinary words cannot. It's not for nothing they are described as "strong language".

Neurological evidence for the emotional impact of cuss words

A number of researchers have investigated the mental processes that support people's emotional responses to taboo words, some assessing the impact of expressions via techniques such as electrodermal monitoring (a kind of polygraph testing). For example, in Bowers and Pleydell-Pearce (2011) participants read aloud swearwords, euphemisms of the swearwords and also neutral stimuli at the same time as their emotional reactions were measured by electrodermal activity; the key finding was that swearwords evoke stronger skin conductance responses than either the sweet-smelling euphemisms or neutral stimuli.

There has also been considerable investigation into the effects of arousal on memory (e.g. MacWhinney et al. 1982; MacKay et al. 2004); again findings reveal that taboo words are always more stimulating than non-taboo words and people remember them better than neutral words. In a 2004 report, for example, MacKay and his colleagues describe the results of a psychological test known as the Stroop task. Different words (including taboo words) were displayed in salient colours, and participants were asked to name the colour and ignore the word. There were three telling effects. People could better remember colours associated with taboo words, and they had better recall of the words themselves. However, they were slower in naming the colour of taboo words. We infer from this that they were distracted by the disturbing nature of these words (Steven Pinker 2007 has described this as "an involuntary boggle"). Interestingly, this effect diminished with word repetition, which is consistent with what we've known for a long time – words wear out and emotional words are particularly prone to burnout.

The results for bilingual speakers provide an additional perspective. Research going back to Gonzalez-Regiosa (1976), Anooshian and Hertel (1994), and more recently Harris et al. (2003), corroborates that the most emotional reactivity is to taboo words in both languages, but stimuli will elicit greater emotional arousal (and better recall) in the first language. But why would the language learned early in life, especially emotive expressions such as dirty words, elicit stronger physiological responses than language learned later in life? The scandal in July 2015 of the cussing Minions sheds some light on how this happens.

At this time, McDonald's was giving out free Minion toys with its Happy Meals. The toys were speaking Minionese (nonsense prattle), but outraged parents heard swearwords: "Well I'll be damned" and "What the fuck" (https://youtube.com/watch?v=hgl3eiu8evw). Those thousands of others who clicked on the link heard them too, and the more they listened, the clearer these obscenities became. People will perceive meaningful patterns in meaningless bursts of noise, just as they will perceive meaningful images in meaningless blobs of ink. And given the saliency of these expressions, it's not surprising parents heard obscenities when their brains were searching for patterns in the auditory inkblots. Concerned parents then confiscated the toys from their children, and asked McDonald's to take them out of circulation. This is precisely how young children pick up the emotive components of these words at such a young age. Dirty words come with social rewards ("Look, everyone is paying attention to my Minion toy!") and of course they come with penalties ("Oh no, they're taking away my Minion toy!"). When the McDonald's promotion was concluded, many young minds were switched on to the power of these special words. But when acquired by late bilinguals, these very same words lack the cultural imprint of the forbidden. Hence, the expressive force is always much weaker in second-language swearwords; in fact, subjects often report feeling nothing when they hear or utter taboo words and phrases in their second language.

Linguistic evidence for the emotional impact of cuss words

> Cunt is an utterly grotesque word […] it's just a guttural, ghastly, nasty word.
>
> (Woods 2007)

In the case of swearwords, people make a very real connection between sound and sense, as if the form of the expression somehow communicates the essential nature of what it represents. It is the reason these words are branded with the label "dirty" and why they are so often described as unpleasant or ugly sounding. It is this perceived relationship between sound and meaning that forms the very basis for the distinction between an unmentionable taboo word (*cunt*) on the one hand, and its mentionable euphemistic alternative (*vagina*) on the other. Taboo words are felt to be intrinsically nasty and this is why they can be so powerful and so disruptive.

Hence, taboo senses have a saliency that dominates and will typically quash the other senses of any language expression recruited as euphemism. Existing vocabulary is abandoned as speakers create new expressions, or find new meanings for old expressions. The attention-grabbing nature of these words can have the effect of eliminating even unrelated expressions simply because of their phonetic proximity (e.g. the demise of monosyllabic <f—k> words in English like *feck* 'efficiency'; the disappearance of the French title *count* – both *count* and *cunt* originally shared the short vowel [ʊ] of modern *pud*; see Burridge and Benczes 2019).

Clearly the swearwords that draw from the pool of dirty words are anything but meaningless words that fail to communicate an effective message. As Jay (2000: 91, 137) has described, "[c]ursing intensifies emotional expressions in a manner that inoffensive words cannot achieve". Take the example of a simple insult. It might pick on a person's physical appearance, mental ability, character, behaviour, beliefs, family, race and so on, and of course, it doesn't have to involve swearwords – *You dag!* can be an insult, but it is not a swearword. However, abusive language that involves taboo words will always have that extra layer of emotional intensity and extra capacity to offend. When Aurelio Vidmar, the coach of soccer team *Adelaide United*, lashed out (in the wake of the Reds' 4–0 loss to Melbourne Victory in February 2009) and described Adelaide as a "pissant town", he used an unusual insult that embraced both an insect and one of the tabooed bodily effluvia – an effective double-whammy to invoke something inconsequential, irrelevant and worthless.

In fact, the beneficial effects of swearwords over neutral vocabulary go well beyond the colour and spice this language might add to an utterance. Much recent research has revealed the various therapeutic aspects of swearing, in particular the surprising upsides of automatic speech such as expletives (*Fuck!*). This kind of emotional language shares functions with other (often involuntary) vocalizations such as laughter, crying and screaming, all of which can make us feel better, improve our focus and cope with stressful and even painful situations.

Swearers lead less stressful lives

> [...] those who swear are likely to suffer less from stress than those who do not swear.
>
> (Montagu 1968: 88)

Evidence abounds that swearing is an emotion-based coping mechanism that makes us feel more resilient. Speaking on her book *Swearing is good for you*, Emma Byrne is quoted as saying "[s]tudies show that when you put people in stressful situations and tell them they cannot swear, their performance goes down and their experience of stress is much greater" (https://health.com/mind-body/benefits-of-cursing).

Many studies have shown that swearing will diminish dramatically under extremely stressful circumstances. Writing of the use of *fuck* by British soldiers in World War I, Brophy and Partridge (1931: 16f) reported that to omit the word was an effective way of indicating emergency and danger ("...if a sergeant said, 'Get your -ing rifles!' it was understood as a matter of routine. But if he said, 'Get your rifles!' there was an immediate implication of emergency and danger"). Helen Ross (1960) examined swearing among British zoologists in the Norwegian Arctic during continuous daylight; she reported that swearing increased noticeably when people were relaxed and happy, but diminished significantly at times of severe stress:

[T]here seemed to be two types of swearing: "social" swearing and "annoyance" swearing. Social swearing was intended to be friendly and a sign of being "one of the gang"; it depended upon an audience for its effect, while annoyance swearing was a reaction to stress […] Under conditions of serious stress, there was silence.

(Ross 1960: 480f)

In a more recent analysis of swearing by psychiatric ward personnel at staff meetings over a six-month period, Gallahorn (1971) reported expletive usage reduced when ward tension was intense. And while the disturbing recordings of air-crash pilots show plenty of swearwords early on in the recording, they are often absent from the final utterances just before the black box flight recorder cuts out (http://planecrashinfo.com/lastwords.htm).

Swearing helps alleviate pain and makes you stronger

In certain trying circumstances, urgent circumstances, desperate circumstances, profanity furnishes a relief denied even to prayer.

(Mark Twain, cited in Paine 1912: 213–14)

Stephens and colleagues were responsible for the now famous "Ice Water" experiment, showing convincingly that swearing helps us endure pain (Stephens et al. 2009). Participants were asked to plunge their hand into a tub of ice water and hold it there for as long as possible while repeating a single swearword of their choice. They then repeated the experiment, but this time they were only able to say an everyday word, one that could be used to describe a table (such as *wooden* or *round*). The majority of participants were able to keep their hands in the ice water for a considerably longer period of time when using the swearword, supporting the link between swearing and a higher pain threshold. Significantly, however, this effect was diminished for habitual swearers. Recall the research that clearly shows how frequent use bleaches a term such as *fuck* of its taboo quality; so it's not surprising that "overuse of swearing in everyday situations lessens its effectiveness as a short-term intervention to reduce pain" (Stephens and Umland 2011: 1278).

New research from Stephens and colleagues also revealed a positive effect of swearing on strength (Stephens et al. 2018). These researchers found that when people cursed their way through the half-minute bike challenge, their peak power rose by 24 watts on average according to the study, and in the ten-second grip task (where they had to squeeze a hand dynamometer), swearers boosted their strength by the equivalent of 2.1kg.

The burning question is of course: could performance be improved or pain be modulated by "more proper" vocalizations such as *Aahhh!*, *Ow!* or *Ouch*?

Certainly, Swee and Schirmer (2015) found similar results to Stephens' ice water experiment – "Ow!" or some similar exclamation decreased people's perception of pain and increased their tolerance to it. However, the very fact that a term is taboo would improve its value as auto-cathartic: the breaking of the taboo is after all an emotional release. Recall the psycholinguistic studies reported earlier that showed the potency of taboo words (*Fuck! Shit!*) over their euphemistic remodellings (*Fudge! Shucks!*).

Abusive swearing replaces physical violence

> It has been said that he who was the first to abuse his fellow-man instead of knocking out his brains without a word, laid thereby the basis of civilization.
>
> (Jackson [1879] 1958: 179)

Swearing is an emotion-based coping mechanism that makes us feel more resilient. But what about the link between hostility and forbidden words in abusive swearing? In this less heroic function, cuss words provide that bonus layer of emotional intensity and added capacity to offend in curses, name-calling or any sort of derogatory comment directed towards others to insult or wound them. It is difficult to imagine there is any plus side to this linguistic behaviour.

However, prominent British neurologist John Hughlings Jackson offered an interesting perspective on this type of swearing. Among his ideas (many of which became the basis of modern scientific neurology) was the suggestion that swearing (verbal aggression) came to replace physical aggression. As Finkelstein (2019) describes in her account of swearing and the brain, this suggestion has some support from the behaviour of non-human primates. Reporting on the observation of primatologist Frans de Waal, Finkelstein describes an incident involving a group of female chimpanzees attempting to prevent an alpha male from attacking another male – had the barking not stopped the attack, there is no doubt physical violence would have ensued. "Maybe in aggression, as in pain, swearing 'steals' resources from physical violence and replaces them with symbolic, verbal, aggression or aggressive vocalization" (136). In other words, when we vent spleen or blow off steam, those cascading cuss words allow us to express our anger or frustration towards someone or something symbolically, rather than through physical behaviours. (Appropriately, the physical link with aggression is part of the etymology of the word *insult* – it derives from the Latin word *in* + *sultare* meaning literally 'to jump on'.)

Even those not convinced by this argument should remember that abuse is the least usual type of swearing. The discussion of social swearing above showed how cuss words more typically act as in-group solidarity markers within a shared relaxed and colloquial style. Like the "incorrect" language of non-standard grammar, these words fall outside what is good and proper, and help to define the gang. They can be a cultural indicator, a sign of endearment (*G'day you old bastard*), a part of steamy pillow talk and, in many societies, an important component of humour. Indeed, humour involves all sorts of things that speakers generally do not cope with and, combined with swearing, provides one of the main ritual contexts for taboo violation today.

Swearers and their vocabularies

> We cannot help but judge others on the basis of their speech. Unfortunately, when it comes to taboo language, it is a common assumption that people who swear frequently are lazy, do not have an adequate vocabulary, lack education or simply cannot control themselves.
>
> (Jay and Jay 2015: 251)

So swearing does appear to have a number of useful functions – what does this then mean for the popular perception of swearers as having underdeveloped vocabularies? This is a notion that researchers Jay and Jay (2015) have dubbed the "poverty-of-vocabulary" assumption – the idea that people resort to taboo words because they can't find better words with which to express themselves. Measuring people's overall linguistic fluency and correlating this with their taboo language use is not an easy task, but what research has been carried out does not support the popular view in any way.

McEnery and Xiao (2004), for example, examined the distribution pattern of *fuck* in all its forms (no less than 4806 examples in the 100,000,000-word British National Corpus) taking into account age, social class and education level. Certainly their findings didn't suggest there was any correlation between taboo words and IQ/lexicon size. In fact, they reported that those of the highest social rank in terms of UK socio-economic classifications (e.g. those with professional occupations and higher managerial positions) used *fuck* way more than those lower down the social scale. So this contradicts another popular assumption that links taboo language with a working class culture.

Jay and Jay's (2015) research, quoted above, also doesn't suggest swearing is any indicator of limited vocabulary or low intelligence. Using a test known as the Controlled Oral Word Association Test (COWAT), these researchers asked volunteers to come up with as many animal words and taboo words as they could beginning with a specific letter, such as A, F and S; participants were allowed one minute for the spoken test and two minutes for the written test. It's true that this work did only measure people's ability to produce words in a certain category (animals), and drew on the student population of a small liberal arts college (so perhaps not your stereotypical swearers). However, the overall finding of the study was clear: swearing fluency correlated overall with general verbal fluency in both spoken and written formats. As Jay and Jay conclude "fluency is fluency".

People who swear aren't necessarily otherwise inarticulate, and, arguably, a good taboo lexicon may be considered a complement to the lexicon as whole, ideally a mechanism for emotional expression of all sorts: anger, frustration, and derogation, but also surprise and elation.
(Jay and Jay 2015: 8)

Swearwords as discourse particles

> Swearing is like mustard; a great ingredient but a lousy meal. We need that part of language to keep its potency, its slightly risky nature, otherwise it wouldn't be swearing.
> (Byrne 2017: 200–1)

There is one final category of swearword that needs attention – those swearwords that are used with such regularity it is hard to imagine there is any auto-cathartic value in them at all.

Lashings of obscenities have become the earmark of celebrated chef and restaurateur Gordon Ramsay, so much so that one of his television cooking series is called *The F-Word*. A single episode of an earlier series, *Ramsay's Kitchen Nightmares*, featured some version of this F-word on no less than 80 occasions over a 40-minute period. An ABC program reporting on the backlash provided the following sample:

(13) GORDON RAMSAY: Would you like it whole or diced? F**ken appetisers. You're not a f**ken cheerleader because that is f**ken embarrassing because it is a f**ken disgrace. (https://abc.net.au/pm/content/2008/s2198990.htm)

Ramsay is using obscenities here as discourse particles (words and phrases that have a role in managing the flow and structure of spoken language) – where other people might use *like*, *well*, *I mean*, *you know* and the like. Their frequency contributes significantly to people's negative perceptions of swearing, as well as the assessment that someone like Ramsay has a stunted vocabulary (he would probably do well to heed the warning by *Vogue* editor Joan Campbell [1986: 11] that "nothing is more deadening to the taste buds than a flavour repeated too often").

This is not to suggest that such bleached swearwords are empty. Like other discourse particles, these expressions convey subtle nuances of meaning and can have complex effects on utterances (Wierzbicka 2002, for example, describes the various meanings of *bloody* in Australian English and shows how they provide important clues to Australian attitudes and values). Yet, one must presume that under such circumstances the auto-cathartic value of both the expletives and the epithets is reduced, and that either alternative expressions will be invented, or some other form of catharsis will be sought – research shows quite clearly that with frequent use a term, such as *fuck*, will lose its standard force. Recall too those studies that confirm swearing will diminish under very stressful circumstances, suggesting that if Ramsay's swearing is indeed annoyance swearing, television viewers never get to see the very worst of what goes on in his kitchen.

Conclusion

> *Hamlet*: Why, then, 'tis none to you, for there is nothing either good or bad, but thinking makes it so.
>
> (*Hamlet*, Act 2, Scene 2)

Andersson and Trudgill (1990: 6) cite a Swedish study on swearing which revealed that 75% of the adults surveyed disliked swearing, and yet 75% of those surveyed also admitted to swearing themselves. Their book had examined different forms of what is perceived by many as "bad language" (including slang, dialects, accents, jargon and of course cussing) and this was a recurring theme – people continue to engage in linguistic behaviour that they take strong exception to. As the authors conclude, there must always be something good about this so-called "bad language" or it simply wouldn't endure.

There is no research to support the idea that the 75% of Swedes using bad language do so because of a limitation in their vocabulary, and there is no basis for the branding of swearers with such labels as "ignorant", "uneducated", "lazy" or "stupid". In fact, Jay and Jay (2015: 8) conclude that "a voluminous taboo lexicon may better be considered an indicator of healthy verbal abilities rather than a cover for their deficiencies". The brains of these Swedes want to swear for good reasons and these include relieving stress, coping with pain, increasing strength and endurance, and bonding with friends and colleagues. These socio-cultural and psychological benefits go way beyond the simple satisfaction that comes from transgression and the liberating effects of violating linguistic taboos. They offer strong motivation that no doubt accounts for the consistent historical failure of legislation and penalties against swearing. History makes clear that censorship and repression, whether they amount to full-blown sanctions or merely social niceties, seem only ever to coincide with more exuberant times of swearing (Hughes 1998). Swearwords appear to flourish all the more vigorously on a diet of individual censoring and public disapproval. Clearly, we are not looking at just some nasty habit that people can be broken of, like smoking in restaurants or nail-biting.

Further reading

Jay's works are among the first serious and extensive examinations of swearing from both a linguistic and psychological point of view; e.g. Jay (1992) addresses the relationship between cursing and such things as language acquisition, gender stereotypes, anger expression and offensiveness (using data from field studies and laboratory-based experiments). Stephens (2013) is a summary of recent research on the psychological functions of swearing, including the author's own experiments assessing swearing as a response to pain; see also Pinker (2007), Allan and Burridge (2010) and Adams (2016). McEnery (2009) uses corpus data to shed light on the typology and sociolinguistics of swearing, and Dewaele (2010) gives the multilingual perspective on swearwords and taboos. The various publications by Hughes offer valuable historical accounts of foul language around the English-speaking world; for example, Hughes (2006) is both an encyclopedia and social history of swearing; its entries cover everything from Anglo-Saxon flyting ("the fine art of savage insult") through to the modern insult-trading rap battle.

References

Adams, Michael. (2016). *In praise of profanity*. Oxford: Oxford University Press.
Adams, Phillip and Patrice Newell. (1994). *The Penguin book of Australian jokes*. Ringwood: Penguin.
Allan, Keith and Kate Burridge. (2006). *Forbidden words: Taboo and the censoring of language*. Cambridge: Cambridge University Press.
Allan, Keith and Kate Burridge. (2010). Swearing and taboo language in Australian English. In Pam Peters, Peter Collins and Adam Smith (eds.), *Comparative grammatical studies in Australian and New Zealand English*, 295–347. Amsterdam and Philadelphia: Benjamins.
Allen, Wendy F. (1987). *Teenage speech: The social dialects of Melbourne teenagers*. B.A. Honours Thesis. Linguistics Department, La Trobe University, Melbourne.
Andersson, Lars-Gunnar and Peter Trudgill. (1990). *Bad language*. Harmondsworth: Penguin.
Anooshian, Linda J. and Paula T. Hertel. (1994). Emotionality in free recall: Language specificity in bilingual memory. *Cognition and Emotion*, 8(6), 503–514. DOI:10.1080/02699939408408956
Bowers Jeffrey, S. and Christopher W. Pleydell-Pearce. (2011). Swearing, euphemisms, and linguistic relativity. *PloS one*, 6(7). DOI:10.1371/journal.pone.0022341
Brophy, John and Eric Partridge. (1931). *Songs and slang of the British soldier: 1914–1918*. 3rd edn. London: Routledge & Kegan Paul.
Burridge, Kate and Réka Benczes. (2019). Taboo as a driver of language change and lexical obsolescence. In Keith Allan (ed.), *The Oxford handbook of taboo words and language*, 180–99. Oxford: Oxford University Press.

Byrne, Emma. (2017). *Swearing is good for you: The amazing science of bad language*. London: Profile Books.
Campbell, Joan. (1986). *Vogue entertaining*. Australia: Octopus Books.
Dewaele, Jean-Marc D. (2010). *Emotions in multiple languages*. Basingstoke: Palgrave Macmillan.
Fägersten, Kristy Beers and Karyn Stapleton. (2017). Introduction: Swearing research as variations on a theme. In Kristy Beers Fägersten and Karyn Stapleton (eds.), *Advances in swearing research: New languages and new contexts*, 1–16. Amsterdam: Benjamins.
Finkelstein, Schlomit Ritz. (2019). Swearing and the brain. In Keith Allan (ed.), *The Oxford handbook of taboo words and language*, 108–39. Oxford: Oxford University Press.
Gallahorn, George E. (1971). The use of taboo words by psychiatric ward personnel. *Psychiatry*, 34(3), 309–21.
Gonzalez-Regiosa, Fernando. (1976). The anxiety arousing effect of taboo words in bilinguals. In Charles Donald Spielberger and Rogelio Diaz Guerrero (eds.), *Cross-cultural anxiety*, 89–105. Washington, DC: Hemisphere.
Harris, Catherine L., Ayse Ayçiçegi and Jean B. Gleason. (2003). Taboo words and reprimands elicit greater autonomic reactivity in a first language than in a second language. *Applied Psycholinguistics*, 24(4), 561–79. DOI:10.1017/S0142716403000286
Haugen, Einar. (1972). *The first grammatical treatise: The earliest Germanic phonology*. London: Longman.
Hughes, Geoffrey. (1998). *Swearing: A social history of foul language*. London: Penguin.
Hughes, Geoffrey. (2006). *An Encyclopedia of swearing: The social history of oaths, profanity, foul language, and ethnic slurs in the English-speaking world*. London: Sharpe.
Jackson, John H. (1958). *Selected writings of John Hughlings Jackson*. Vol. I. New York: Basic Books.
Jay, Timothy B. (1992). *Cursing in America: A psycholinguistic study of dirty language in the courts, in the movies, in the schoolyards and on the streets*. Amsterdam: Benjamins.
Jay, Timothy B. (2000). *Why we curse: A neuro-psycho-social theory of speech*. Amsterdam and Philadelphia: Benjamins.
Jay, Kristin L. and Timothy B. Jay. (2015). Taboo word fluency and knowledge of slurs and general pejoratives: Deconstructing the poverty-of-vocabulary myth. *Language Sciences*, 52, 251–9. DOI:10.1016/j.langsci.2014.12.003
Jay, Timothy B. and Kristin Janschewitz. (2008). The pragmatics of swearing. *Journal of Politeness Research. Language, Behaviour, Culture*, 4(2), 267–88. DOI:10.1515/JPLR.2008.013
MacKay, Donald G., Meredith Shafto and Jennifer K. Taylor. (2004). Relations between emotion, memory, and attention: Evidence from taboo Stroop, lexical decision, and immediate memory tasks. *Memory and Cognition*, 32(3), 474–88. DOI:10.3758/BF03195840

MacWhinney, Brian, Janice M. Keenan and Peter Reinke. (1982). The role of arousal in memory for conversation. *Memory and Cognition*, 10(4), 308–17. DOI:10.3758/BF03202422

McEnery, Anthony. (2009). *Swearing in English: Bad language, purity and power from 1586 to the present*. London: Routledge.

McEnery, Anthony and Zhonghua Xiao. (2004). Swearing in modern British English: The case of *fuck* in the BNC. *Language and Literature*, 13(3), 235–68. DOI:10.1177/0963947004044873

Montagu, Ashley. (1968). *The anatomy of swearing*. New York: Macmillan.

Musgrave, Simon and Kate Burridge. (2014). Bastards and buggers – Historical snapshots of Australian English swearing patterns. In Kate Burridge and Réka Benczes (eds.), *Wrestling with words and meanings: Essays in honour of Keith Allan*, 3–32. Melbourne: Monash University Publishing.

O'Connor, James. (2000). *Cuss control: The complete book on how to curb your cursing*. New York: Three Rivers.

Paine, Albert Bigelow. (1912). *Mark Twain, a biography: The personal and literary life of Samuel Langhorne Clemens*. 2 Vols. New York: Harper and Brothers.

Pinker, Steven. (2007). *The stuff of thought: Language as a window into human nature*. New York: Penguin.

Rawson, Hugh. (2003). *Dictionary of euphemisms and other doublespeak: Being a compilation of linguistic fig leaves and verbal flourishes for artful users of the English language*. Pittsford: Castle Books.

Ross, Helen E. (1960). Patterns of swearing. *Discovery*, 21(November), 479–81.

Stephens, Richard. (2013). Swearing – The language of life and death. *The Psychologist*, 26(9), 650–3.

Stephens, Richard, John Atkins and Andrew Kingston. (2009). Swearing as a response to pain. *Neuroreport*, 20(12), 1056–60. DOI:10.1097/WNR.0b013e32832e64b1

Stephens, Richard, David K. Spierer and Emmanuel Katehis. (2018). Effect of swearing on strength and power performance. *Psychology of Sport and Exercise*, 35, 111–17.

Stephens, Richard and Claudia Umland. (2011). Swearing as a response to pain – Effect of daily swearing frequency. *Journal of Pain*, 12(12), 1274–81. DOI:10.1016/j.jpain.2011.09.004

Strauss, Valerie. (2005). More and more, kids say the foulest things: Anti-swearing efforts falling on deaf ears. *Washington Post*, Tuesday, April 12, A12.

Swee, Genevieve and Annett Schirmer. (2015). On the importance of being vocal: Saying "Ow" improves pain tolerance. *The Journal of Pain*, 16(4), 326–34. DOI:10.1016/j.jpain.2015.01.002

Tannen, Deborah. (2010). *When mere words aren't enough* (New York Times blog: Room for debate). https://roomfordebate.blogs.nytimes.com/2010/04/12/why-do-educated-people-use-bad-words

Wierzbicka, Anna. (2002). Australian cultural scripts: *Bloody* revisited. *Journal of Pragmatics*, 34(9), 1167–209. DOI:10.1016/S0378-2166(01)00023-6

Woods, Pete. (2007). *The C word: How we came to swear by it*. (30/7/2007). http://www.bbc.co.uk/programmes/b007sj0x

5 Is written grammar better than spoken grammar?

Andreea S. Calude

Introduction

It is with great fondness and excitement that I will read just about any prose written by Zadie Smith, Amitav Ghosh or Jhumpa Lahiri. These master story-spinners and English language virtuosos have the ability to transport me across time, space and culture into completely new worlds by their mere, yet expertly-assembled, word sequences. Take the opening sentence from *The hungry tide* by Amitav Ghosh for example:

> Kanai spotted her the moment he stepped onto the crowded platform: he was deceived neither by her close-cropped black hair, nor by her clothes, which were those of a teenage boy – loose cotton pants and an oversized white shirt.

And now compare it with the following transcript from a portion of spontaneous, spoken conversation recorded in the late 1990s in New Zealand:

Speaker A: pub crawls real ones <laughs>
Speaker B: do you not have them here?
Speaker C: <laughs>
Speaker A: too much work
Speaker C: there was one in what um <longer pause> in the first term? or the end of the second term
Speaker A: the kayak club was going to have one down the Avon river through town
Speaker C: speaking of that I went and saw Brian today down in the um h v lab they've got pairs whole lot of rafts there that he was blowing up checking for leaks and patching them up <pause> it was quite I think must be him and the postgrads going white water rafting or something
Speaker A: yeah yeah oh right oh yeah

Speaker C: mm <pause> getting right into it
Speaker A: yeah John when I was talking to John the other day he's into kayaking eh he says oh yeah we're going to go for a kayak <longer pause> don't know what river the Motu or somewhere I suppose out that way yeah

It is no wonder that some people conclude spoken language has no real grammar or structure and is generally "inferior" to the glorious written word. The written sentence is eloquently crafted into a carefully manicured collection of well-planned prose. In contrast, the speech extract is jagged and abrupt, full of false starts and repetitions, overlapping speech and people talking while still composing their thoughts. But it wasn't always so! Compared to speaking, writing is a recent innovation. In 1935, one of the most respected grandfathers of linguistic theory, Leonard Bloomfield, wrote that written language was in fact nothing more than a mechanism for recording spoken language (the true and primary archetype of language) and not really worth studying in and of itself. How the tables have turned!

Today, the view of the written word as superior to the spoken one has become so ingrained, that linguist Per Linell termed it "the written language bias", and he went on to write an entire book on the subject. It is not uncommon to stumble upon the even more extreme view, that "spoken grammar" is itself a myth and a contradiction in terms (as a PhD student studying aspects of spoken New Zealand English grammar, I was often faced with stunned expressions from people baffled by their perceived lack of my object of study; I also remember once exchanging views with a heliophysicist who received similarly stunned expressions related to his research area, "Maybe all I do is get up each morning and check that the sun still shines, but at least the sun does exist", he would commiserate). But is there any truth to the view that the grammar of written language is *better* than the grammar of spoken language?

Written and spoken language – a tale of beauty and the beast

Despite the fact that the terms "spoken language" and "written language" imply a dichotomy, in reality, this is not the case. They form a continuum with some genres at the more "spoken" end (spontaneous unplanned conversation, telephone conversations), and other genres at the more "written" end (written academic texts, legal documents). In the middle of the continuum, there are intermediate genres which share properties with both speech and writing, such as spoken news broadcasts (which despite being spoken are planned and edited, like written language), or written diary entries (which despite being written, are off-the-cuff and unedited, like spoken language). The genres at the opposite ends of the continuum differ in major respects, ranging from how they are acquired, produced, accessed and used. It is for these reasons that linguists resort to the term "medium" when distinguishing between speaking and writing, and reserve the term "genre" for specific types of language uses, such as diary entries, newspaper articles and scientific prose. Let's consider five of these now.

Spoken language is relatively **easy and quick** for young (hearing) babies to acquire, and for the most part, babies do not even remember doing so. While the acquisition process is slightly more gruelling for the parents witnessing it, there are sufficient exciting and endearing milestones to distract them along the way. For example, the moment children spot patterns and are able to generalize them, they run wild with the new knowledge. It is therefore common to hear English-speaking children express their ideas using phrases like: *Look! The sheeps are sleeping*; *I bringed it*; *You deaded the spider, mummy*; *This book is gooder than that one*. But these delicious moments are short-lived and soon enough, children will conform to the more accepted language patterns they hear around them.

Unlike the relatively wide access to spoken language, written language has historically not been available to all members of society, with many countries still retaining low literacy rates today. In the past, it was only priests and high-ranking members of society who had access to education and were therefore in the privileged position of being *able* to read and write. Thankfully, with education reforms and changes in social policies, literacy spread within Western societies. But even then, as most school and university students will attest, unlike learning to speak, learning to write is not an easy process and mastering the skill takes time and effort – for many, it remains an elusive and scary pursuit. It also involves various stages, including learning to form and shape letters (or pictorial diagrams, depending on the language), stringing well-formed phrases and sentences together, and eventually, building longer units of prose. Neither of these stages is easy or forgettable for many of us.

Any given language tends to be strongly linked to its speakers – we cannot fathom a language without bringing to mind those who use it. This link highlights a parasitic characteristic of language: the reliance of language on its speakers. In fact, Nicholas Chater and Morten Christiansen (2008) have gone further to show that it is language which evolves to adapt to our brains, rather than vice versa. The strong connection between language and its speakers carries the equally strong transfer of values from speaker onto language. So it is that the language of the educated, the erudite and the privileged members of society – i.e. written language – has itself become elevated and superior in status by its very association with its users. Conversely, the language variety that is cheap to acquire and widely acquired – spoken language – is treated like an invisible commodity with little prestige. Yet imagine what life would be without it!

In English, we talk of "the gift of writing" which someone might be said to mystically possess in their ability to produce writing of exceptional stylistic quality. But when praising someone's speaking ability, we refer to "the gift of the gab" which does not imply a mysterious genius, but an inclination towards talking for the sake of talking, of being able to while time away chatting, or of being able to influence or entertain others (a useful skill on occasion but not quite on the same academic pedestal as the writing gift).

A second aspect of spoken language is its **immediacy**. What we think of as typical speech, (not pre-recorded, rehearsed or scripted language) happens off-the-cuff, with little or no planning, more or less straight out of our heads. This makes speech cognitively taxing because in a conversational setting, our minds have to deal with both parsing what the other person is saying and formulating a reasonable response – all in real time. So high is the cognitive burden of the process that for beginner second language learners, it becomes an impossible task, with many reporting that by the time they are able to formulate their response, the conversation has long moved on to a different topic.

Written language is generally less immediate. We can obviously rush to write a quick text message, a Tweet or Facebook post or even an email, but other types of writing take much longer to mould into shape. Writing this very chapter took several months and several waves of editing, by a number of people. Reading it will probably also take some time, especially for some people. As the old saying goes, "good things take time", and writing is similarly appreciated over speaking because of the time and effort required to produce it.

Directly related to the effort and time involved in generating a written text is the degree of **precision** of a text. Writers need to consider the needs of a reader in advance and anticipate any potential ambiguities which might creep into their texts. Speakers need not bother with this aspect because listeners are able to ask questions to resolve potential ambiguities at the time of the interaction. Achieving precision and eliminating vague or incomprehensible language in a written text goes some way towards explaining the lack of immediacy of this medium.

It may come as a small relief in certain circumstances that many of us are blessed with not being able to remember exactly what someone has said even a few minutes prior. We do remember the gist of their contribution, but most people I know will not be able to recall the exact wording of it, or even the language it was uttered in. The **impermanence** of spoken language can be a problem, however, in cases when we might want to analyse its structure or lexical content, or in cases when we might want to remember what was said, such as in an interview, or a university lecture.

Conversely, written language is by its very nature preservable and therefore more permanent. This quality has also gone some way towards increasing its status. The gap between the impermanence of speaking and the preservability of writing is being filled somewhat by the ease of recording and storing speech on mobile phones and tablets (at least in some parts of the world), and by the Internet, which has made written language less permanent, with online content becoming more fluid and easier to change.

Finally, spoken language is used largely to **moderate relationships** and comparatively less so for imparting informational content. Written language is more likely to involve higher referential content, and less affective language. There are exceptions, as written diary entries tend to be full of affective content, and televised news broadcasts are (at least supposedly) highly dense in informational content. However, we find that at the more "spoken" end of the continuum between speech and writing, spontaneous conversation is intrinsically affective, while at the more "written" end of the continuum, academic and legal language are rich sources of information.

In summary, speech and writing are really two different beasts. Speech is quickly acquired, and largely widely available to all members of society. It is used for communicating affective content, it is immediate and impermanent, and it lacks attention to precision. Writing takes longer to acquire and is not necessarily readily accessible to all members of society; it is generally more long-lasting and precise, it necessitates more time and effort to produce, and its function is oriented towards the exchange of information. The qualities of the two mediums are connected to value judgements and opinions which are transferred onto the language medium itself, giving rise to biases against spoken language as an "inferior", poorer cousin of written language.

The misconception that speech has no grammar

Grammar can itself be seen from prescriptive and descriptive perspectives – as described in more detail in Chapter 6 of this volume, by Lyle Campbell and Russell Barlow. I limit the discussion to a single example here. Through prescriptive eyes, grammar is understood as a perfectly formed, more or less invariant, set of logical rules which set out "good" principles for producing well-formed discourse (language), for which there is wide-reaching agreement in a community of native language-users. For example, *There's so many people in this supermarket queue* would immediately raise prescriptive eyebrows for its perceived incorrect use of *'s* instead of the plural form of the verb *to be*: *There are so many people in this supermarket queue.* However, undeniably, the sentence is still decodable, even by hardened prescriptivists. What is at stake here is not communication and intelligibility alone, but the form which endows the linguistic transaction with the desired amount of dignity and style.

In contrast, theoretically cognitive-leaning linguistic scholars, viewing language through a descriptive lens, describe grammar as a set of recurrent patterns whose purpose is to facilitate communication by providing conventions which make language production and language comprehension possible. You know who is doing what because subjects of sentences occur in the same place in a given sentence; be it before the verb or after, depending on the language – the details do not really matter as long as consistency is achieved. It is this consistency that allows for ease of communication. In a sentence like *John rang Mary*, it is important to distinguish who is doing the action (the subject, *John*) and who is the receiver of the action (the object, *Mary*). Note that crucially, changing the nouns within grammatical roles (*Mary rang John*) changes the meaning of the sentence altogether. Not every sentence lends itself to a real protagonist subject – consider for instance the Internet meme *It's easy to identify people who can't count to ten (they are in front of you at the supermarket express checkout)*; *it* at the beginning of this sentence is not acting deliberately, is not an agent, and yet is the subject of the sentence. The pattern of subject followed by verb followed by object is so routinized in English that English sentences will ideally have an expressed subject, resorting to a mere placeholder if no "doer" can be found. Du Bois (1985: 363) summarized this position as: "grammars do best what speakers do most". In this view, grammar is thus more like a useful set of habits than a rigid set of rules. Descriptive views of grammar are comfortable admitting the existence of variation across speakers and genres with regard to what is perceived as "grammatical" or allowed by the system. In contrast, prescriptive views of grammar gloss over or even deny such variation, assuming instead an overall homogeneity of grammatical forms. The goal of grammar from this standpoint is to restrain the exuberance of speakers so that they can be better understood.

Moreover, the power of grammar consists not just in making communication easier by illuminating grammatical roles, but also in its flexibility, enabling the backgrounding of those things we do not want brought forward. For example, in the Air New Zealand safety instruction briefing *In case of low cabin pressure, oxygen masks will be released from the ceiling*, the masks will be released by someone or some mechanism if required, so there is no need to keep looking for the masks from the start of the journey or to panic that they are not there at the time of instruction, nor should one worry about who exactly is going to release them, or whether or not they may have the time and ability to do so in a real emergency. All of that negative talk is spared us by the use of a sly passive – in English, the verb *be* together with the past participle from of the verb *release*.

The two views of grammar have important consequences for how speech and writing, and their respective grammars, are understood and analysed. Owing to the properties discussed earlier, written texts have a more predictable structure, a more complex one, and largely a greater adherence to the consistencies captured by current theories of grammar. For instance, subjects are readily found in written text, but not always in spoken language. It is not uncommon to hear exchanges such as:

Speaker A: now where did I put my hat?
Speaker B: maybe in the cupboard?

The response provided by speaker B is short and to the point, and is not a full clause, missing its subject for the good reason that it can be recovered from the preceding turn. But even missing subjects do not provide the limit to reductions. There are various other fragmented utterances: *because life*, *just coz*, false starts and repetitions, and combinations of constructions which start out as one type of construction and end up as another (termed anacolutha or syntactic blends). The term "construction" is used by grammarians to discuss particular clusters of words which hang together and turn up in various contexts but always have the same basic function. Their function can be quite vague and hard to capture in concrete terms. Although the primary function of questions might be to elicit information, an apparent question like *Why do they always slam that door*? seems to function more as a statement of the speaker's feelings. Another example is the question *You do realise that oven is still hot, don't you?*, which functions as a warning and is similarly not eliciting information.

Returning to syntactic blends, one such type of construction is what I term the "double cleft" (there are other names which are used to describe them, such as, "that's X is Y", "double BE", or "intrusive BE"). I have spent many a dinner trying in vain to convince friends that *That's what I am doing is writing my linguistics thesis* is a valid construction in spoken English and not a grammatical error. Such constructions are "valid" because first, they recur in speech, and in fact not just in New Zealand English (the variety I was studying) but also in other varieties of English, for instance in Canadian and American English. Secondly, speakers hearing double clefts seem to have no problems understanding them, and never question the speaker about their use.

Alas, the phenomena observed in (especially) spontaneous spoken language have driven some linguists to completely banish the medium from linguistic analysis, perhaps most famously, Noam Chomsky himself.

Adding to the negative attitudes which have coloured the view of spoken language, a historical accident seems to have further encouraged the misconception of spoken language as lacking a grammar system. Studying spoken language became even more questionable as an enterprise given that, methodologically, it was impossible to achieve reliable recall of the spoken word. I return to this point in the next section. As a result, grammatical theory turned its attention exclusively to written language. It is hence not surprising that current theories of grammar are unable to successfully fit spoken data. As in other fields of inquiry, the instruments developed are biased by contextual factors present at the time of their devising. Were history different and were we concerned with the analysis of spoken language first and foremost, we might have ended up with entirely different theories of grammar.

By the 1980s, another historical development was to bring about an unexpected change. A boom in technical innovation regarding computer storage and recording equipment opened up new avenues for research in many fields, including linguistics. Having invested a reasonable amount of effort in the analysis of written language, the question facing contemporary linguists had now become: how should they go about analysing spoken language? The body of work which followed has led to the emergence of two schools of thought, which linguist Geoffrey Leech described as the "sameness of spoken vs. written grammar hypothesis" and the "differentness of spoken vs. written grammar hypothesis". Crudely speaking, the *sameness* camp maintains that the grammars of speech and writing are overwhelmingly the same, and largely overlapping, with some differences in frequencies of various constructions; some constructions occur more in speech, others more in writing. The two grammars are in essence two sides of the same coin, as is also evidenced by the fact that people do not consciously notice holding two distinct grammar systems in their heads (when speaking the same language). Conversely, the *differentness* camp takes the more radical stance that the grammar of speech is so different from that of writing that in fact, the two are two distinct grammatical systems, with some non-trivial overlap – yes, as literate beings, you and I hold (at least) two grammar systems in our heads, and even more if we speak more than one language (no wonder I can never remember where I put my keys!). The differences between the two systems are not superficial, as evidenced by the difficulty in mastering a good command of written language ("proper" written language of the prescriptive type), beyond forming/typing letters on a page.

The grammar of speech

The first set of recordings collected purposely for linguistic study was the London-Lund Corpus which was originally founded in the 1980s as a cooperation between linguists from London and linguists from Lund, in Sweden. This corpus informed the *Survey of English Usage* project which produced the first large modern contemporary description of English, a well-cited and much-celebrated volume, *A grammar of contemporary English* (written by Randolph Quirk, Sidney Greenbaum, Geoffrey Leech and Jan Svartvik). This pioneering effort paved the way for the building of other corpora which followed shortly after, such as the The British National Corpus, The Cambridge International Corpus, The Santa Barbara Corpus of Spoken American English, The Wellington Corpus of Spoken New Zealand English and others which continue to be built today. I use the word "built" because indeed, putting a spoken corpus together is no mean feat, nor is it a quick one. Spoken-corpus building is a long-term project. Because there is, to date, no reliable way of automating the transcription process, it remains largely a laborious and costly one, in both time and money. It is also said among researchers that it is easier to obtain blood samples than language samples from people – that is, humans are very conscious of the conclusions one might draw about them based on their language use and this makes them reluctant to come forward to offer these up for dissection. This is how, almost 50 years later, we still know lots about a small part of society, namely about the spoken language of academics, often our own colleagues or our students, and very little, comparatively, about everyday people one is likely to meet in the street.

Despite difficulties in creating spoken corpora, the current resources available have allowed linguists to get a sense of what spoken language and its grammar might be like. So what does spoken grammar actually look like? The first observation is that spoken grammar has its own internal organisation and recurrent, consistent patterns. It is not the case that speakers can just spout out any chaotically-ordered word sequence and expect to make themselves understood. Whether written or spoken, the following is plain gibberish: *The have one kayak was to club going Avon down the town river through*. Yet some constructions which appear consistently in written grammar are conspicuously absent in spoken grammar. The following are some examples.

Structuring speech: noun phrases are short and simple

There are two types of phrases which rule the grammatical landscape: noun phrases, that is phrases which denote entities (*the blue house*, *I*, *this marvellous chapter*, *the river flowing under the new highway*, *London*), and verb phrases, phrases which denote actions and events (*go home early*, *waiting for the perfect man*, *is out*, *can easily read this chapter*). Both of these can in principle be "grown" to infinity because we can go on adding more words to a given noun or verb phrase, but practically speaking, that would be silly because we would forget what we started out from in the first place.

Linguists Jim Miller and Regina Weinert have compared the occurrence of the different types of noun phrases in different language mediums. They found that in conversation, both English and Russian, noun phrases tended to be shorter and less complex in structure, typically containing personal pronouns, such as, *I, you, he*, or simple nouns, such as, *books, London, John*. If the nouns had any additional detail, this was kept to a simple structure too, *the book I read, the car that I bought*. In contrast, newspaper articles had a preference for longer, more complex noun phrases in both languages: *numbers that are not attributable to a specific line in the UK constitution*, or *the appalling manner in which the new provisions have been presented to Parliament*. While marvelling at the dense and complex information related in the latter examples, you might wonder whether speakers are robbed by their grammar of the ability to discuss complex information. Rest assured, there are ways around it. Speakers will simply spread the information over multiple clauses (which are groups of words that represent a single idea and contain a subject and a predicate, the verb and anything else strongly linked to it), one chunk at a time. In speech, the previous noun phrase example may look something like:

I heard about the new provisions [new clause] that were talked about in Parliament [new clause] it was appalling [new clause] the way [stranded noun phrase] they were presented [new clause]

In the same way that languages whose structures preclude them from expressing certain ideas will develop alternative means for getting around these constraints, it turns out that different mediums within the same language variety will also have ways around any limitations, by presenting speakers with alternative strategies for accommodating their communicative needs.

Interestingly, the types of noun phrases that Miller and Weinert found in spoken English and Russian seem to share structural similarities with those described by Australian linguist Bob Dixon in the Aboriginal languages of Diyari and Bgiyambaa. These Aboriginal languages have never been written down, being exclusively spoken varieties. Even though their grammars are said to allow combinations of nouns and multiple adjectives (describing words, like *red, big, sweet*), in the data that Dixon analysed, it is rare to find more than one adjective together with any given noun, let alone three or four. The similarities between spoken varieties of English and Russian and completely unrelated, never-written-down languages like Diyari and Bgiyambaa point to an overarching adaptation of the spoken medium, regardless of language, to cognitive constraints limiting processing and production capabilities.

Structuring speech: subjects are light

Staying in the company of noun phrases, those phrases which function as clausal subjects, that is, phrases which denote what the clause is about, tend to also exhibit important differences in structure across language mediums. Miller and Weinert report that not only are complex noun phrases generally absent from conversation, but their data shows that this absence is particularly pronounced in relation to subjects. *That complex subjects might occur in spoken language is a possibility never realized* is a sentence unlikely to be heard in speech. The starting point of the clause, *That complex subjects might occur in spoken language*, is a full clause in its own right because it contains a subject (*complex subjects*) and a predicate (*might occur in complex language*). The planning required in order to produce such a complex starting point for a sentence is highly cognitively taxing. Miller and Weinert found no occurrences of such subjects in their conversational data. Speakers avoid them entirely – with one exception: if the speaker happens to be someone exposed to so much writing that they are essentially speaking like a book. If I was speaking rather than writing this, the grammar of spoken English will provide me with alternative means for expressing the idea captured by my earlier example, namely an extraposition construction: *It is never the case that complex subjects occur in spoken language*. By shifting the difficult material to the end of the utterance, a simple subject pronoun (*it*) can be used, therefore easing the cognitive load of the speaker and hearer.

Structuring speech: subordinate clauses are isolated from main clauses

Clauses are powerful building blocks in grammar: functionally, they express one idea or proposition, and structurally, they involve a subject and its corresponding predicate. They come in two main flavours: main clauses and subordinate clauses. Main clauses are vital because without them – so the written language theory goes – it is next to impossible to figure out the message, as it is main clauses that carry the full(er) information, main verb type, and other vital information required to decode intended meaning. In a written sentence like *I will study linguistics if I find the right course*, interpreting the conditional subordinate clause *if I find the right course* is difficult in absence of the accompanying main clause *I will study linguistics*. The subordinate clause *if I find the right course* relies on the main clause for the crucial event described (*study linguistics*), and it would be odd to see it in the discourse all by itself.

It turns out that Italian speakers are not plagued by such issues. They habitually use certain conditional clauses to express recurrent and consistent meanings, thus rendering the main clause redundant. Vallauri (2004) explains that in the conversational Italian excerpts he analysed, *se* clauses (*if*-clauses) can occur by themselves, with no main clause in sight. Their meanings come from a specific subset of possibilities which include "no problem, it's fine", "it's out of our hands", "but, wait that's not true", and some other specific idiomatic meanings, all of which can be understood from the context. Here are some examples from his data of clauses which occur by themselves: *se me lo fa avere* ("if you can get it for me") or *se sapessi* ("if only you knew").

Italian speakers are not alone either! Ritva Laury has also written extensively about conditional clauses in Finnish and Swedish (with colleagues Camilla Lindholm and Jan Lindström), showing that isolated conditionals occur in spoken grammar without their accompanying main clauses, and function as directives, instructing the listener to do something. For example, in Swedish one might hear: *Om du kan åka å hämta mej då?* ('if you can come and pick me up then?'); or in Finnish: *Niij jos tota, te maksasitte sittem meille takas* ('so if um, you would pay us back then'). These more polite, softened requests have acquired a life of their own in spoken grammar, having their own specific function and structural independence. And in case you are wondering, English has not escaped the opportunity to allow its conditional clauses to reign free in speech either, as illustrated by the work of Lesley Stirling (for example, *Okay, if you'd like to take a seat now*).

Structuring speech: old words, new functions

The final example discussed in this chapter comes from Australian English, though it is by no means exclusive to this English variety. In an article published in 2017, Isabelle Burke carefully exemplifies new uses of the word *which* in spontaneous Australian conversation. *Which* is a versatile and frequent word with a heavy presence in English grammar already (making it a "function" word), among which (here is one!) is its widely acknowledged relativizer role – *The book which I read last night* (here, it introduces the relative clause *I read last night* that provides additional information about the *book*). As a relativizer, *which* introduces clauses that rely on the presence of the noun they elaborate on; in other words, these clauses are subordinate, not main. Because *which* has already been functioning as a function word for centuries, contributing towards the organization of grammar, much like road signs contribute to the road layout, it is not surprising to witness an expansion of its use to other grammatical roles. Users of English often do not notice these function words because they focus on the content words (nouns, verbs, adjectives and adverbs) which convey the main part of the meaning; but the hard-working function words provide the scaffolding to support the content words.

Burke shows that in her data, *which* can signal the intended continuation with a current topic and desired hold of the speaking-floor.

Speaker A: well Mum wants to go Cambodia.
Speaker B: um.
Speaker A: **which** I was hoping to go along depending when she choose to. Um, 'cause I, I think she's really interested in teaching somewhere else.

Alternatively, *which* may act as a means for introducing the speaker's stance, opinion or evaluation of what was previously said:

> I guess she's leaving now so she won't really be needing to deal with it. But like, yeah, she's all for, having interviews and stuff, **which** I, I don't know I think interviews are important.

Here is another opinion introduced by *which*:

> And no one'll … I mean say, for instance with … insurance, I mean you have to be insured … **which** we don't mind bein' insured really but it does cost a lot … But you have to comply – there's all sorts of compliance.

Crucially, the clauses introduced by *which* in the above examples are not dependent on any other clauses per se; they function as separate statements, expressing ideas related to but not reliant on any other chunks of discourse. In other words, they function like main, not subordinate, clauses.

A second observation about the novel uses of *which* in conversation is the fact that it is in conversation that these new uses arise. Spoken language is not just another language medium but is the very arena in which linguistic innovations have the opportunity to flourish and potentially stick, driving language change. Owing to a relaxed attitude to speech generally, away from editorial eyes and prescriptive pens, speech is an open playground for those interested in watching the evolution of language unfold.

Written grammar and spoken grammar serve different functions equally well

From humble beginnings, stereotype and stigmatization, spoken grammar is turning out to overturn much of the negative baggage it has attracted over the years. As Giles and Niedzielski write in the *Language myths* book "pleasantness or unpleasantness of a language variety is a time-honoured social convention" and the "pleasantness, or otherwise, of a language (and hence the emotive qualities associated with it) are contingent on social attributes of the speakers of it". Their comments are as applicable to different language mediums (within the same language) as they are to different languages or distinct language varieties.

The short tour of grammatical constructions presented in this chapter was intended to show that the grammars of various spoken languages, not only English and its varieties, but also Russian, German, Italian, Finnish, Swedish, Diyari and Bgiyambaa are worthy of being labelled "grammars" in their own right. These grammars are excellently adapted to the spoken context and equipped to serve the needs of those who use them. It is not that the grammar of speech is "better" than that of writing, or conversely, that the grammar of writing is "better" than that of speech – they each fit a different purpose and are both equally "good" at doing what they are adapted to achieve. And while I will probably always love reading Zadie Smith, Amitav Ghosh and Jhumpa Lahiri, it is equally satisfying and entertaining for me to hear the spoken words of Eddie Izzard, Jack Whitehall or Ben Hurley in their stand-up routines!

Acknowledgements

I thank the NZ Royal Society Marsden Grant for their generous financial support and David Trye and Gerry Delahunty for their readings of the chapter.

Further reading

For prescriptive and descriptive views of language, watch: "Does Grammar Matter", TED ED Lesson, which can be viewed at: https://ed.ted.com/lessons/does-grammar-matter-andreea-s-calude.

For a survey of the development of spoken language corpora see Leech (2000) (the quote included in the chapter was from 687–692).

For shorter research articles on constructions found in spoken grammar see Burke (2017), Lindström, Lindholm and Laury (2016) and Vallauri (2004).

For a linguistic overview of spoken and written grammar see Miller and Calude (2020) and for a longer analysis of the grammar of spoken language, see Miller and Weinert (2009).

References

Bloomfield, Leonard. (1935). *Language*. London: Allen & Unwin.
Burke, Isabelle. (2017). Wicked which: The linking relative in Australian English. *Australian Journal of Linguistics*, 37(3), 356–386. DOI:10.1080/07268602.2017.1298398
Chater, Nicholas and Morten Christiansen. (2008). Language as shaped by the brain. *The Behavioral and Brain Sciences*, 31(5), 489–509. DOI:10.1017/S0140525X08004998
Du Bois, J. W. (1985). Competing motivations. In J. Haiman (ed.), *Iconicity in syntax*, 343–365. Amsterdam: Benjamins.
Ghosh, Amitav. (2004). *The hungry tide*. Harper Collins.
Giles, Howard and Nancy Niedzielski. (1998). Italian is beautiful, German is ugly. In Laurie Bauer and Peter Trudgill (eds.), *Language myths*, 85–93. London: Penguin.
Leech, Geoffrey. (2000). Grammars of spoken English: New outcomes of corpus-oriented research. *Language Learning*, 50(4), 675–724. DOI:10.1111/0023-8333.00143
Lindström, Jan, Camilla Lindholm, and Ritva Laury. (2016). The interactional emergence of conditional clauses as directives: Constructions, trajectories and sequences of actions. *Language Sciences*, 58, 8–21. DOI:10.1016/j.langsci.2016.02.008
Linell, Per. (2004). *The written language bias in linguistics: Its nature, origins and transformations*. London and New York: Routledge.
Miller, Jim and Andreea Calude. (2020). Spoken and written language. In Bas Aarts and April McMahon (eds.), *Handbook of English linguistics*. 2nd edition. Oxford: Blackwell/Wiley.
Miller, Jim and Regina Weinert. (2009). *Spontaneous spoken language: Syntax and discourse*. 2nd edition. Oxford: Oxford University Press.
Quirk, Randolph, Sidney Greenbaum, Geoffrey Leech and Jan Svartvik. (1972). *A grammar of contemporary English*. London: Addison-Wesley Longman.
Vallauri, Edoardo Lombardi. (2004). Grammaticalization of syntactic incompleteness: Free conditionals in Italian and other languages. *SKY Journal of Linguistics*, 17, 189–215.

6 Is language change good or bad?

Lyle Campbell and Russell Barlow

Introduction

Is language change good or bad? Versions of this question are frequent on the Internet, in newspaper columns and in letters to the editor, in various books by wannabe language pundits, in coffee shops and in high school English classrooms. The popular attitude towards change in language is mostly negative. The changes are often seen as corruption, decay, degeneration, deterioration, the product of laziness and a threat to morality and even to national security. We read that this linguistic deterioration reflects social decay, that our language is embattled, being destroyed and reduced to an almost unrecognizable remnant of its former and rightful glory – described by words such as "bad", "ugly", "wrong", "incorrect", "unacceptable" and a host of others that express negative attitudes. And the guilty parties who are to be blamed for the current (bad) state of language? They are variably reported to be the youth with their sloppy language use, parents, teachers, poor educational policies, the media, popular culture, modern technology, politicians, globalization, America, moral decline and neglect of religion. Laments like these are found throughout history, and are not limited to English. Jonathan Swift (famed author of *Gulliver's travels* and "A modest proposal") attributed language decline to the "Licentiousness which entered with the *Restoration* [1660], and from infecting our Religion and Morals, fell to corrupt our Language" (in his *A proposal for correcting, improving and ascertaining the English tongue*, 1711–1712). Even from the brothers Grimm, famous both as historical linguists and as collectors of fairy tales, we read:

> The farther back in time one can climb, the more beautiful and more perfect he finds the form of language, [while] the closer he comes to its present form, the more painful it is to him to find the power and adroitness of the language in decline and decay.
>
> (Jacob and Wilhelm Grimm 1854: iii)

As Thomas Lounsbury, a 19th-century professor of Language and Literature at Yale University, put it:

> There seems to have been in every period of the past, as there is now, a distinct apprehension in the minds of very many worthy persons that the English tongue is always in the condition of approaching collapse, and that arduous efforts must be put forth, and put forth persistently, in order to save it from destruction.
>
> (Lounsbury 1908: 2)

America is often deemed the culprit for the assumed ongoing degeneration of the English language. The American journalist Edwin Newman, for example, wrote *Strictly speaking: Will America be the death of English?* (1974). British newspapers report complaints of the corrupting American influence in the UK pushing out traditional British pronunciations in words like *adver**TISE**ment* for *ad**VERT**isement* and *paytriotic* for *patriotic*, and for *schedule* being pronounced now as *skedule* rather than *shedule*. *Controversy* earlier was pronounced as *CONtroversy* in Britain and shifted only relatively recently for many speakers there to *conTROversy*. People there complained of an unfortunate American influence when they heard *conTROversy* on the radio, though it has never been pronounced in America with the stress on that syllable (Copping 2011).

Concerns for the presumed negative effects of language change are a large part of what led to the establishment of language academies – to protect languages from decay and to foster their purity. French has the Académie française, Spanish has the Real Academia Española and German has the Rat für deutsche Rechtschreibung. English is one of the few major languages that have no language academy attempting to protect them from unwanted change.

In the debate about the harms versus benefits of language change, one thing that all agree on is that language change happens – it cannot be prevented or avoided. All languages change all the time (except dead ones). In spite of concerns, life always goes on with no obvious ill-effects in the wake of linguistic change. The language we speak today is no less able to serve our communicative needs than the language our ancestors spoke. Today's language is entirely adequate for creating "beautiful poetry, literary pieces, and expressions of love and awe and all other human feelings" (Zanuttini 2015). The changes taking place today that so distress purists and prescriptivists are the same in kind and character as past changes about which there was once much complaint but whose results today are held to have enriched the modern language.

Languages are always changing, adapting to accommodate the needs of their users. If English had not changed since, say, around 1980, we would not have the words to talk about things like *bling, blogs, cyberstalking, googling, mansplaining, meh, road rage, selfies, sexting, turduckens, unfriending, wannabes* and scads of technical and scientific topics. As language users' needs change, language change follows.

What *is* language change?

So, what exactly *is* language change? There's a popular conception of linguistic change as something abrupt and sporadic, whether brought on by major events (such as the Norman conquest of England) or minor ones (like the innovation of texting). To be sure, social, political and economic changes do play a part in language change. Many types of language change are possible: lexical (losing, borrowing or coining new words), phonological (changes to pronunciation), syntactic (loss or addition or modifications of grammatical structures) or semantic (change in meanings).

People notice most easily the changes that bring new words or new meanings. New words are usually easy to spot. Sometimes words enter a language when its speakers come into contact with other languages (loanwords). Thus, it must have been obvious to speakers of English that new words like *genre, lingerie, rendezvous* (from French), *angst, kindergarten, waltz* (German), *guerrilla, macho* (Spanish), *paparazzi, pizza* (Italian), *tsunami, sushi* (Japanese) and *taboo* (Tongan) were changes in English. Vocabulary changes that come along with technological innovations appear to be obvious as well. Along with the development of computers and the Internet came *blog, download, emoji, google* and hosts of other new words. People have long noticed that words come and go. As the Roman poet Horace wrote in the 1st century BC:

> Multa renascentur quae iam cecidere, cadentque quae nunc sunt in honore vocabula, si volet usus, quem penes arbitrium est et ius et norma loquendi.
>
> (*Ars Poetica*, Horace)
>
> 'Many words which have fallen will revive, and many which now are respected will fall, if custom wishes, in whose power is the judgement and law and principle of language.'

Another noticeable kind of change, semantic change, is also one of the most common sources of ire about language usage. Purists are wont to become galled over the changes in meanings of words. Thus we hear complaints about *unique* now meaning 'special' or 'unusual' and not 'single' or 'solitary' as it used to; or *literally* now being used to intensify a sentiment (as in,

Is language change good or bad? 83

I literally died when I heard the news). *Nice*, an often mentioned example, has left us an interesting trail of meaning changes. It started with Latin *nescius* 'ignorant, unaware', derived from *nescire* 'not to know, to be ignorant' (*ne-* 'not' + *scire* 'to know', the root from which we also get *science*). Old French inherited this as *nice*, having changed its meaning from Latin to 'careless, clumsy, weak' and also 'poor, needy' and 'simple, stupid, silly, foolish'. English took *nice* as a loanword from French in the late 13th century in the meaning 'foolish, stupid, senseless', changed this to 'fussy, fastidious' and then to 'dainty, delicate' (c. 1400), on to 'precise, careful' (by the 1500s, as preserved in *nice and early*), changing to include 'finicky, very particular' in the 16th century, to 'agreeable, delightful' (attested in 1769), to 'kind, thoughtful' (by 1830), including also 'pleasant, agreeable', and then also 'respectable' in the 19th century (https://etymonline.com/word/nice).

Although new words and new meanings are perhaps the most noticeable changes that a language can undergo, often the most drastic changes come – gradually – through changes in pronunciation. The great discovery of the Neogrammarians (the German school that dominated historical linguistics from the late 19th century onward) was that the sounds in languages do not change in chaotic fashion, but rather sound changes are regular – they affect all relevant words, without exception. Sound changes, more than anything else, account for the difference in speech varieties and how these can develop into separate languages. Thus, because Vulgar Latin spoken in Spain and in France changed gradually over the centuries, each in different ways, we now have the two separate languages, Spanish and French, each having undergone many sound changes.

There are lots of ideas about *why* the sounds in languages change over time. Sensational anecdotes – like the urban legend that Castilian Spanish pronounces *z* with a *th* sound because people adopted the speech patterns of a lisping king – certainly do not explain sound change. While the story of the Castilian lisp is apocryphal, it is nevertheless possible for external, social factors to influence sounds and cause them to change. People may adopt a more prestigious-sounding pronunciation or avoid stigmatized sounds. New sounds can also be borrowed from other languages, such as the *zh* sound which came into English from French in loanwords like *rouge*, *bourgeois* and *massage*. Internal, linguistic factors in particular motivate sound change. A change in pronunciation might enable speakers to move their speech organs more easily and rapidly, or it might facilitate greater clarity for listeners, say, by further differentiating two similar sounds, making the distinction between them easier to perceive. Sound change is natural; it happens all the time in spoken languages. Therefore, compared to regular sound changes – that generally occur systematically and gradually over time and which often result in very marked overall changes to a language – the changes that seem to bother people the most are rather small, sporadic and – crucially – perceived as recent.

Defining "good" and "bad" in language change

Dictionary definitions of "good" and "bad" vary hugely from source to source, though all characterize these words as involving value judgements, subjective assessments based on one's standards, principles or beliefs, but not based on facts that can be checked or proved. Language change is not good or bad by any objective measure. The beauty or ugliness that comes from language change is in the eye (or the ear) of the beholder. This raises the question: by what standards, principles and beliefs, and whose, could languages' goodness or badness be judged? Here, we avoid the philosophical and moral quagmires surrounding value-judgement terms, and instead concentrate on linguists' take on positive or negative aspects of language change. In this way, we take "good" to mean "good for some particular purpose" – and the purpose we are considering is communication. Language change would thus be "good" if it aids communication – that is, makes the transfer of information more efficient, clearer or more precise. And language change would be "bad" if it somehow impairs communication, making it less efficient, less clear or harder to process. Of course, language is a lot more than just a utilitarian tool for communication; it can, for example, serve poetic functions – but, to avoid aesthetic judgements and other complications, for our purposes here we concentrate on the effects of language change on communication.

In language change, what is good for the goose can at times be terrible for the gander. Change that might be argued to contribute to greater efficiency in one part of the language can have deleterious consequences for other parts of the language. That is, "good" or "bad" in language change is relative and contextually restricted. There is a constant trade-off between what is good for speaking versus what is good for understanding, where a particular change can simultaneously be good for one of these poles of language but bad for the other. Changes that simplify pronunciation (facilitate speech production) can obstruct understanding (language processing).

Take for example the sound change that deletes final *t* and *d* in certain consonant clusters in many varieties of English. In many words, this loss does not make understanding very much more difficult, for instance in *firs' thing*, *las' thing*, *slep' soundly*, *san' castle* ('sand castle'), *lef' school*, *mus' be*. However, when the lost final *t* or *d* in the cluster represents the past tense of verbs, its deletion can compromise comprehension. For example, in *I ask Peter*, the *ask* could be present tense *ask* (as in *I ask Peter all the time*) or past tense (*I asked Peter*); in *they rol' past him*, the *rol'* could be past *rolled* or present *roll*. This simplifying sound change that makes such words easier to pronounce harms the grammar by eliminating the distinction between present tense and past tense in cases such as these.

That change in one area can have negative consequences for other areas is easy to see in pairs of words where a sound change can make them no longer distinct from each other, leading to confusion. An often-cited example involves the two words of English, *quean* 'disreputable woman, prostitute' (now lost from most dialects of English) and *queen*, where the vowel of *quean* had a lower "e", distinct from the higher "e" of *queen*. The difference in pronunciation disappeared nearly everywhere after these two vowels merged in Middle English. However, in the southwestern area of England, the two vowel sounds remained distinct in words generally and both these words, *quean* and *queen*, still survive there, where they are not homophonous; *quean* did not survive elsewhere where the two words became homophonous – it was intolerable that the word for the queen should sound exactly like the word for a prostitute (Campbell 2013: 330–1). There is a bit more to the story. In a very few places instead of just abandoning the word *quean* to avoid the homophony of *quean* and *queen*, an initial "wh" was substituted for the "qu" of *quean* (but not for *queen*), and both words survive, different in pronunciation. The conflict caused by the merger of the vowels was avoided through this sporadic change to deflect from the problem. In another case, English *shut*, from Old English *scyttan*, would have become *shit* by the regular sound changes, a homophony apparently too pernicious to abide – so the vowel of *shut* was deflected to avoid the homophony (Campbell 2013: 332). Such cases show how a regular sound change, often thought to be "good" because it makes pronunciation easier, can simultaneously be "bad" where it causes loss of distinction between words of different meanings or loss of grammatical distinctions as in the case of the present and past tenses with final consonant-cluster reduction.

The relative good and bad of language change is illustrated also in the interplay between sound change and analogy, two major kinds of language change. Analogy is a process whereby something in a language changes to be more like something else in the language with which it is somehow associated, to which it bears a similarity. The interaction between sound change and analogy is summarized in the slogan (sometimes called "Sturtevant's paradox"): sound change is regular and causes irregularity; analogy is irregular and causes regularity. A regular sound change applies to the words that have the sound in the contexts that are affected by the change. Such sound changes, however, can create alternate forms of words. For example, the change called umlaut changed "back vowels" (like *o* and *u*) to "front vowels" (like *e* and *i*) whenever there was a front vowel in a following syllable, as in *elder*, from *old* + *-er* (the front vowel *e* of *-er* 'comparative' caused the *o* of *old* to front to *e*, giving *eld-er*). The regular umlaut change left *old* with two variant forms, *old* and *eld-*. English had many words with alternations of this sort. However, analogical change later changed *elder* to *older* on analogy with non-alternating comparative forms, for example *tall/taller*. This analogical change was irregular in that it applied only here and there, to individual cases; it undid the irregularity of *elder*, changing it to *older*, thus eliminating the multiple forms (*old* and *eld-*) created by the regular sound change, leaving only a single form, *old*, in both *old* and the comparative *older* (*elder* now survives only in restricted contexts with specialized meaning).

The history of the verb *to choose* in English shows this interaction of analogy and sound change well. The Old English verb meaning 'to choose' had several forms; it had cēosan (pronounced [čēozan]) 'to choose', cēas (pronounced [čǣas]) 'chose [singular]', curon [kuron] 'chose [plural]' and coren [koren] 'chosen'. The different consonants in the Old English forms of this verb (č, k, s, z, r) came about from two sound changes. The *chose* (plural) and *chosen* forms had changed original *s to *z* when the stress followed it (a change called Verner's law); stress later shifted to the first syllable so the conditioning environment of the change was no longer visible in Old English; and then later this *z* between vowels changed to *r* (a change called rhotacism), and this change gave Old English curon and coren. A change (called palatalization) turned *k* into *č* ('ch') before front vowels, giving cēosan ([čēozan]) 'to choose' and cēas ([čǣas] 'chose [singular])'. Together, these regular sound changes left a number of different forms in the paradigm for 'to choose'. Later, analogy levelled out the consonant differences, leaving Modern English *choose* / *chose* / *chosen* uniformly with the same consonants. In this example, the regular sound changes, rhotacism (following Verner's law) and palatalization, created irregularity in the paradigm for 'to choose' in Old English, and subsequent analogical change restored uniformity to the consonants. The sound changes were, it is assumed, motivated by ease of pronunciation, but the result of that was greater complexity in the verb paradigm, the multiple forms being more difficult to process and to learn. Analogy, often motivated by ease of processing and parsing, reduced the complexity that the sound changes had introduced. We may say, then, that the sound changes were good for facilitating production (pronunciation), but were bad for having created many related forms, difficult for processing. While the subsequent (analogical) changes did nothing to improve production, they facilitated processing and learnability by making the consonants of the several forms of 'to choose' the same.

In an often-cited example from Classical Greek, sound change deleted *s* between vowels, but *s* also signalled future tense. The problem was that if the sound change were allowed to delete every intervocalic *s*, it would delete the future tense in many verbs, a harmful outcome for the

Is language change good or bad? 87

grammar – for example, the difference between *poié-s-ō* 'I will do' and *poié-ō* 'I do' would be lost. So, the intervocalic future markers of Classical Greek were simply not lost. This has been interpreted in two ways. One is that the sound change was prevented only where it would raise so much havoc with the tense system, therefore preserving the *s* when it signalled 'future' but losing *s* between vowels in other words that did not involve 'future'. The other view is that Greek did lose its *s* 'future' between vowels in a regular change that deleted all cases of intervocalic *s*, but that the *s* 'future' was later restored on analogy with 'future' verbs that had *s* after consonants (and therefore had not lost the *s* 'future' that was deleted by the change that affected *s* between vowels). Either way, this illustrates the negative consequences that otherwise well-motivated changes can have for other areas of the grammar.

Regular sound change can lead to big changes to the grammar of a language. For example, English – like Latin and Greek – used to have case suffixes on nouns, endings that indicated their role in a sentence. The form of the word 'son' was *sunu* when it was used as the direct object (shown by accusative case) in a sentence (as in *She saw her **son***), but the form was *suna* if the word was used as the indirect object in a sentence (as in *She gave her **son** the apple*). Various sound changes (including a reduction of both final *u* and final *a*) resulted in a loss of case distinctions among these nouns. We might wonder whether this change was good or bad. On the one hand, a language without different case endings is arguably easier to pronounce and to learn. For example, a learner of Polish must learn not just a "singular" and a "plural" form of a given noun, but up to six different versions of a single noun – just in the singular (as in the noun meaning 'girl', which has the singular forms *dziewczyna* [nominative], *dziewczynę* [accusative], *dziewczyno* [vocative], *dziewczyny* [genitive], *dziewczynie* [dative and locative] and *dziewczyną* [instrumental]). For the learner of modern English, it would, however, suffice to learn just *girl* (and *girls* for the plural). On the other hand, these case distinctions can facilitate communication: listeners of Old English received more information, in the form of the case suffixes, about the role of each noun in a given sentence. The regular sound changes in Old English that led to the demise of case endings had the effect of constraining English word order. It used to be possible to structure English sentences such that either the direct object or indirect object could come first, without the need of a preposition or other indication in the grammar, since with case endings the role of each noun was always obvious. For example, an Old-English sentence like *She gave her son the apple* could just as well be phrased as *She gave the apple her son*, without any confusion or comedic effect, since the word meaning 'son' – regardless of its place in the sentence – would be marked as the indirect object (*sun-a*) and the word meaning 'apple' would be marked as the direct object.

Where do notions of correct, pure and good come from, and how do sentiments against language change arise?

So if from a purely linguistic standpoint language change is not inherently good or bad, though often motivated by the pull to make things easier to produce (to pronounce) or to process (to understand and to learn), then where do notions of correct, pure, good language come from and how do attitudes against language change develop? They do not come from the languages themselves, not from purely linguistic facts. Of course, society can assign negative or positive value (stigma or prestige) to things in language, and this does happen very often with new or ongoing changes in language, for various non-linguistic reasons.

Linguists approach language descriptively; they are not concerned with notions of "proper" or "correct" language, rather with describing actual usage instead of prescriptions about assumed proper usage. For linguists, non-standard language is no better or worse than standard language; both adequately serve the communicative needs and goals of their users. There is, however, the tradition of prescriptive grammar – promoted by school teachers and the socially powerful – that is concerned with what it believes to be correct grammar, combatting what it views as incorrect. It is concerned with what it assumes to be "good" or "bad" language usage; it describes the language according to how some people or institutions think it should be used. Typically, such a prescriptive approach favours conservative over innovative usage, although prescriptivists sometimes introduce innovations of their own, such as rules against "split infinitives" and "double negatives".

Linguistically, scientifically, objectively, there is no basis for judging some varieties of language, some ways of talking, as better than others. However, these socially motivated judgements about good and bad in language can have significant social consequences. While linguists do not judge standard varieties of English as better than nonstandard varieties, it is nevertheless necessary to realize that the sort of usage deemed "correct" and "good" by prescriptivists can have consequences for getting jobs in banks, for admission to law school, for adequate performance at university, for successful careers in most professions and so on. Rightly or wrongly, for every aspect of life in which standard English is expected, avoidance of nonstandard or stigmatized language conveys a social advantage.

Ironically, what prescriptivists may consider absolutely bad can be considered good by some sectors of society. For example, some men in the UK give covert prestige to speaking the working-class dialect, which reflects for them the positive attributes of in-group identity or manliness. Standard English is thus judged good by some and bad by others, and, vice versa, non-standard English, though judged negatively by prescriptivists, is judged positively in cases where it has covert prestige. The language changes behind these different varieties of language are thus neither absolutely good nor absolutely bad. It truly does boil down to value judgements that are not based on scientific linguistic facts.

Value judgements about language change appear to be here to stay. Despite the sage counselling of linguists about prescriptivism versus descriptivism, pseudointellectuals continue to decry what they see as the abasement of "their" language. On New Year's Day 2019, a piece called "Speak English!" by Cal Thomas, a well-known and widely syndicated conservative American columnist, appeared in newspapers across the US. In it, Thomas complains about young women's use of *like* and *you know*, saying these "are the language of the ignorant, of a generation that can neither speak well, nor think rationally. Call them Bernie Sanders voters." He writes of listeners wishing to plug their ears when assaulted with *like* and *you know*. He also complains about *pre-boarding* an airplane because it is impossible and about numerous clichés. (Despite his professed hatred of clichés, Thomas served up several, for example starting one paragraph with "Don't get me started on … ".) He asks, "what's the point of speaking English if it can't be properly spoken and understood?" We note here, as in many such laments, that the accusation of ignorance and political wrongheadedness lies in apparent blissful ignorance of over 30 years of valuable linguistic analyses of the focusing and quotative discourse functions of *like* and the contributions of *you know* to communication and understanding. At another point, Thomas boasts of his being "taught never to end a sentence in a preposition". The avoidance of sentence-final prepositions is – in the grand history of the English language – itself a relatively new fad, having arisen it seems in the late 17th century (Shakespeare had no qualms about prepositions stranded at the ends of sentences). In spite of Thomas' prescriptions about prepositions, he uses *between* instead of *among* when he boasts that he was also taught "the difference between there, their and they're" – is there just one difference among the three? The point here isn't to poke fun at his stodgy, conservative linguistic proclamations and preferences, but rather to point out that these laments are based on just that – preferences. There is nothing intrinsically good or bad about sentence-final prepositions or clichéd metaphors – it comes down to taste.

Conclusions

So, no, language change in and of itself is neither good nor bad. It can sometimes be assumed to have beneficial aspects, such as facilitating speech production or comprehension, and it can be thought sometimes to have detrimental consequences, sometimes creating a greater burden for comprehension. However, there is no linguistic, scientific basis for the frequent condemnation of linguistic change as bad, nor for the occasional declaration that it is good. These are social judgements about language change – they depend on prejudices and preferences, not on anything about the languages involved per se.

Acknowledgement

We thank John Van Sickle for the reference to Horace and for the translation.

Further reading

For the wider question of the ways in which languages change, and for the specific question of the supposed virtues or problems of them doing so, Aitchison (2012), Campbell (2013) and Trask (2015) provide valuable and readable introductions.

References

Aitchison, Jean. (2012). *Language change: Progress or decay?* 4th edition. Cambridge: Cambridge University Press. DOI:10.1017/CBO9781139151818

Campbell, Lyle. (2013). *Historical linguistics: An introduction.* 3rd edition. Edinburgh: Edinburgh University Press, and Cambridge, MA: MIT Press.

Copping, Jasper. (2011). The 'conTROversy' over changing pronunciations. *The Telegraph*, February 5, 2011. https://www.telegraph.co.uk/news/newstopics/howaboutthat/8305645/The-conTROversy-over-changing-pronunciations.html

Grimm, Jacob and Wilhelm Grimm. (1854). *Deutsches Wörterbuch.* Leipzig: Hirzel.

Lounsbury, Thomas Raynesford. (1908). *The standard of usage in English.* New York: Harper and Brothers.

Newman, Edwin. (1974). *Strictly speaking: Will America be the death of English?* New York: Warner Books.

Swift, Jonathan. (1712). *A proposal for correcting, improving and ascertaining the English tongue: In a letter to the most honourable Robert Earl of Oxford and Mortimer, Lord High Treasurer of Great Britain.* 2nd edition. London: Tooke.

Thomas, Cal. (2019). *Speak English!* Chicago: Tribune Content Agency. https://calthomas.com/columns/speak-english, released 01/01/2019

Trask, Larry. (2015). *Trask's historical linguistics.* 3rd edition, revised and edited by Robert McColl Millar. Abingdon, Oxon: Routledge. DOI:10.4324/9781315728056

Zanuttini, Raffaella. (2015). Don't fear our changing language. *Pacific Standard*, February 17, 2015. https://psmag.com/social-justice/dont-fear-our-totally-changing-language

7 Are the sounds of languages influenced by climate, environment and biology?

Dan Dediu and Scott R. Moisik

Introduction

It stands to reason to wonder why on Earth there are so many languages being used out there (current estimates are in the range of 7,000 or so; Hammarström et al. 2018) and why a single one wouldn't suffice.[1] To push it to the other extreme, why aren't there as many languages as there are humans on the planet (thus about 7.5 billion)?

While it is apparently easy to dismiss both (one language per speaker would not do much for communication, would it?[2] And good luck convincing everybody to switch to just one language and stick to it across conflicts, divisions and generations!), the question is actually extremely profound: why do we have this particular patterning of linguistic diversity? Why are there about 7,000 languages, very unequal in their geographic spread and number of speakers (compare the few "big" languages, such as Mandarin Chinese, Spanish and English, used by hundreds of millions of speakers each, with the "median" languages used by a few hundred to a few thousand speakers, and with those that seem to still manage with some tens of speakers[3]), distributed among about a few hundred very unequal language families (ranging from the massive Austronesian, Indo-European or Niger-Congo/Atlantic-Congo each with hundreds to thousands of languages, to the families that have only one surviving member, such as Basque)? Would, say, 500 languages in four families (one per continent) work? Would 25,000 languages in 1,000 families describe a possible alternative history?

Such questions bear a striking resemblance to those asked about biological diversity and, more recently, about other forms of human cultural diversity, and it is becoming generally accepted that a proper answer must contain some form of evolutionary dynamics. More precisely, *cultural evolution* is fundamental in shaping linguistic diversity (Richerson and Christiansen 2013; Tamariz and Kirby 2016), and a vast research programme is under way aiming to understand the whole range of phenomena, from the individual-level biases (Culbertson and Kirby 2016), to the repeated use and transmission of cultural traits (Tamariz and Kirby 2016), to fundamental evolutionary concepts (Croft 2008) and the reconstruction of cultural and linguistic phylogenies (Atkinson and Gray 2005). Essentially, cultural systems, such as language are seen as full-blown evolutionary systems which change across time (and space) following principles such as *inheritance with modification* from a shared ancestor (explaining why there are families of genealogically related languages, such as French, Italian and Romanian, all obviously similar due to their shared origins from Latin less than 2,000 years ago) and *adaptation* to various selective pressures (explaining why, for example, more frequent words tend to be shorter).

When it comes to *language universals* and *universal tendencies* (or statistical universals), it has long been accepted that they must emerge from some sort of *biases*, *constraints* and what are technically known as *affordances* due to the way humans acquire, use and transmit language, ranging from proposals in the vein of Chomsky's Principles and Parameters framework where "universal" linguistic properties are a direct and unmediated expression of our genome (Behme 2014), to more realistic proposals of how, for example, articulation and acoustics shape phonetics and phonology (Ohala 1989; Yu 2013), or how properties of face-to-face interaction shape communication (Levinson 2016). However, when it comes to the other side of the coin, namely *linguistic diversity*, until very recently, the "received wisdom" pretty much ruled out *adaptation* to selective pressures from outside language itself, arguing instead that randomness is a sufficient explanation. Such randomness is represented, for example, by *sociolinguistic* factors that associate one variant with high status irrespective of its "intrinsic" properties (a famous example is the low status in New York of not pronouncing post-vocalic [r], while in England, non-rhotic pronunciation is a marker of high status – Milroy and Gordo, 2008: 140), *errors* of production, perception or learning (Ohala 1989) or one-off *historical accidents*. Adaptation does sometimes play a role, in the sense that some aspects of a language might change in response to changes in others, as, for example, in grammaticalization[4] (Hopper and Traugott 2003), but the idea that selective pressures from *outside language itself* may shape different languages differently was seen as somehow problematic, without explanatory power, and relegated to the "fringes" of the language sciences. But is it so?

This chapter explores the "fringe" proposal that things *outside* language, in what we call the language's *wider environment* (Dediu, Janssen and Moisik 2017), do affect different languages differently, helping to explain why the observed linguistic diversity is distributed the way it is. More than that, however, the real importance of this idea goes beyond the aspects of diversity it helps to explain, by freeing language and languages from the

Platonic world of ideas and rooting them back into reality, into the body of the speakers, and into the climate, geography and cultures these speakers inhabit. In the following, we will focus mostly on the sounds of languages (i.e. their phonetics and phonology), so as to narrow the discussion and to capitalize on the preponderance of examples published to date, as well as on our own expertise, but these ideas apply to all levels and aspects of language – this is an area of research ripe for investigation!

The wider environment part I: geography, climate and ecology

Language learning and use do not happen in a void or in a Platonic world of ideas, but in the *real* world, where physics, chemistry and biology apply. The language learners and users themselves are (and have always been) biological organisms inhabiting, adapting to and using this real world, with its myriad constraints and affordances. Thus, it is almost obvious that language and speech must be shaped by this environment, either in themselves (e.g. the acoustic waves carrying most of the spoken information obey the laws of physics) or through their learners and users (e.g. to produce acoustic waves humans have to move, in a highly coordinated manner, various parts of their vocal tract), resulting in various *universals*, *universal tendencies* and *design features* of language and speech (Hockett 1963; Maddieson 1996).

However, the idea that *variation* in some aspects of this environment might affect different languages differently is very hard to test, and there were few serious such proposals – see, for example, the discussion in Everett, Blasi and Roberts (2016) and the accompanying comments. Fortunately, this has changed due to the recent explosion in large *databases* of language features and classifications, such as WALS (Dryer and Haspelmath 2013), AUTOTYP (Bickel et al. 2017), PHOIBLE (Moran, McCloy and Wright 2014), Glottolog (Hammarström et al. 2018) and Ethnologue (Lewis 2009), which can be *computationally processed* and *linked* to other databases containing geographical, environmental and biological information. Other factors facilitating this new focus are advances in *statistical methods* (such as multilevel regression and phylogenetics), *computer power* and (relatively) user-friendly *programming/data analysis environments* (such as R and Python). Here, due to space constraints and consistency, we will focus on a small selection of such recent proposals that, nevertheless, highlight the main paradigms, methods and results.

We will begin with a surprising proposal back in 2013, that suggested a causal connection between the *altitude* at which a language is spoken and the probability that it has *ejective consonants* in its phonological inventory:

the higher the altitude, the higher the probability (Everett 2013). What we find particularly interesting about the paper, is that it provides two lines of evidence, one statistical and one articulatory/acoustic, arguing that they converge in supporting the proposal. The statistical argument rests on a relatively large dataset of 567 languages – 92 with phonemic ejectives and 475 without – and tests the probability of the presence of ejectives depending on various relations to altitude (e.g. their own altitude or being less than 500km away from regions higher than 1500m – see Everett 2013). The second line of argumentation rests on the peculiar articulation of ejectives, which are produced by compressing air supra-glottally, followed by its release: it is argued that the lower air pressure at higher altitude would reduce the effort needed to articulate these sounds (but, on the other hand, it would also reduce their salience). All in all, the jury is still out on this proposal (and no new analyses have been published to our knowledge), but even if it is ultimately falsified, this paper was one of the first to use a large database to statistically test a principled hypothesis connecting a clearly-defined aspect of language (the presence or not of phonemic ejectives) with a clearly-defined aspect of the environment (altitude) through a plausible causal mechanism (articulatory effort).

The same fundamental paradigm was extended a few years later and applied to explain the apparent scarcity of *tone* languages in (hot and cold) *deserts* around the world (Everett, Blasi and Roberts 2015) – for more on tones and tonal languages, see Chapter 12 in this volume by Paul Warren. Here, the sample is much larger, consisting of two databases – WALS with 527 languages, and the World Phonotactics Database (Donohue et al. 2013) with 3,756 languages – and the statistical analysis is much more refined and multi-faceted (using different techniques applied at various levels of aggregation) with proper controls for increased similarity between related languages due to shared inheritance from their proto-language (known as "Galton's problem" – Mace and Pagel 1994) and contact (see, for example, Ladd, Roberts and Dediu 2015 for details and approaches to these issues). With these methods and data, they found that languages spoken in dry places (both hot and cold) have a lower probability of being tone languages. Complementing this statistical evidence, the authors discuss as a potential mechanism the idea that air dryness negatively affects the vocal folds, reducing the capacity to achieve the fine control needed for the production of linguistic tone (in some ways, also a manifestation of articulatory effort). This proposal has generated very mixed reactions (for a good sample, see the comments in issue 1 volume 1 of the *Journal of Language Evolution*), but for our purposes here it illustrates very well the kind of questions being asked (environmental variation influencing linguistic diversity), the data and methods that can be used (large-scale databases, advanced statistics and mechanistic reasoning) and the wider implications (language is not insulated from the wider world, but an integral part thereof).[5]

All these examples and many more – see Lupyan and Dale 2016, Dediu, Janssen and Moisik 2017 – explore the idea that variation in aspects of the wider environment (climate, ecology, culture, etc.) affects certain aspects of language (phonetics/phonology, morpho-syntax, lexicon) differently in different languages, depending on the particular environment a particular language inhabits. Thus, languages in arid climates will tend to simplify or altogether renounce their tone systems (if they had one) or not develop one in the first place, to pick one example, and these tendencies affect languages more or less in similar ways (of course, taking into account other properties of the languages and their socio-cultural context). Thus, this is a way for environmental diversity to shape what is sometimes called the *structural* or *typological* diversity of languages (Nettle 1999; Nichols 1999).

However, there is yet another way in which the environment affects language, namely by influencing how languages spread and differentiate to form *language families*, and how they are *distributed* across the surface of our planet. Concerning the first, there is a striking observation to be made about the few hundred families in existence (Lewis 2009; Hammarström et al. 2018), namely that they differ greatly in the *number of languages* that comprise them (from one in the case of the language isolates to more than a thousand for Austronesian and Atlantic-Congo), the *geographic area* over which they are spread (from one or a few villages to large portions of entire continents) and their *number of speakers* (from tens to billions). This highly skewed distribution of families, with most being rather small and geographically circumscribed, while a few are huge and of continental (or even global) spread, is explained by many factors (see Diamond 1998 for a highly readable and still relatively up-to-date account), one of them being represented by the environment. Bentz et al. (2018) have recently applied methods borrowed from evolutionary biology to determine quantitatively the way in which a number of extra-linguistic factors (including climate, latitude, longitude and altitude) have interacted with the differentiation and spread of a large set of language families. More precisely, they computed the *phylogenetic signal* of each such factor in each language family, which gives an estimate of how similar the factor is among closely related languages. The main finding is that the spread and diversification of most families is *not* independent of such factors, with the geographical location (longitude and latitude) and climate being among the most important overall (but with large variation between families). For example, while the large families of Eurasia and Africa tend to show strong signals for longitude, those of the Americas have a strong signal for latitude (both findings supporting the ideas in Diamond 1998), and others (e.g. Sino-Tibetan) show a strong signal for altitude. Taken together, these findings seem to suggest that the spread of languages and their later differentiation into families are conditioned by preferences and constraints resulting from the fit of "cultural packages" (such as agricultural techniques) to relatively specific ecoclimatic zones. Finally, climate, and in particular *ecological risk* (Nettle 1999), seems to drive the distribution of linguistic diversity (Hua et al. 2019), with many small languages in areas of low risk and few large ones spread across areas of high risk.

Thus, it is clear from this brief review of some recent work that *climate*, *ecology* and *geography* play a largely-neglected role in explaining the distribution of linguistic diversity at many levels, from the *structural* (i.e. why do some languages have feature X while others don't), to the *genealogical* (why are some language families distributed the way they are) and to the unequal *density* of languages across the globe. The mechanisms involved are quite diverse (from aerodynamic to physiological to cultural adaptations and strategies against ecological risk), but, in most cases, we are just beginning to understand the intricacies of the multi-level interactions between language learning, use and transmission, and the constraints and affordances provided by the environment. However, compared to one and a half decades ago, these ideas are becoming widely accepted, and the methodology that needs to be used for identifying and testing such proposals is becoming continuously refined, involving large databases, advanced statistics/data science and mechanistic accounts (Ladd, Roberts and Dediu 2015; Everett, Blasi and Roberts 2016).

The wider environment part II: human biology

While the "wider environment I" (geography, climate, ecology …) is seeing growing attention and acceptance, with several high-profile publications and discussions that have pushed the field forward, the "wider environment II", namely our biology, seems to raise more fundamental problems and more resistance, not only scientifically, but also in terms of its perceived ideological, moral and ethical implications. The horrors of racism, sexism and discrimination in general, culminating in the evils perpetrated during the second world war by Nazism in the name of ideologies of "race purity" (unfortunately, still enduring in various forms), are very strong collective traumas and warning signs. Thus, understandably, there is a strong reaction against anything perceived as (even remotely) leading to similar ideas and, in particular, against anything remotely resembling the old "race science". Unfortunately, modern genetics and the study of inter-individual and inter-group differences seem to be seen in this light, as nothing else but a new way of dividing people and placing them in immutable hierarchies of "value", based on ancestry, the way they look, the way they behave or their sex, among others (Roberts 2011; Saini 2019).

While these are entirely legitimate concerns and we should all fight against repeating the horrors of history, modern genetics and the understanding of variation are among the best weapons we have in this fight. More precisely, it is because of genetics that we have such a deep and clear understanding of how complex human ancestry is, of how messy history (recent and ancient) was, and of how hollow various claims of "specialness" are (Jobling et al. 2013; Reich 2018), but, as forcefully argued by many (e.g. Reich 2018), if we do not discuss these findings, others will, usually with a more or less hidden agenda, usually picking only those aspects of science that fit their preconceived ideologies. Moreover, variation (biological as well as cultural) is probably one of the most important resources of humanity, as it allowed us to colonize the whole planet and to build civilizations so varied (and yet, deep down so similar) that made us (for better or worse) the top life form on the planet: uniformity begets boredom, stagnation and extinction. Finally, one of us has experienced first-hand the horrors of the other extreme of the pendulum swing: the claim that there are no differences between people, that each one is but a cog in the social machine, a cog that can be shaped any way a higher force (the state/the "party") so desires for the good of the "people" – the other great evil of the 20th century, communism. So, we hope that this digression does what we intend it to do: bring this discussion into the open, with all its pros and cons, so we can freely judge the merits and dangers of studying human variation.

But where does this variation come from and how is it patterned? It ultimately originates in us being biological organisms, products of evolution, a process that cannot exist without variation and that produces variation. On the other hand, we are a global species with a relatively recent origin (currently, the oldest anatomically modern human is about 300,000 years old – Hublin et al. 2017) and a very messy history (repeated spreads, admixture with other groups including the Neanderthals, local extinctions and recolonizations, mass population movements, local persistence, etc. [Jobling et al. 2013; Pääbo 2014; Reich 2018]), which explains several – at first sight surprising – facts about us. First, and foremost, we are very similar to each other, even when compared with the chimps (orders of magnitude less numerous and geographically much less spread out than us – Bowden et al. 2012). Second, we are not clones, and there is inter-individual and inter-group variation emerging from this history (Barbujani and Colonna 2010; Jobling et al. 2013; Reich 2018), with the most diverse human populations being in Africa, where we have evolved for the longest and from where we recently expanded across the world, forming continuous clines of decreasing diversity the farther away one looks from Africa, both genetically and phenotypically (Betti et al. 2009; Barbujani and Colonna 2010). Third, on this broadest canvas, most of the variation is roughly distributed not between continental groups (~10%), not between populations (~10%), but between individuals (~80%) (Lewontin 1972; Jobling et al. 2013), though there is huge variation between genetic loci, with some carrying very strong ancestry signals in some contexts (Nassir et al. 2009; Jobling et al. 2013; Reich 2018). Fourth, while most of this variation is distributed continuously and clinally (i.e. there are no sharp boundaries), at many loci simultaneously and without correspondence to the many (sometimes contradictory and always vague and ideologically charged) "racial classifications" (Barbujani 2005; Rattansi 2007), there is a historical signal carried by our genes, sometimes striking (as in the recovery of the map of Europe from genetic data by Novembre et al. 2008) but always revealing a palimpsest of bewildering complexity that goes against any simplifying -isms of "us" versus "them". Fifth, the variation between groups is generally highly multivariate, continuous, statistical and overlapping.

It is against this background that we must understand that there is widespread (but heavily underestimated and understudied) inter-individual and inter-group variation in the biological bases of speech and language, and, particularly relevant here, in the anatomy, physiology and control of the speech organs (or the vocal tract), including the tongue, the lips, the hard and soft palate and the larynx (Gick, Wilson and Derrick 2013). Due to many factors, not least the use of anatomy by "racial classifications" and the overtly racist comments about the languages of the native populations in the past (see, for example, de Voogt 2019 for click languages), but also the "universalist" turn in the language sciences, serious research about the effects of this variation on cross-linguistic diversity (as opposed to its effects on individual speech, especially in the rich speech pathology literature) is lacking. Nevertheless, this is changing, and we will summarize here a few recent publications (for other reviews, see Ladd, Dediu and Kinsella 2008; Dediu, Janssen and Moisik 2017).

Using structural MRI and 3D intraoral optical scan data from a sample of more than 100 participants from four broad ethno-linguistic groups, Dediu, Janssen and Moisik (2019) show that the anatomy of the hard structure of the oral vocal tract (jaws, dentition and hard palate) contains enough information to statistically differentiate those four ethno-linguistic groups when the information about appartenance was given, and the classification of particular individuals to their group was better than chance but far from perfect. Thus, as expected from the discussion above, the anatomy of the vocal tract shows statistical, continuous, multivariate and overlapping distributions between groups. The origins of this variation are far from

Is language influenced by environment? 99

obvious, most probably involving complex interactions between genetics, and environmental and cultural factors; and their effects on speech, phonetics and phonology must be even more complex.

Focusing on cultural factors, Blasi et al. (2019) study the cross-linguistic variation in the occurrence of the so-called labiodental sounds (sounds produced using the lower lip and the upper teeth, such as [f] in *ferry* and [v] in *very*). They show, using a variety of methods and converging evidence, that (a) labiodentals tend to occur more frequently in the languages of populations that practice agriculture than of those that practice hunting and gathering, (b) that the typical types of food consumed by these two types of populations affect the dentition and jaw, resulting in different types of bite (overjet and overbite for the first, and "edge-to-edge" for the latter), and (c) that overjet and overbite favour (biomechanically) the production of labiodentals. Thus, here we have a case where a cultural change in food production (from hunting and gathering to agriculture), triggers a change during the lifetime of the individual (no genetic variation here!) in the configuration of the teeth and jaw, that alters the probability that labiodentals are produced and integrated into the language (see Blasi et al. 2019 for discussion).

However, in most cases, we do not know why the inter-individual and inter-group variation in vocal tract anatomy exists,[6] but we can ascertain it using various experimental techniques (e.g. MRI, intraoral optical scans, X-rays, dental casts, etc.), and then try to understand what effects such variation might have on speech, phonetics and phonology. For example, Janssen, Moisik and Dediu (2019) use a realistic geometric computer model of the vocal tract – a customized version of the VocalTractLab v2 (http://vocaltractlab.de/; Birkholz 2013) – to study the influence of a range of plausible positions of the larynx on the production of vowels. This is a relatively "hot topic" in the literature on the evolution of language, as it has been controversially claimed that a "pre-modern" position of the larynx (i.e. a larynx higher in the throat than in modern humans) in archaic humans, such as the Neanderthals, might have interfered with their capacity to produce the "full" vowel space, especially the vowels [i] and [u] (Lieberman and Crelin 1971; Boer and Fitch 2010; Lieberman 2012),[7] but the main interest was rather to model the effect of variation in larynx position within the modern human range (Janssen, Moisik and Dediu 2019). The main findings were that while there are relatively large differences in vowel production due to the larynx position, these differences are smaller than one would have expected, being actively compensated by other articulators, so that even extreme positions might be compatible with the full vowel space.

Dediu, Janssen and Moisik (2019) focused on the more subtle effects of the shape of the hard palate: using shapes actually observed in human MRI scans injected into the VocalTractLab v2 model, they simulated the learning and production of five cross-linguistically frequent vowels when the agents had one of those shapes of the hard palate. As the resulting variation was rather small, they placed the agents in an Iterated Learning Model where successive generations of naive agents (with the same hard palate shape) learn their vowels from the previous generation, and they observed that not only is this small influence of hard palate shape on vowels not lost, but that it is, in fact, amplified as more rounds of learning occur across more generations. This suggests that the cultural transmission of language might be effective in amplifying small biases emerging from anatomy to the level of cross-linguistic variation (Dediu, Janssen and Moisik 2017).

A different type of modelling might help us to better understand where some of these weak biases are coming from. Moisik and Dediu (2017) tackle the long-standing question of why some types of speech sounds (here, click consonants) are phonologically rare in the world's languages, and, particularly in the case of clicks, are also geographically constrained (e.g. Engstrand 1997; Güldemann 2007; Moisik and Dediu 2019, but see also de Voogt 2019), by testing an old observation by Traill (1985). This observation (see also Engstrand 1997; Traunmüller 2003) suggests that a rather "smooth" alveolar ridge – found at higher frequencies among the native speakers of the so-called "click languages" of southern Africa than in other populations (Moisik and Dediu 2017) – might favour the production of clicks. Moisik and Dediu (2017) clarify and operationalize what this "favouring" might mean, by constructing a biomechanical model of the articulation of a generalized lingual click using ArtiSynth (https://artisynth.org; Lloyd, Stavness and Fels 2012), which showed that a "smoother" alveolar ridge reduces the total muscle effort required to articulate a click and might also increase the click's acoustic distinctiveness. This might allow clicks, which are widespread in paralinguistic use, to become phonologised through the repeated use and learning of language.

But how about real people (as opposed to computer models)? Dediu and Moisik (2019) analyse MRI (static, sustained articulation and real-time), intraoral and acoustic data, collected from a large multi-ethnic sample, concerning the articulation of the North American English /r/. This sound is somewhat of a celebrity in phonetics as (arguably) the same acoustic output can be produced using several articulatory strategies that have no visible correlates (the two "classic" ones being the so-called "tip-up" and "bunched" articulations), which offers the perfect natural experiment on how learners settle on a way of producing a sound without cues on how to produce it (see Smith et al. 2019 for discussion). The data from Dediu and Moisik (2019) shows, first, that there is a continuum of articulatory strategies used by the speakers, and, second, that these articulatory strategies correlate with the anatomy of the anterior part of the vocal tract (the hard palate in particular).

Conclusions

Thus, while these studies are clearly just the beginning, and some (or all) might need to be amended by future work, taken together they paint a clear picture in which language and speech are not some abstract constructs divorced from the world they inhabit. In fact, they are influenced by their wider physical and biological environment, including climate, ecology and the anatomy of the speakers themselves, producing either universals (and universal tendencies) when these external factors are the same across all humans, or linguistic diversity when these factors vary across populations. This view of language and speech, not just *embodied* but more generally *rooted* in the world, opens new ways of understanding how language originated, how it evolved, why it is the way it is and how it is learned, perceived, processed and produced, all of obvious theoretical import, but also with potential practical implications for speech and language pathologies, and more natural human-computer interactions.

However, some outstanding issues remain to be solved (Everett, Blasi and Roberts 2016; Dediu 2017; Dediu, Janssen and Moisik 2017; Dediu and Moisik 2019): first, we need more cases of such influences (and we must replicate and dissect those we already have) before we can be sure of the strength, type and conditions under which such effects exist. Second, we need to understand the origins of these biases, be they rooted in the environment and mediated by acoustics, physiology, biomechanics or cognition, or coming from our own biology. Third, we need good theories of how such biases are amplified (or dampened) by the processes of language use and transmission in highly complex, structured and dynamic speech communities. Finally, we must find ways to tackle the extremely complex, multi-level and cross-disciplinary causal links between such weak biases and their manifestation as linguistic universals and diversity.

We hope that this chapter managed to kindle interest in these exciting new topics, where the language sciences interact intimately with data science, genetics, anatomy, geography, ecology and human biology (to name just a few). And, to end, we would say that the answer to our rhetorical question in the title must be a tentative "yes" …

Acknowledgements

We wish to thank the ArtiVarK participants. DD was supported by an IDEXLyon (16-IDEX-0005) Fellowship grant (2018–2021).

Notes

1 In fact, it has been famously claimed that "a visiting Martian scientist would surely conclude that aside from their mutually unintelligible vocabularies, Earthlings speak a single language" (Pinker 1994: 232) cited in (Evans and Levinson 2009: 429).
2 If we are willing to relax the definition of "language", one might argue that each person's language use is highly individual, so that there are at least as many idiolects as speakers (as quite a few people are multilingual).
3 See the *Glottolog* (https://glottolog.org/; Hammarström et al. 2018) and the *Ethnologue* (https://ethnologue.com/16/ethno_docs/distribution/).
4 For example, the loss of inflections and grammatical gender in Middle English resulted in a fixed word order and a reliance on particles in modern English (Millward and Hayes 2011: 162). See Campbell and Barlow's chapter in this volume for more detail.
5 This was later generalized to the proposal that languages spoken in drier climates tend to use fewer vowels (Everett 2017).
6 When it comes to pathological variation (such as cleft palate or dental abnormalities) quite a good deal is known about the genetic and environmental factors (see, for example, OMIM https://omim.org/), but when it comes to normal variation, not much is currently known about the interplay between genes and environment.
7 Emphatically, this has little to do with their capacity for language (Lieberman and Crelin 1971; Lieberman 2012).

Further reading

A must-read for understanding the issues concerning linguistic diversity is Evans and Levinson (2009) and a good introduction to (articulatory) phonetics is Gick, Wilson and Derrick (2013). For human evolution and history (through the lens of genetics), two popular and up-to-date books are Pääbo (2014) and Reich (2018), and a lucid modern view on racism is Roberts (2011). A good source for the influence of environmental factors on language is Everett, Blasi and Roberts (2016) plus the accompanying comments and authors' response. For selection versus drift in language, Lupyan and Dale (2016) is a very good general discussion, and Bentz et al. (2018) is an empirical study covering a large set of language families and factors. For the biology of the vocal tract, see Dediu, Janssen and Moisik (2017) for a general manifesto, and Dediu and Moisik (2019) for a discussion in the context of sound change; those seeking a historical perspective might look at Dediu and Ladd (2007) which pretty much started this line of inquiry, and at Brosnahan (1961) for a much earlier (and independent) similar insight.

References

Atkinson, Quentin D. and Russell D. Gray. (2005). Curious parallels, curious connections – Phylogenetic thinking in biology and historical linguistics. *Systematic Biology*, 54(4), 513–526.

Barbujani, Guido. (2005). Human races: Classifying people vs understanding diversity. *Current Genomics*, 6(4), 215–226.
Barbujani, Guido and Vincenza Colonna. (2010). Human genome diversity: Frequently asked questions. *Trends in Genetics*, 26(7), 285–295. DOI:10.1016/j.tig.2010.04.002
Behme, Christina. (2014). A 'Galilean' science of language. *Journal of Linguistics*, 59(3), 671–704. DOI:10.1017/S0022226714000061
Bentz, Christian, Dan Dediu, Annemarie Verkerk and Gerhard Jäger. (2018). The evolution of language families is shaped by the environment beyond neutral drift. *Nature Human Behaviour*, 2(11), 816. DOI:10.1038/s41562-018-0457-6
Betti, Lia, François Balloux, William Amos, Tsunehiko Hanihara and Andrea Manica. (2009). Distance from Africa, not climate, explains within-population phenotypic diversity in humans. *Proceedings of the Royal Society. Series B, Biological Sciences*, 276(1658), 809–814. DOI:10.1098/rspb.2008.1563
Bickel, Balthasar, Johanna Nichols, Taras Zakharko, Alena Witzlack-Makarevich, Kristine Hildebrandt, Michael Rießler, Lennart Bierkandt, Fernando Zúñiga and John B. Lowe. (2017). The AUTOTYP typological databases (Version 0.1.0). GitHub database. *The AUTOTYP typological databases (Version 0.1.0)*. https://github.com/autotyp/autotyp-data/tree/0.1.0
Birkholz, Peter. (2013). Modeling consonant-vowel coarticulation for articulatory speech synthesis. *PloS one*, 8(4), e60603. DOI:10.1371/journal.pone.0060603
Blasi, Damián E., Steven Moran, Scott R. Moisik, Paul Widmer, Dan Dediu and Balthasar Bickel. (2019). Human sound systems are shaped by post-Neolithic changes in bite configuration. *Science*, 363(6432), eaav3218. DOI:10.1126/science.aav3218
Boer, Bart de and W. Tecumseh Fitch. (2010). Computer models of vocal tract evolution: An overview and critique. *Adaptive Behavior*, 18(1), 36–47.
Bowden, Rory, Tammie S. MacFie, Simon Myers, Garrett Hellenthal, Eric Nerrienet, Ronald E. Bontrop, Colin Freeman, Peter Donnelly and Nicholas I. Mundy. (2012). Genomic tools for evolution and conservation in the chimpanzee: Pan troglodytes ellioti is a genetically distinct population. *PLoS Genetics*, 8(3), e1002504. DOI:10.1371/journal.pgen.1002504
Brosnahan, Leonard Francis. (1961). *The sounds of language: An inquiry into the role of genetic factors in the development of sound systems*. Cambridge: Heffer.
Croft, William. (2008). Evolutionary linguistics. *Annual Review of Anthropology*, 37(1), 219–234.
Culbertson, Jennifer and Simon Kirby. (2016). Simplicity and specificity in language: Domain-general biases have domain-specific effects. *Frontiers in Psychology*, 6, 1964. DOI:10.3389/fpsyg.2015.01964. Accessed 23/11/16 from http://www.ncbi.nlm.nih.gov/pmc/articles/PMC4709471/
Dediu, Dan. (2017). From biology to language change and diversity. In Nick Enfield (ed.), *Dependencies in language: On the causal ontology of linguistics systems* (Studies in Diversity Linguistics 99), 39–53. Berlin: Language Science Press.
Dediu, Dan, Rick Janssen and Scott R. Moisik. (2017). Language is not isolated from its wider environment: Vocal tract influences on the evolution of speech and language. *Language and Communication*, 54, 9–20. DOI:10.1016/j.langcom.2016.10.002

Dediu, Dan, Rick Janssen and Scott R. Moisik. (2019). Weak biases emerging from vocal tract anatomy shape the repeated transmission of vowels. *Nature Human Behaviour*, 1–9. DOI:10.1038/s41562-019-0663-x

Dediu, Dan and D. Robert Ladd. (2007). Linguistic tone is related to the population frequency of the adaptive haplogroups of two brain size genes, ASPM and microcephalin. *Proceedings of the National Academy of Sciences of the United States of America*, 104(26), 10944–10949.

Dediu, Dan and Scott R. Moisik. (2019). Pushes and pulls from below: Anatomical variation, articulation and sound change. *Glossa: A Journal of General Linguistics*, 4(1), 7. DOI:10.5334/gjgl.646

Diamond, Jared. (1998). *Guns, germs and steel: A short history of everybody for the last 13,000 years*. London: Vintage.

Donohue, Mark, Rebecca Hetherington, James McElvenny and Virginia Dawson. (2013). World phonotactics database. Department of Linguistics, The Australian National University. http://phonotactics.anu.edu.au

Dryer, Matthew S. and Martin Haspelmath (eds.). (2013). *WALS online*. Leipzig: Max Planck Institute for Evolutionary Anthropology. http://wals.info/

Engstrand, Olle. (1997). Why are clicks so exclusive? *Proc. of Fonetik-97, Umeå University, PHONUM*, vol. 4, 191–194. Accessed 3/12/12 from http://referenc e.kfupm.edu.sa/content/w/h/why_are_clicks_so_exclusive_116050.pdf

Evans, Nicholas and Stephen C. Levinson. (2009). The myth of language universals: Language diversity and its importance for cognitive science. *The Behavioral and Brain Sciences*, 32(5), 429–448. DOI:10.1017/S0140525X0999094X

Everett, Caleb. (2013). Evidence for direct geographic influences on linguistic sounds: The case of ejectives. *PLoS one*, 8(6), e65275. DOI:10.1371/journal. pone.0065275

Everett, Caleb. (2017). Languages in drier climates use fewer vowels. *Frontiers in Psychology*, 8. DOI:10.3389/fpsyg.2017.01285. Accessed 28/11/17 from https:// www.frontiersin.org/articles/10.3389/fpsyg.2017.01285/full

Everett, Caleb, Damián E. Blasi and Seán G. Roberts. (2015). Climate, vocal folds, and tonal languages: Connecting the physiological and geographic dots. *Proceedings of the National Academy of Sciences*, 201417413. DOI:10.1073/ pnas.1417413112

Everett, Caleb, Damián E. Blasi and Seán G. Roberts. (2016). Language evolution and climate: The case of desiccation and tone. *Journal of Language Evolution*, 1(1), 33–46. DOI:10.1093/jole/lzv004

Gick, Bryan, Ian Wilson and Donald Derrick. (2013). *Articulatory phonetics*. Malden: Wiley-Blackwell.

Güldemann, Tom. (2007). *Clicks, genetics, and "proto-world" from a linguistic perspective*. Leipzig: University of Leipzig Papers on Africa 29.

Hammarström, Harald, Sebastian Bank, Robert Forkel and Martin Haspelmath. (2018). *Glottolog, 3.2*. Jena: Max Planck Institute for the Science of Human History. http://glottolog.org

Hockett, Charles F. (1963). The problem of universals in language. In Joseph H. Greenberg (ed.), *Universals of language*, 1–29. Cambridge: MIT Press.

Hopper, Paul J. and Elizabeth Closs Traugott. (2003). *Grammaticalization*. Cambridge: Cambridge University Press.
Hua, Xia, Simon J. Greenhill, Marcel Cardillo, Hilde Schneemann and Lindell Bromham. (2019). The ecological drivers of variation in global language diversity. *Nature Communications*, 10(1), 2047. DOI:10.1038/s41467-019-09842-2
Hublin, Jean-Jacques, Abdelouahed Ben-Ncer, Shara E. Bailey, Sarah E. Freidline, Simon Neubauer, Matthew M. Skinner, Inga Bergmann, et al. (2017). New fossils from Jebel Irhoud, Morocco and the Pan-African origin of Homo sapiens. *Nature*, 546(7657), 289–292. DOI:10.1038/nature22336
Janssen, Rick, Scott R. Moisik and Dan Dediu. (2019). The effects of larynx height on vowel production are mitigated by the active control of articulators. *Journal of Phonetics*, 74, 1–17. DOI:10.1016/j.wocn.2019.02.002
Jobling, Mark A., Edward Hollox, Matthew Hurles, Toomas Kivisild and Chris Tyler-Smith. (2013). *Human evolutionary genetics*. New York: Garland.
Ladd, D. Robert, Dan Dediu and Anna R. Kinsella. (2008). Languages and genes: Reflections on biolinguistics and the nature-nurture question. *Biolinguistics*, 2(1), 114–126.
Ladd, D. Robert, Seán G. Roberts and Dan Dediu. (2015). Correlational studies in typological and historical linguistics. *Annual Review of Linguistics*, 1(1), 221–241. DOI:10.1146/annurev-linguist-030514-124819
Levinson, Stephen C. (2016). Turn-taking in human communication – Origins and implications for language processing. *Trends in Cognitive Sciences*, 20(1), 6–14. DOI:10.1016/j.tics.2015.10.010
Lewis, M. Paul (ed.). (2009). *Ethnologue: Languages of the world*. 16th edition. Dallas: SIL International. http://www.ethnologue.com/
Lewontin, Richard C. (1972). The apportionment of human diversity. In Theodosius Dobzhansky, Max K. Hecht and William C. Steere (eds.), *Evolutionary biology*, vol. 6, 381–398. New York: Springer. https://link.springer.com/chapter/10.1007/978-1-4684-9063-3_14
Lieberman, Philip. (2012). Vocal tract anatomy and the neural bases of talking. *Journal of Phonetics*, 40(4), 608–622. DOI:10.1016/j.wocn.2012.04.001
Lieberman, Philip and Edmund S. Crelin. (1971). On the speech of Neanderthal man. *Linguistic Inquiry*, 2, 203–222.
Lloyd, John E., Ian Stavness and Sidney Fels. (2012). ArtiSynth: A fast interactive biomechanical modeling toolkit combining multibody and finite element simulation. In *Soft tissue biomechanical modeling for computer assisted surgery*, 355–394. Berlin and Heidelberg: Springer. Accessed 30/7/15 from http://link.springer.com/chapter/10.1007/8415_2012_126
Lupyan, Gary and Rick Dale. (2016). Why are there different languages? The role of adaptation in linguistic diversity. *Trends in Cognitive Sciences*, 20(9), 649–660. DOI:10.1016/j.tics.2016.07.005
Mace, Ruth and Mark Pagel. (1994). The comparative method in anthropology. *Current Anthropology*, 35(5), 549–564.
Maddieson, Ian. (1996). Phonetic universals. *UCLA Working Papers in Phonetics*, 92, 160–178.

Millward, Celia M. and Mary Hayes. (2011). *A biography of the English language*. Boston: Cengage.
Milroy, Lesley and Matthew Gordon. (2008). *Sociolinguistics: Method and interpretation*. Malden: Wiley.
Moisik, Scott R. and Dan Dediu. (2017). Anatomical biasing and clicks: Evidence from biomechanical modeling. *Journal of Language Evolution*, 2(1), 37–51. DOI:10.1093/jole/lzx004
Moisik, Scott R. and Dan Dediu. (2019). The ArtiVarK click study: Documenting click production and substitution strategies by learners in a large phonetic training and vocal tract imaging study. In Bonny Sands (ed.), *The handbook of clicks*. Leiden: Brill.
Moran, Steven, Daniel McCloy and Richard Wright (eds.). (2014). *PHOIBLE online*. Leipzig: Max Planck Institute for Evolutionary Anthropology. http://phoible.org
Nassir, Rami, Roman Kosoy, Chao Tian, Phoebe A. White, Lesley M. Butler, Gabriel Silva, Rick Kittles, et al. (2009). An ancestry informative marker set for determining continental origin: Validation and extension using human genome diversity panels. *BMC Genetics*, 10, 39. DOI:10.1186/1471-2156-10-39
Nettle, Daniel. (1999). *Linguistic diversity*. Oxford: Oxford University Press.
Nichols, Johanna. (1999). *Linguistic diversity in space and time*. Chicago: University of Chicago Press.
Novembre, John, Toby Johnson, Katarzyna Bryc, Zoltán Kutalik, Adam R. Boyko, Adam Auton, Amit Indap, et al. (2008). Genes mirror geography within Europe. *Nature*, 456(7218), 98–101. DOI:10.1038/nature07331
Ohala, John J. (1989). Sound change is drawn from a pool of synchronic variation. In Leiv E. Breivik and Ernst Håkon Jahr (eds.), *Language change: Contributions to the study of its causes*, 173–198. Berlin: Mouton de Gruyter. Accessed 3/3/2018 from http://www.linguistics.berkeley.edu/~ohala/papers/pool_of_synchronic_var.pdf
Pääbo, Svante. (2014). *Neanderthal man: In search of lost genomes*. New York: Basic Books.
Pinker, Steven. (1994). *The language instinct*. New York: Morrow.
Rattansi, Ali. (2007). *Racism: A very short introduction*. Oxford: Oxford University Press.
Reich, David. (2018). *Who we are and how we got here: Ancient DNA and the new science of the human past*. Oxford: Oxford University Press.
Richerson, Peter J. and Morten Christiansen (eds.). (2013). *Cultural evolution: Society, technology, language, and religion* (Strungmann Forum Reports), vol. 12. Cambridge, MA: MIT Press.
Roberts, Dorothy E. (2011). *Fatal invention: How science, politics, and big business re-create race in the twenty-first century*. New York: New Press.
Saini, Angela. (2019). *Superior: The return of race science*. London: HarperCollins.
Smith, Bridget J., Jeff Mielke, Lyra Magloughlin and Eric Wilbanks. (2019). Sound change and coarticulatory variability involving English /ɹ/. *Glossa: A Journal of General Linguistics*, 4(1), 63. DOI:10.5334/gjgl.650

Tamariz, Monica and Simon Kirby. (2016). The cultural evolution of language. *Current Opinion in Psychology*, 8, 37–43. DOI:10.1016/j.copsyc.2015.09.003

Traill, Anthony. (1985). *Phonetic and phonological studies of !Xóõ Bushman*. Hamburg: Buske.

Traunmüller, Hartmut. (2003). Clicks and the idea of a human protolanguage. *PHONUM*, 9, 1–4.

Voogt, Alex de. (2019). Clicks in language evolution: A call for clarification. *Journal of Language Evolution*. DOI:10.1093/jole/lzz001. Accessed 30/6/19 from https://academic.oup.com/jole/advance-article/doi/10.1093/jole/lzz001/5424270

Yu, Alan C. L. (2013). *Origins of sound change: Approaches to phonologization*. Oxford: Oxford University Press.

8 Can you tell someone's sexuality from the way they speak?

Evan Hazenberg

As a sociolinguist who works at the intersection of language, gender and sexuality, I get asked this a question a lot. It's an interesting question, and something close to it is what drew me into this field in the first place; but the way that it's worded is almost as interesting as the question itself. When someone asks, "Can you tell someone's sexuality from the way they speak?" what they're really asking is, "Can you tell if someone is *gay* from the way they speak?" Or even more precisely, they're asking, "Can you tell if a *man* is gay from the way he speaks?" It's not a question about sexuality in the abstract, but rather about a particular style of a particular kind of sexuality, presented in a particular way that is culturally meaningful.

Why do we ask our specific question in such a roundabout way, rather than coming out with it and asking about gay men, if that's who we're really interested in? There are a couple of possible reasons for being so circumspect. One might be that we're socially conditioned to try not to sound too nosy or judgemental, and by phrasing the question so broadly and generally, we're taking the sting out of it. Rather than pointing to an identifiable group of people and putting them under a proverbial microscope, we cast our net wide enough that we might be asking about everyone. On those occasions when I try to answer in the broadest sense – to actually talk about sexuality in the general terms – there's almost always an immediate series of follow-ups, and before long, we're talking about gay men.

Another reason for being roundabout, related to the first, could have to do with our sensitivity to loaded words. My mother tends to refer to me and my friends as *homosexuals*, which never fails to make me cringe, while my use of *queer*[1] to describe myself makes her distinctly uncomfortable. We've had different experiences of those two words, and they mean different things to each of us. Rather than accidentally picking the wrong word, one with unintended political or social baggage, we may choose to ask about the more neutral *sexuality*, which is non-specific enough that people are unlikely to take offense. It's a safe way to ask a potentially awkward question.

A third possibility has to do with *markedness*: the extent to which we notice differences and measure those differences against a background "normal". If I say hello to someone at a bus stop, I almost don't notice it if they say hello back, because it's expected. I *do* notice it if they turn their back on me, or start shouting insults, because that's not following the social script of normalness that I'm expecting. Echoing a polite greeting is *unmarked*, anything else becomes *marked*. In most of the world, heterosexuality is unmarked, and so goes unnoticed, and unquestioned. We don't feel the need to interrogate and understand unmarked things, because they're so taken for granted that they're common-sense, obvious even. A woman holding hands with a man doesn't warrant closer inspection or classification, because it seems perfectly "normal" and "natural". In contrast, two women or two men holding hands – especially two men – is marked enough that it sticks out to us. The same is true of how we use language: people who sound straight, whatever that means, go unnoticed and uninspected; they sound more or less like we expect them to. But anyone who deviates from that draws our attention, and with it our curiosity. We're not interested in what it means to sound "straight" in the same way that we're not interested in someone saying "hi" back to us – it's normal, so who cares? What we're interested in are the places where things and people don't follow the script we're expecting.

Scripts and expectations

Western societies, for better or worse, have a lot of scripts about gender and sexuality. They're not the same from place to place, and intercultural miscommunications are quite common. My sister worked for a while in western Canada with a colleague who was visiting from Italy, and he couldn't understand why none of the women he met seemed interested in him, despite his best efforts at being charming and seductive. What was happening was that his flamboyant Italian machismo – which indexed heterosexual masculinity in Italy – was being interpreted by Canadian women as gay; his attempts at seduction came across as camp rather than passionate, and so his attempts at seduction weren't taken seriously. Similarly, when I first moved from Canada to New Zealand, it took me a while to realize that short rugby shorts with pastel shirts meant hipster-sporty, rather than queer. The point here is not the particulars of cultural customs, or of the differences between them, but rather that these social scripts for masculinities and femininities (both heterosexual and otherwise) exist in the first place. We are constantly taking in endless small cues about identity and knitting them together into an understanding of people's social identities.

So what about sexuality and language? The way that someone speaks is one of the cues that we pay attention to when we're figuring them out.

We take what they actually do – what they say and how they say it – and hold it up against the scripts in our head for comparison. At this level, we're mostly talking about stereotypes: how close does a given person come to the idealized notions we carry around with us? We all carry models of different types of women and men in our heads, based on our own experiences of actual human beings that we've met in the world, but also on what we're shown through media channels. If you've never actually met and interacted with a gay man, for example (that you know of), then your understanding of what "gay men" as a group look, sound and act like will be heavily influenced by what you've seen on television and in movies. If you've got gay friends, on the other hand, then you may be attuned to a broader range of gay masculine identities than the relatively narrow tropes shown in the media. And if you yourself are part of a queer community, your awareness will be even more nuanced still.

When any new show comes on with queer principal characters, my friends tend to have one of two responses: half of them celebrate the visible representation of people who look and sound like them, while the other half roll their eyes and complain about the perpetuation of stereotypes. The queer identities that end up on our screens are often a simplistic line-drawing of a very complicated social space: it's not that they're wrong exactly, but they're only showing part of the story. There are dozens of ways to be gay – dozens of different subcultures with their own identities and presentations – but only a handful of those ways are clearly interpretable to people outside of queer communities. Those queer identities that are easily interpretable are the ones that people grab onto and use as a guide to making sense of queer identities more generally.

Stereotypes also play a part in research on language and sexuality. For one thing, they can help identify the really salient aspects of language that highlight sexuality – the things that people notice about how gay men speak, for example, give us a good place to start in investigating differences in language use. How different is different enough to be noticed? What happens with differences that don't get noticed? Stereotypes also tell us something about how we socially classify the language that we encounter. There was a really neat experiment done in Michigan, along the US-Canada border, that looked at the effect of social filters on the perception of language variation (Niedzielski 1999). There's a particular pronunciation of some vowels that is a stereotype of Canadian English, but that is also widespread in Michigan, although people from Michigan don't know that. What Niedzielski found was that people from Michigan only perceived the Canadian-like pronunciation when they were told that they were hearing a recording of a Canadian. When they were told that they were listening to someone from Michigan, they didn't perceive the Canadian pronunciation. What this means for us is that there are probably some linguistic features that have become stereotypically associated with the speech of gay men, even though they're also present in the speech of other groups of people, but we only notice them when our social filters tell us to. We can use stereotypes to help investigate similarities in language use as well as differences.

Of course, similarities and differences exist between any two groups, as they do between any two individuals. In one sense, individuals scale up into groups, and groups decompose into individuals. But that individual-group dynamic isn't always very straightforward: what seems true of a group isn't necessarily equally true of all of the individuals in that group, and the things that make people individuals get distorted when we start grouping them together. This can pose a methodological problem for language and sexuality research, or indeed any research that aims to understand complex social phenomena such as identity, and what effect those phenomena have on behaviour. If we want to understand the relationship between language and sexuality, should we be looking at the group, or at the individual?

On the one hand, we form impressions about groups of people based on patterns that we notice. If, for instance, I meet one left-handed person who sneezes a lot, I might not read too much into that: I might file those two observations (that she is left-handed and sneezes a lot) as two independent facts about her as an individual. But if I then meet another ten left-handed people who also sneeze a lot, I might start to make an unconscious association between left-handedness and sneezing. And that, in turn, is likely to affect both my perception of people who sneeze (I might decide that they're probably left-handed) and my expectation of left-handed people (I might start to look for reasons why someone *isn't* sneezing as much as I expect them to). And in fact, once I've got that association in my mind, meeting one or two left-handed people who don't sneeze won't necessarily shift my perception of that left-handedness/sneezing relationship: I can classify them as non-sneezing exceptions to the pattern that I've already identified, without having to rethink the fundamental basis of my classification system. Our perceptions of social phenomena are affected by our experiences (the things that we've noticed about the world around us), and we average out our multiple individual experiences according to the social categories relevant to those experiences (categories such as left-handed people, or gay men). Ultimately, we end up with a kind of generalized set of expectations about the behaviours of groups of people, and we use those expectations in interpreting what people do. Viewed from that perspective, then, it makes sense to study groups of people as a way to understand how we come to have the expectations that we do.

On the other hand, those averaged-out generalizations don't actually represent the specific behaviours of individuals, so they're not a very useful tool for understanding what people actually do. For one thing, averaging out can selectively ignore meaningful differences, which is one reason why it's so easy to misrepresent statistics. My favourite cautionary tale on that point is the following "statistic": the average human being has one ovary and one testicle. Mathematically, that's not inaccurate – if you added up all of the ovaries, and then separately added up all of the testicles, and divided each number by the total number of people, you would end up with an average distribution of one of each per person. But that ignores the reality of the distribution of ovaries and testicles, which is that for the most part, they come in mutually exclusive sets of two. The way that we calculated our "average" erases an extremely relevant real-world distinction which significantly impacts on the plausibility of the thing that we've just calculated. A further problem with reporting "averages" is that there are (at least) two distinct meanings of the word *average*: the first is a mathematical average, which is the adding-up-and-dividing exercise we abused a few seconds ago. The second is something closer to *normal* or *common*. It's not always obvious from a sentence which of those two meanings is intended: "Testicles and ovaries have a mean distribution of one of each per person" is *not* the same as "Normal people have one ovary and one testicle", but "The average person has one ovary and one testicle" casually invites both readings.

When we're talking about something that is as obviously incorrect as the ovary-testicle example, where each of us has strong enough independent evidence to refute the conclusion, we can laugh about how ridiculous it is. But when we're trying to understand something that isn't as easily and straightforwardly observable, we have to trust what research tells us, which in turn means that we have to trust that the research does what it says it's doing. The scientific peer review process helps with this, but good researchers are also careful about what they claim that their research shows. That doesn't mean that they don't have confidence in what they've studied, but rather that they've given a faithful account of what they've done, and they're aware of its limitations. This kind of self-reflective practice can lead to changes in methodologies and approaches, which can lead to changes in understanding. In language and gender studies, for example, there has been a massive shift in the past two or three decades from thinking about "women" and "men" as fixed and unmoving demographic categories to recognising that femininities and masculinities are emergent social identities that are shaped by social expectations, and that simultaneously help to shape what those expectations are. There has been a similar shift in language and sexuality studies, from trying to understand what "gay men" do with language to trying to understand how social identities of queer masculinity emerge through language use. Stereotypes are a starting point for that kind of research, but we also have to look further than what our intuitions tell us.

In the next few sections, we'll look at some of the stereotypes that exist about queer men's speech, and then at some of the research that's been done by linguists to investigate and push past those stereotypes. Then we'll think about the speech of queer women, ask ourselves why there are far fewer stereotypes about "sounding lesbian" than there are about "sounding gay", and take a look at some more research around queer women and language. Finally, with a more fleshed-out understanding of some of the basics, we'll circle back to the question that started this whole conversation: can you tell someone's sexuality from the way they speak?

Sounding gay: masculine identities

There's an exercise I often do with undergraduate students in language and gender classes: I give them a sheet of paper, and two minutes to write down as many stereotypes as they can about how gay men speak. At this point we're not looking for political correctness or accuracy – I want them to produce a list of the conventional expectations and social norms that circulate in their communities and in the media that they consume. This gives us a baseline of popular perceptions of masculine sexualities, which is a great starting point for our subsequent discussions. In fact, I invite you try it out yourself: give yourself two minutes and a blank sheet of paper and write down anything and everything that springs to mind about men who sound gay.

After their two minutes are up, I put my students into small groups and ask them to compare their lists. There are two things that I want them to realize. The first is the richness of the stereotypes that they're aware of, once they start thinking about it. Most people can come up with a list of ten to twenty different stereotypes without too much effort, covering different dimensions of language (from pronunciation of certain sounds, to word choices, to things they do with their voices more globally). The second thing that I want my students to notice is how similar their lists are to those of their classmates. Not only are there a lot of specific stereotypes in circulation, but it seems that they come together to form a remarkably coherent package. The particular kind of gay masculinity that these stereotypes address is usually pretty consistent: it's almost always white, generally quite young and urban, and more often than not interested in fashion and interior design. These are the stereotypes that we absorb from television and film, and although they're not representative of the full range of queer masculinities that exist, they do tell us something about what we as a society notice, and how we understand the social relations between different kinds of people.

One of the persistent stereotypes about how gay men talk is that they are somehow using "women's language", or at least speaking in a feminine way.

This association between queer men and femininity has been around for a long time, possibly linked to the flamboyance of particularly camp personas or to a more general classification of non-heterosexual men as being more effeminate overall. It's hard to put a date to this association, partly because in Western societies, homosexuality was historically not widely discussed or documented outside of criminal records. In England, it wasn't really until Oscar Wilde's trial in 1895 that the homosexual man became an identifiable type of person; prior to that, men might engage in specific sexual acts deemed unacceptable, but those sexual acts weren't linked to personal traits such as being educated and articulate, soft-spoken, or interested in cultural, artistic or aesthetic pursuits. Wilde's conviction produced a new social focus on masculinity, and a new interpretative lens for particular types of behaviour and mannerisms. Being different took on a new social meaning.

This link between effeminacy and gay male sexuality can be reflected on a linguistic level in things like the perception of word usage: gay men are said to be more descriptive than straight men (and so come closer to stereotypical women's language), particularly with respect to colours – words like *magenta* and *periwinkle* are thought of as feminine, and by extension when used by men, they seem gay. Robin Lakoff's 1973 article (and later book) called "Language and Woman's Place", which more or less launched the academic field of language and gender, noted that "if a man should say ['The wall is mauve'], one might well conclude he was either imitating a woman sarcastically, or a homosexual, or an interior decorator" (Lakoff 1973: 49). Lakoff's point here is that colour precision marks either feminine attention to detail, or masculine technical specificity. This feminine attention to detail (presumably superfluous detail, since if it isn't superfluous then it would be considered a technical specification of a sort) is also linked to stereotypes of both women and gay men using more "empty" or over-the-top expressions, such as *divine*, *fabulous*, *super* and *oh my God*. Of course, they aren't really "empty" at all, since they serve various communicative functions (showing emotional affect, aligning yourself with another speaker's position, showing that you're paying attention, etc.), but since those roles in a conversation are stereotypically seen as feminine, men who take up those roles may also be seen as effeminate. Another example of bleed-through from femininity into stereotyped gay masculinity can be found in terms of address. The phenomenon of gay men using feminine pronouns and titles (such as calling each other *girlfriend* and *Miss*, as in *Miss Jason is in a mood today*) has a similarly long track record: Gershon Legman's (1941) glossary *The Language of homosexuality* mentions it explicitly, and it continues to circulate in film and television to this day.

On a smaller language scale, the "gay lisp" is also a long-standing stereotype – gay men are *thaid* to turn their *etheth* into TH *thoundth*. The precision and specificity of this observation make it a relatively easy one to examine linguistically. The difference in articulation between an S sound (which linguists represent with the symbol [s]) and a TH sound (which we represent as [θ] when it's the sound in words like *thing*, and [ð] when it's the sound in words like *this*) is basically about tongue position. For [θ] and [ð], the tip of your tongue is touching your upper teeth, and for [s] your tongue is touching a bit further back in your mouth, on the bony ridge behind your teeth. These two different places of articulation produce air friction at two different bands of frequencies, so we can figure out how far back in the mouth the tongue is positioned by recording someone's speech and analysing the acoustic characteristics in the recording. With fricatives (sounds like [s], [θ] and [ð]), the further front in the mouth the tongue is, the higher that band of frequencies is going to be; further back means lower frequencies. Generally speaking, men produce [s] sounds with a lower frequency than women: Jongman, Wayland and Wong (2000) reported mean peak frequencies of around 7.5 kHz for women, and 6.1 kHz for men. This pattern has been found in many varieties of English, and although the specific frequencies vary from place to place, women generally have significantly higher frequencies for [s] than men.

This doesn't happen in all languages, though – the effect is negligible in Japanese (Heffernan 2004) and German (Fuchs and Toda 2010), for instance – so it's not a product of biological or anatomical differences. It's a social and stylistic practice for signalling particular masculinities and femininities in English, and there have been some fairly robust differences reported between straight-sounding and gay-sounding men. Research in California (Zimman 2013; Podesva and Van Hofwegen 2016), Ontario (Hazenberg 2016) and New Zealand (Hazenberg 2017) has shown three things fairly consistently. First, there is a lot of variability in /s/ production by gay men, with some producing an /s/ that is phonetically indistinguishable from straight men, while others produce something much closer in frequency to what women produce. Given the multiplicity of gay male identities and styles, this variation shouldn't really come as a surprise. Second, there are regional differences in how /s/ is produced – in other words, sounding gay doesn't mean the same thing everywhere. The social meaning of language variation is always locally conditioned. An interesting example of this comes from Copenhagen (Maegaard and Pharao 2016): depending on whether you speak the more "standard" Copenhagen Danish or the more non-standard "street" Copenhagen variety, a fronted /s/ can signal gay masculinity (standard) or toughness and immigrant masculinity (street). Being able to recognise *gay* or *tough* masculinity in Copenhagen comes down to whether or not you can differentiate between standard and street Danish – local knowledge, in other words. Finally, these acoustic studies of /s/ tell us that, even though we *call* it a "gay lisp", and we exaggerate the frontness (*frontneth*) of /s/ when we stereotype gay-sounding men, it never is actually pronounced as /θ/ or /ð/. It moves forward into the range of /s/ as produced by women, but we don't have a stereotype of women lisping. We're over-generalizing and over-shooting when we perceive a "gay lisp". This is because we filter what we hear against what we expect to hear – so when we hear a man producing /s/ at a higher-than-expected frequency, we "overhear", and map it to stereotypes that we already have in our minds.

Things like /s/, *darling* and *fabulous* are clearly part of our stereotypes about how gay men speak, but we sometimes get a strong (and often accurate) sense that a man is gay even when we don't hear such obvious linguistic cues. The fact that we can't identify what we think we're hearing makes it hard to figure out what it might be, and so makes it trickier to study. *Tricky* doesn't mean impossible, though, and there's a group of researchers in Toronto who spent several years trying to untangle that particular knot (see Smyth and Rogers 2002 for a summary of some of their findings). They examined a range of linguistic phenomena, including: /s/ frequencies and duration; how clearly articulated certain consonants are; the relative spacing of some vowels in terms of how close to each other they're articulated; vowel duration; and voice pitch. Several other researchers have also taken a stab at the question of how a perceptually gay persona is created and understood, particularly around voice pitch and intonation (see Gaudio 1994; Levon 2006; Podesva 2006 for some examples). It seems that people are generally pretty good at inferring sexual orientation from men's speech, but that the relationship between the pitch properties of their speech and how their sexuality is categorized isn't straightforward. Those pitch properties – such as the range of frequencies that a speaker uses, how much pitch variation there is overall, and how quickly and dramatically the pitch changes – don't correlate neatly with perceptual ratings in terms of femininity, homosexuality or other personal traits linked stereotypically with gay men.

So the picture that emerges overall from these studies is a complicated one. When we try to isolate and study linguistic phenomena in isolation, we get messy and contradictory results. What seems to be going on is that there is a whole range of linguistic resources that people can deploy to create a gay-sounding voice, and any combination of those features will produce the same perceptual effect. But there's no particular reason why two people would choose the same subset of features, so studies that look at averages across communities are losing sight of the specific strategies that people are actually using. Most contemporary research on language and sexuality falls under what Eckert (2012) would class as the "third wave" approach to language variation, which is to look at individuals across multiple contexts, examine what they're doing and how they're doing it, and then make indexical links between the context and the social meanings that the speaker is drawing on. It's a labour-intensive approach, but it pays off in terms of the degree of detail we're able to learn about how we present our social identities through language.

Sounding lesbian: feminine identities

We started our discussion of gay-sounding speech with a brainstorming exercise, which also seems like a good place to launch this section. Get yourself another sheet of paper, reset your timer for two minutes, and jot down all of your stereotypes about how lesbians talk.

Most people have a lot more trouble coming up with clear stereotypes about lesbian and queer women than they do about queer men, so your second list is probably shorter than your first. There also tends to be less agreement among different people. The most common response I come across has to do with voice pitch: lesbians are said to speak with a lower voice than straight women, but that generalization is nowhere near as prevalent as a lot of the stereotypes that we have about gay men. While a lower pitch is also generally true of how men talk, it's actually surprisingly uncommon for anyone to explicitly jot down "lesbians talk like men". While there may be some kind of tenuous association between lesbians and masculinity that parallels the link between gay men and femininity, it is nowhere near as clear or conscious.

So why this difference? Why aren't the two lists basically mirror images of each other? For some reason, we just don't have as clearly defined stereotypes of lesbians as we do of gay men. Partly this may be because women remain generally peripheral to men across most domains, which pushes queer women even further from the center, out into the periphery of the periphery, as it were. There are also differences in how queer men and women position themselves; Zwicky (1997) observes that gay men construct identities in opposition to straight men, but that lesbians construct identities through greater affinity with women, not through opposition. And since we tend to notice difference more than similarity, social identities built on difference are unsurprisingly more noticeable than those built on solidarity. Queen (2014) points out that there *are* tensions between groups of women, including between some lesbians and some straight women, but those tensions have failed to produce any coherent stereotypes; possibly because they are more locally-defined, they fail to pick up enough traction to become widely circulated. Historical differences in access to public space (Cameron 2011) may also have played a role in the lack of recognizably lesbian speech styles comparable to those available to gay men.

From a linguistic perspective, pitch – the frequency at which we speak – is quite straightforward to study, and so has been looked at periodically over the course of a couple of decades. In one of the earlier studies of lesbian speech, Moonwomon-Baird (1997) compared pitch characteristics of two lesbians and two straight women and found little evidence of pitch as a marker of sexuality. She tentatively concluded that lesbian identities are constructed through discourse rather than phonetic details, unlike what we see with queer men. A later study (Waksler 2001) found no evidence that pitch range was indicative of sexuality for women, and Lutzross (2010, cited in Podesva and Kajino 2014) compared perception and production data, finding that although female voices with digitally-lowered pitch ranges were rated as more lesbian-sounding, there was no evidence that lesbians actually made use of that perceptual property when they were speaking. Much as we saw with the speech of gay men, what we hear (or what we think we hear) does not necessarily reflect reality; we are categorizing as we listen, and to some extent, hearing what we want to hear. And, of course, lesbian identities are no more universal than those of gay men; just as there are different ways of being a gay man, which may be invisible to outsiders but which are nevertheless salient within the community, there are different ways of being a lesbian. Levon (2011) looked at pitch properties among two groups of lesbian women, arguing that their use of higher pitch in particular contexts reflected their divergent gender ideologies. More work needs to be done on different communities of queer women, in a way that has started to be done with queer men (see Rusty Barrett's 2017 book *From drag queens to leathermen*).

The lack of clear stereotypes does not mean, of course, that there isn't social marking going on in the speech of lesbians; it just means that we're not very good at identifying what we're attuning to. I have definitely met women who "sound lesbian" to me, and so have most of the lesbian and queer women that I know. Although much less research has been done on the speech of lesbians than on the speech of gay men, researchers (for example: Waksler 2001; Pierrehumbert et al. 2004; Munson et al. 2006; Podesva and Van Hofwegen 2016) have tackled many of the same areas, such as the acoustic properties of certain vowels and consonants, and prosodic qualities, like speech rate and segmental duration. As before, research shows varying degrees of difference between straight- and lesbian-sounding women, and very little consistency within groups of lesbian women.

As with gay-sounding men, then, it would seem that the properties of lesbian-sounding speech are hard to pin down to one or two salient features. Indeed, the situation is very likely the same as with gay men: there is a resource pool consisting of a number of linguistic features and forms which are to some extent associated with non-heterosexual femininities, and any given individual woman can draw on some subset of those resources to encode her identity through language. Which women choose which resources will depend on a number of factors, such as which style of queer femininity they want to present, where they live and how interpretable they want their identity to be – whether they want their identity recognized by everyone, or only by people in their close-knit communities.

The linguistic evidence for the existence of lesbian-sounding speech styles is about as strong as that for gay-sounding styles; although it has been studied less often, the patterns in the findings are quite similar. The principle difference between the two situations is one of social salience. While there are a number of strong stereotypes about gay men, there are very few about queer women, and those that do exist aren't nearly as widely-spread as those of gay men.

Can you tell someone's sexuality from the way they speak?

So we come back to where we started: *can* you tell someone's sexuality from the way they speak? The short answer is: *it depends*.

It depends on whether they're presenting an identity that aligns with our expectations of what queer people sound like. If we're relying on a handful of stereotyped features popularized in the media, and someone isn't ticking those particular boxes, our intuitions may be unreliable. It also depends on how familiar we are with the range of possible identities that they might be presenting. Our knowledge of different communities – gay, lesbian, queer, online or in the real world – influences how we make sense of someone's presentation. There are straight cultures and communities that we might not be able to categorize accurately, either – so it depends on whether we have enough local knowledge to tease sexuality apart from other dimensions of their identity. We are always presenting multiple identities, and there may be bleed-through from one into the other. Think of my sister's Italian colleague, whose European flamboyance was misunderstood as Canadian gay masculinity.

Ultimately, whether or not we can tell someone's sexuality from their language depends on whether they're choosing to make their sexuality known to us. Although we may have a strong nosy urge to categorize people's sexuality, they are under no obligation to fill us in.

Note

1 The use of the term *queer* gets a lot of people in trouble. I'm using it here as an umbrella term to refer to identities other than strictly heterosexual. In the past, people have preferred initialisms such as LGB (Lesbian, Gay, Bisexual)

or LGBT (Lesbian, Gay, Bisexual, Transgender) or LGBTQ (Lesbian, Gay, Bisexual, Transgender, Queer *or* Questioning) – that initialism can get very long, and inevitably excludes identities (which is why it keeps getting longer). We're living in a time when identity labels are proliferating rapidly, so having an inclusive term to encompass everyone is a useful shorthand for a chapter like this. That said, I freely acknowledge that *queer* does not sit well with everyone, and in using it as I do, I'm not trying to push it as the only acceptable term for talking about the collective community of non-heterosexual people. It's just the one that *I* use.

Further reading

For the general question of the way in which language might reflect sexuality, see Barrett (2017), Cameron and Kulick (2003) and Livia and Hall (eds.) (1997).

References

Barrett, Rusty. (2017). *From drag queens to leathermen: Language, gender, and gay male subcultures*. New York: Oxford University Press.

Cameron, Deborah. (2011). Sociophonetics and sexuality: A discussion. *American Speech*, 86(1), 98–103. DOI:10.1215/00031283-1277537

Cameron, Deborah and Don Kulick. (2003). *Language and sexuality*. Cambridge and New York: Cambridge University Press.

Eckert, Penelope. (2012). Three waves of variation study: The emergence of meaning in the study of sociolinguistic variation. *Annual Review of Anthropology*, 41(1), 87–100. DOI:10.1146/annurev-anthro-092611-145828

Fuchs, Susanne and Martine Toda. (2010). Do differences in male versus female /s/ reflect biological or sociophonetic factors? In Susanne Fuchs and Martine Toda (eds.), *Interface explorations: Turbulent sounds: An interdisciplinary guide*, 281–302. Berlin: Walter de Gruyter.

Gaudio, Rudolf P. (1994). Sounding gay: Pitch properties in the speech of gay and straight men. *American Speech*, 69(1), 30–57. DOI:10.2307/455948

Hazenberg, Evan. (2016). Walking the straight and narrow: Linguistic choice and gendered presentation. *Gender and Language*, 10(2), 270–294. DOI:10.1558/genl.v10i2.19812

Hazenberg, Evan. (2017). *Liminality as a lens on social meaning: A cross-variable study of gender in New Zealand English*. PhD thesis. Wellington, New Zealand: Victoria University of Wellington.

Heffernan, Kevin. (2004). Evidence from HNR that /s/ is a social marker of gender. *Toronto Working Papers in Linguistics*, 23(2), 71–84.

Jongman, Allard, Ratree Wayland and Serena Wong. (2000). Acoustic characteristics of English fricatives. *Journal of the Acoustical Society of America*, 108(3), 1252–1263. DOI:10.1121/1.1288413

Lakoff, Robin. (1973). Language and woman's place. *Language in Society*, 2(1), 45–80. DOI:10.1017/S0047404500000051

Legman, Gershon. (1941). The language of homosexuality: An American glossary. In Reprinted in Deborah Cameron and Don Kulick (eds.), (2006), *The language and sexuality reader*, 19–32. Abingdon and New York: Routledge.

Levon, Erez. (2006). Hearing "gay": Prosody, interpretation, and the affective judgments of men's speech. *American Speech*, 81(1), 56–78. DOI:10.1215/00031283-2006-003

Levon, Erez. (2011). Teasing apart to bring together: Gender and sexuality in variationist research. *American Speech*, 86(1), 69–84. DOI:10.1215/00031283-1277519

Livia, Anna and Kira Hall (eds.). (1997). *Queerly phrased: Language, gender, and sexuality*. Oxford: Oxford University Press.

Lutzross, Auburn. (2010). *You sound like a lesbian: Sociophonetic stereotypes of lesbian speech*. Unpublished BA thesis. Amhurst: Hampshire College.

Maegaard, Marie and Nicolai Pharao. (2016). /s/ variation and perceptions of male sexuality in Denmark. In Erez Levon and Ronald Beline Mendez (eds.), *Language, sexuality, and power*, 33–104. New York: Oxford University Press.

Moonwomon-Baird, Birch. (1997). Toward the study of lesbian speech. In Anna Livia and Kira Hall (eds.), *Queerly phrased: Language, gender, and sexuality*, 202–213. New York: Oxford University Press.

Munson, Benjamin, Elizabeth C. McDonald, Nancy L. Deboe and Aubrey R. White. (2006). The acoustic and perceptual bases of judgments of women and men's sexual orientation from read speech. *Journal of Phonetics*, 34(2), 202–240. DOI:10.1016/j.wocn.2005.05.003

Niedzielski, Nancy. (1999). The effect of social information on the perception of sociolinguistic variables. *Journal of Language and Social Psychology*, 18(1), 62–85.

Pierrehumbert, Janet B., Tessa Bent, Benjamin Munson, Ann R. Bradlow and J. Michael Bailey. (2004). The influence of sexual orientation on vowel production. *Journal of the Acoustical Society of America*, 116(4), 1905–1908.

Podesva, Robert J. (2006). Intonational variation and social meaning: Categorical and phonetic aspects. *University of Pennsylvania Working Papers in Linguistics*, 12(2), 189–202.

Podesva, Robert J. and Sakiko Kajino. (2014). Sociophonetics, gender, and sexuality. In Susan Ehrlich, Miriam Meyerhoff and Janet Holmes (eds.), *The handbook of language, gender, and sexuality*. 2nd edition, 103–122. Hoboken: John Wiley & Sons.

Podesva, Robert J. and Janneke Van Hofwegen. (2016). /s/exuality in smalltown California: Gender normativity and the acoustic realization of /s/. In Erez Levon and Ronald Beline Mendez (eds.), *Language, sexuality, and power*, 168–188. New York: Oxford University Press.

Queen, Robin. (2014). Language and sexual identities. In Susan Ehrlich, Miriam Meyerhoff and Janet Holmes (eds.), *The handbook of language, gender, and sexuality*. 2nd edition, 203–219. Hoboken: John Wiley & Sons.

Smyth, Ron and Henry Rogers. (2002). Phonetics, gender, and sexual orientation. *2002 Canadian Linguistics Association Proceedings*, 299–311.

Waksler, Rachelle. (2001). Pitch range and women's sexual orientation. *Word*, 52(1), 69–77. DOI:10.1080/00437956.2001.11432508

Zimman, Lal. (2013). Hegemonic masculinities and the variability of gay-sounding speech. *Journal of Language and Sexuality*, 2(1), 1–39. DOI:10.1075/jls.2.1.01zim

Zwicky, Arnold M. (1997). Two lavender issues for linguists. In Anna Livia and Kira Hall (eds.), *Queerly phrased: Language, gender, and sexuality*, 21–34. New York: Oxford University Press.

9 Is learning a signed language easier than learning a spoken language?

Sara Pivac Alexander and George Major

Is sign language universal (one or many)?

Wherever you find communities of Deaf[1] people, all around the world, you are likely to find a sign language. You might see people moving their hands in precise ways as they communicate with each other and if you look closer, you might also notice that they are using some interesting facial expressions and body movements as they talk. If you have used a spoken language your whole life, relying on your ears and mouth to communicate, then the idea of learning to talk in this completely new way can be an exciting thought. Imagine being able to chat with your friends using sign language in a loud café, through a window or even in a library where everyone has to be quiet – but you can chat, because you can sign without making a noise.

So, is learning a signed language easier than learning a spoken language? After all, you only need to make some pictures with your hands and these will represent the spoken words you already know, right? Not quite! Sorry to be the bearers of bad news, but learning a new signed language is, in fact, very hard work and not linguistically easier than learning a new spoken language. Those facial expressions and body movements are not random; they are actually used in quite specific ways to create certain meanings. Learning a signed language is a bit different to learning a spoken language though, something which we will explore in this chapter.

Our perspective that sign languages are challenging to learn is not actually new at all. In 1978, Roger Brown wrote an article in which he debunked this myth. Mike Kemp (1998: 257) wrote that sign language learning can be "difficult and even gruelling". Although we are saying much the same thing, we hope to update this perspective, based on our experiences of the sign language classroom in the current day. But before we get stuck into those details, we'll first briefly touch on sign languages around the world, and on some of the reasons people might be drawn to take a sign language class in the first place.

Contrary to a pervasive myth that sign language is "universal", there are many unique sign languages around the world. It is very hard to pin down the exact number. The online Ethnologue (www.ethnologue.com) lists 144 different sign languages, though researchers think that the numbers are probably greater than this (Woll, Sutton-Spence and Elton 2010). The World Federation of the Deaf website (http://wfdeaf.org/our-work/) says there are "300+ sign languages" although they don't explain where this number comes from. Signed languages are not just representations of the spoken languages around them, so for example, even though English is spoken in both the USA and Australia, the signed languages in those countries are very different from each other (see Woll, Sutton-Spence and Elton 2010 for a more detailed discussion about how different sign languages relate to each other). This is important to keep in mind because in this chapter we are attempting to talk about "sign language" in general, but of course just like spoken languages, signed languages can be vastly different to each other.

Thanks to the pioneering work of researchers in the late 20th century, such as William Stokoe (1960, 1978), sign languages have been recognized as true languages in their own right, and not just the mime and gesture that they were once thought to be (more on this soon). With this recognition, a more global awareness of sign languages and Deaf communities has developed, and in some countries, there has been a bit of an explosion in the numbers of hearing people wanting to learn to sign. The United States is one example of a place where numbers of sign language class enrolments have increased dramatically (Kemp 1998; Quinto-Pozos 2011; Rosen 2008). It is curious, though, that as more and more hearing people learn signed languages, the myth that they are somehow "easier" to learn than spoken languages still exists as it did when Brown wrote his chapter more than 40 years ago.

Sign language learning is on the rise!

It must help that there are more video clips showing sign languages on social media these days, and that sign language interpreters are becoming more visible on television and in the public domain. Sign languages are very visual, and it's not too hard to be distracted and then perhaps utterly fascinated by the movements and facial expressions of an interpreter in a news briefing, or a Deaf person signing beautifully to music in a viral video. Some of our students have enrolled in sign language courses after seeing interpreters on the news during natural disaster coverage. And there are a whole host of other reasons to learn to sign – to communicate with Deaf family, friends and colleagues, to become a sign language interpreter or work in Deaf education, or just simply for a fun class to learn a cool new language.

In some countries "baby sign" has become very popular, whereby young hearing babies and their parents learn signs to be able to communicate with each other. It is true that babies as young as six months often can physically produce signs before spoken words. This is because the ability to form shapes with the hands usually comes earlier than the fine motor skills required to form spoken words. So baby sign is a useful communication tool for families, and we have seen around the world that whole companies are built upon this craze. These classes focus on basic vocabulary, however, and often use American Sign Language (ASL) even in countries where ASL is not a language used by the local Deaf community. Enthusiasm for baby sign generally wanes when babies start to pick up spoken language. We wonder if baby sign creates the sense that if it is so easy for babies, it must be easy for adults to learn too! Several students have told us they took sign language at university because they thought it would be very easy credits compared to other papers.

Speaking with your hands – how hard can it be?

One of the most common misconceptions is that sign languages must be easy to learn because they are just "pictures on the hands". There is actually a good reason for this – or at least we understand why this is the case, linguistically speaking. Compared to spoken languages, signed languages have a much higher degree of iconicity (signs that have pictorial qualities, which means that the sign in some way represents the form of the actual thing). A good example in many sign languages is the sign for *table* (Figure 9.1), in which the hands trace the physical outline of a flat table-top and then down the sides to represent legs.

The opposite of an "iconic" sign is an "arbitrary" sign where the form of the sign does not in any way represent the shape or qualities of the entity. Sign languages have a lot of arbitrary signs too, for example the sign for *sister* (Figure 9.2) in New Zealand Sign Language (NZSL).

Spoken languages actually have iconicity too – it is called "onomatopoeia", where the word closely represents the actual thing (*boom*, *crack*, *splat*)! But the very interesting thing is that signed languages have much more of it, and this is likely where the misconception comes from. Does it mean sign languages are less sophisticated? Not at all – it just means that as visual languages, they make use of this whenever possible! Why use an abstract sign for *table* when elements of the actual thing can be shown and it is very clear and efficient?

When new students start learning a sign language, they will often start with highly iconic vocabulary, such as *sit*, *write*, *book*, *drink*. These signs look a lot like the action or the thing, so they are quite easy to learn and the myth that sign languages are easier to learn stays intact for a little while.

Figure 9.1 TABLE in many sign languages. All images are from the NZSL Online Dictionary (https://nzsl.nz) by Deaf Studies Research Unit, Victoria University of Wellington, and are licensed under Creative Commons BY-NC-SA 3.0.

Until students start learning a bit more, and they realise that many signs are not iconic at all, and beyond that there are many complex grammatical constructions to get their heads around. At some point the sheer amount of new and challenging aspects of learning to sign can be a bit of a shock. It can even be quite overwhelming for some students.

Three challenges unique to learning a sign language

To begin with, learning to talk in a new language modality, and using the whole upper body, instead of just mouth and ears, to communicate, can be mentally and physically very tiring. Students are not only learning to

Is it easier to learn a signed language? 127

Figure 9.2 Sister in NZSL.

use their hands in articulate and precise ways, they also need to use facial expressions to get meanings across, and this is a new territory for many. It's as if someone has been a right-handed person all their life and they start a new class – suddenly they're required to write only using their left-hand. Early classes can leave students feeling a range of emotions, as well as just physically exhausted – our students talk of getting headaches at the end of a two-hour class or feeling like their "eyes are going to fall out".

The initial shock can extend beyond producing the language too. In many (but not all) countries the majority of sign language teachers are Deaf themselves. This means most sign language classes are full immersion in the language from the first day, and a number of classrooms (like ours) have a "voice off" rule. Some students sign up for classes not knowing that they will have a Deaf teacher and unaware that they will be asked to switch their voices off completely. Some students are delighted and invigorated by this new way of communicating in a classroom, while others can experience a significant cultural shock. Kemp (1998, citing Brown 1978) describes this cultural shock in detail, noting that it can take some time for students to recover from this and to gain confidence in the new language. He suggests a "reality check" may be needed for learners who think sign language is very easy to learn in a short amount of time.

As well as getting used to a new way of moving the hands, face and body to communicate, the immersive sign language classroom involves learning appropriate ways to behave in a signed conversation, like getting attention through waving or tapping someone's shoulder, and holding eye contact with others. Students cannot really look away to utter a sentence or two in sign language – they have to lock eyes with the person they're talking to, in order to communicate and get their point across. Some students come from cultural backgrounds where prolonged and direct eye contact is considered inappropriate, and many are used to a lifelong behaviour where they can look away while speaking. So it can feel uncomfortable or embarrassing to have to hold someone's gaze for quite a considerable amount of time. These sorts of things are very normal for the Deaf teachers but can feel quite weird for new students and they need time to get used to it. We do not find that this puts students off in the long run but it can definitely be a challenge to begin with.

Cultural shock aside, initial sign language learning can feel like students are making very quick progress as lots of new and fun vocabulary is learnt. However, Kemp (1998: 255) points out that "like all languages, it is not mastered easily beyond a basic level. Mastery requires extensive exposure and practice". As students start to learn more grammatical structures, and start to learn more abstract and complex ways of making meaning, the challenge intensifies.

The nuts and bolts of learning a sign language

There are four different components that make up a sign and need to be produced correctly: handshape, orientation of the palm, location (on or near which part of the body), and movement of the sign. These components are like sounds in spoken languages – the sounds need to be right for a word to make sense. Some signs are one-handed, and some are two-handed. Two-handed signs may have the same or different handshapes, and they may either move in the same (symmetrical) or in a different (non-symmetrical) way. Sign language students have more difficulties producing signs that have multiple parts to them (Ortega and Morgan 2015).

Did you also know that there are different types of signs? Most signs are made primarily with the hands, though rare signs are made with facial expression alone. Then there are some unique signs that involve both hands and particular facial expressions and they actually don't make sense if one of these components is missing. They're a bit like slang words and they are deeply rooted in Deaf culture. They don't follow any spoken language mouth patterns and so it can be very puzzling for hearing students to see Deaf people using mouth patterns like that. To use New Zealand

Sign Language as an example, a mouth pattern that looks like *whoof*, along with a specific sign to accompany it, means 'flash' or 'excellent', *bif* means 'oh really' and *baba* means 'that's unusual' (Figure 9.3). To really start to understand these types of signs, students have to look at context, and see it repeated over and over in real interaction between fluent signers.

And like learning any other language, understanding is one thing but producing these types of complex signs is quite another. Even when students try really hard, it is so difficult to produce these in the same way a Deaf signer does, and they may instead produce something that looks a bit funny in the beginning. These types of signs are usually taught at a more advanced level, by which time ideas of sign language being easy to learn are fast evaporating. These "slang" signs we are describing do not always translate easily to spoken languages (or at least they often do not have a one-word equivalent translation), which can also be a bit of a rude awakening.

Specialized and technical vocabulary can be particularly challenging because signed languages generally have much smaller vocabularies than spoken languages. This is partly because they have historically been used less in technical domains (e.g. medicine, science, etc.) compared to more

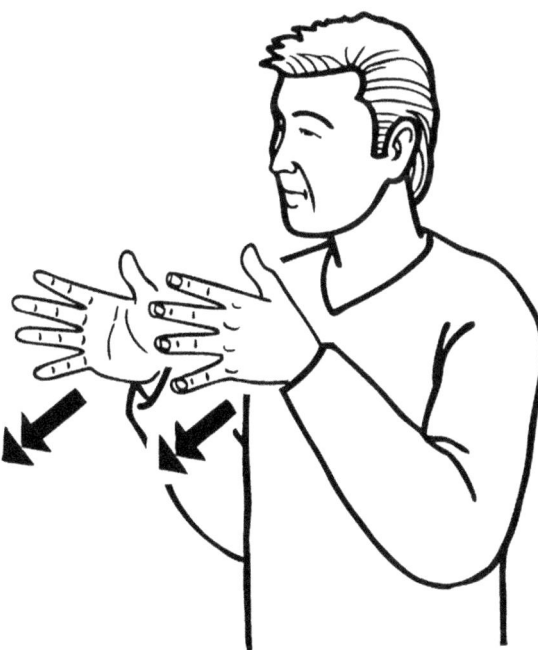

Figure 9.3 UNUSUAL in NZSL.

established majority languages like English, but also partly because sign languages create meaning through other strategies too. For example, there is no verb *to be* in the sign languages that we are familiar with (as in "I *am* happy"; "you *are* happy"). The language is not missing anything here; it just has other ways to express the concept. It can be very hard though for new learners trying to find the signs for *is* and *are*! Technical concepts sometimes require the signer to "circumnavigate", or to find other ways to explain and convey the concept if there is no direct equivalent available.

Once the learner moves beyond simple vocabulary to phrases and sentences, it becomes clear that sentence structure can be very different to other languages. Especially at the advanced levels, the order in which you can put words and ideas can be a lot more flexible than in a language such as English. Students may need to use two or more sentence structure rules (just like other spoken languages) but at the same time they need to think about using more than one specific facial expression to get their intended point across. Raise eyebrows there, neutral eyebrows there, head back slightly, lips narrowed and so on. It can be quite a lot to deal with!

And then there are "classifiers" or "depicting signs", which are very hard to learn. They are another mysterious sphere to sign languages, using some parts of signs (handshapes for example) but in a very visual and creative way. For example, using a flat handshape to represent a car (that handshape is the classifier in this case), this can be moved, accompanied by specific facial expressions that add particular meanings, to show the car going uphill, downhill, speeding erratically, cruising along, driving a bumpy road, skidding, etc. These exact movements are determined by the meaning at the time, so they are never necessarily the same. For this reason, "depicting signs" cannot be looked up in the dictionary, unlike "frozen signs" (like *table*, *sister* above), which can be looked up in the dictionary because they don't change. We say that depicting signs are partly lexical (part real sign) and partly gestural, and in many languages there is nothing that compares.

Space can also be used to show contrast between things, like size, cost and power differences. For example, if a signer was talking about the government, they might place the government in a space that is quite high up, to show that it is a powerful entity. Space is also used to show tense and time, with the past being behind the signer and the future being in front, although space can also be used in more specific ways to show something occurring regularly, sporadically, changes through time and much more. In sign languages, the space in front of you is your stage, your world – you've got to visualize everything to conjure a mental image in your mind, and sign as you imagine it.

Is it easier to learn a signed language? 131

Signing in certain spaces conveys specific information, and changing that space in any way can change the meaning significantly. For example, a signer can talk about flying from Australia to Cuba using just one two-handed sign, as opposed to the whole string of words (a sentence) that would be used to say the same thing in a spoken language. It doesn't mean the sign language is simpler however – a lot of meaning is packed into and around that sign. Firstly, the signer will have already set up Australia and Cuba at specific spots within their signing space. One hand likely points to the space where Cuba has already been established. At the same time the other hand, in an iconic handshape that depicts an airplane, starts in the space where Australia has been established and then moves to show the direction and destination of flight. A specific facial expression with puffed cheeks may be used to show that it is a long flight. Students have to concentrate hard to pick up all the meanings contained in the use of space and facial expression. This is one of the hardest things for students to learn to do well; it takes a lot of practice to be able to understand and use this three-dimensional space consistently and clearly.

You know how some spoken languages have many different pronouns to learn ("he", "she", "it" etc.)? Well in a signed language, you only need to point your finger in space, like little children do … so it should be very easy, right? Again, not quite! Like in the example of Cuba and Australia above, sign languages tend to "place" things in a particular space, in the "signing space" in front of the person signing. Then that space can be pointed at later to refer back to that entity (whether it's a person, animal, place or an idea). If the student forgets where they placed that entity, or mixes the spaces up, it's hard for the person watching to understand what is being talked about (a bit like getting pronouns mixed up). In addition, the act of pointing with an index finger, especially at a person, can be considered rude in some cultures. So this can be quite unsettling for some students, especially when combined with that prolonged eye gaze we talked about earlier.

While we are outlining some key challenges in learning a sign language, fingerspelling deserves a mention too. Fingerspelling, used by some sign languages more than others, is spelling individual letters of the alphabet on the hands, in order to "borrow" spoken language words. For example, if a student doesn't know the sign for a place, they can fingerspell the place name in full. It can also be used for names, and sometimes for when the signer wants to convey a specific spoken language word but doesn't know the sign for it, or one does not exist. It is one thing to learn to do fingerspelling, but quite another to understand other people's fingerspelling, especially when it can be very fast. In order to read fingerspelling the student is required to recognize a whole combination of signs (for letters) and then to put these together to form the word. Of course this is similar to when a new word or a name is said in a spoken language – after all it is just the perception and recognition of symbols – but this comprehension can be a struggle for adult learners (see Quinto-Pozos 2011 for more detailed discussion of this).

Sign languages and language variation

Our final point in the discussion of why signed languages are not easier to learn than spoken languages relates to language variation (e.g. differences in the words people use, and the ways they speak). Most students learn mainly from a sign language teacher and are accustomed to that person's signing style. So then when the student ventures out into the Deaf community, meets Deaf visitors in class or trawls through sign language videos online, they can be amazed to learn not everyone signs in the same way. Some Deaf people may be particularly difficult for students to understand because they use different signs for the same words. They may also have a different communication style when they sign, for instance, they may sign quickly, or in a rambling sort of a way, or using a very small signing space, which can be quite different to the teacher's style that the student is used to. Variation in languages is a natural part of all languages so this in itself is not different to spoken languages. However, with sign languages there can be a lot more variation, and this is mainly because of the ways in which Deaf people learn sign languages.

The majority of deaf children are born to hearing parents. Less than 10% of deaf children are born to signing Deaf parents, from whom they learn the language from birth, as their mother tongue, so to speak. Hearing parents who have deaf babies may or may not have knowledge about sign language or access to learning it, nor an awareness about how important sign language is to young deaf babies. They may be advised to try technological interventions (e.g. cochlear implants) and to focus on learning the spoken rather than signed language. Some other deaf children may have hearing technology as well as exposure to both spoken and signed language around them. Other deaf children may be deprived of any real first language, whether that is spoken or signed, until they are much older and past the age where it is relatively easy to learn a language.

So, within the Deaf community, there is huge variation in the age at which Deaf people come to learn sign language – it could be at birth, later during childhood, or discovering it later as an adult. This means that Deaf communities are made up of a rich mix of native and non-native (second language learner) signers, all of which makes for a massive variation in ways people sign. It is very challenging for students! In our experience this can cause some panic and uncertainly, especially in advanced learners such as sign language interpreting students who may feel stressed to observe that real life sign language can look so different from beginner classes or sign language learning resources.

So is signed language easier than spoken language?

Before bringing this chapter to a close, we do need to acknowledge that some of our advanced sign language students do still genuinely claim that learning a sign language is "easier" for them than learning a spoken language. Let's consider some of the possible reasons for this perception based on what we have seen and on what our students have told us over the years.

Overwhelmingly in our experience, students find sign language classes a lot of fun, because they tend to be very interactive and not book-based. It is really hard to see class as a difficult chore when they have so much fun there and cannot wait for the next class! If class is so much fun, it is naturally easier to practise, to want to do better, and to progress in the language. Some students (probably not those who have experienced the significant culture shock we mentioned earlier!) have told us that it feels easier to immerse themselves in the language because of the change in modality; that is, switching to hands/body/eyes instead of mouth/ears to communicate. They can even ask for new signs they don't know by fingerspelling, so there is no need to use English and this helps them to stay immersed in the new language.

Sign language class also suits some people's learning styles better, for example, if they are quite visual learners, or are already naturally good at communicating in a very gestural sort of way to get their point across. These students may take to sign language classes like ducks to water. Students are a diverse group and so it makes sense that some individuals just naturally excel in learning a signed language (though to be fair, at the same time, others may also more naturally excel in learning spoken languages). And as we mentioned earlier, the iconic nature of some signs is a very helpful jumpstart at the beginner level, especially for those very visual learners, even if that advantage does not carry through to the advanced levels.

Mouth patterns are also an element of sign languages that can help learners, by giving clues in figuring out meanings of unknown signs. Some signs, particularly nouns, are produced with a pattern on the mouth of a corresponding spoken language word. It is important to mention though that the use of these varies widely between different sign languages. Although this doesn't extend in any way to all signs/sign languages, it can still be a helpful tool to some learners: if a student is stuck with a sign, they could look at the lip pattern for clues. This strategy can be especially helpful during test time.

Finally, Deaf people in the community may sometimes be quite forgiving of imperfect signing skills, so students learning the language can feel more confident to give it a go in authentic Deaf community settings. Although we cannot by any means generalize this to all Deaf people/communities, at least in our experience, this is often the case. It may have a lot to do with the fact that Deaf people have spent their whole lives having to accommodate and try to understand people who cannot sign (and having to try to lipread), so they can be extremely skilled at putting together scraps and clues of language and gesture to make meaning. In the early stages, then, when students are doing their best to approximate signs they have seen, it is possible that they feel more competent than they actually are, because Deaf people are just so very good at filling in the gaps.

So to return once again to our initial question: are signed languages easier to learn than spoken languages? We would say that linguistically speaking, they are not. We have seen that there are some valid reasons why students might perceive sign language to be easier in the earlier levels – particularly if they start by learning the iconic signs that do have very pictorial qualities. Also if students have a lot of fun in interactive sign language class, it is of course going to be easier to engage and get better at signing. Other students, however, can experience significant cultural shock from having to communicate in a new way with no voice and different conversation rules. And there is often physical exhaustion from learning to use the eyes, arms, body and face in a completely new way. Regardless of first impressions, progressing beyond beginner level will bring a realization that the grammar of sign languages, including the use of space and facial expression, is complex, rich and vastly different to other languages.

The sign language learning experience itself really depends (like any language learning) on the individual student, their aptitude and motivation, and the teacher's skill in making the class fun and dynamic. If you haven't already learnt a sign language of your local community, we encourage you to find a class, and discover it for yourself!

Acknowledgements

The authors would like to thank David McKee for his input on this chapter.

Note

1 In this chapter we follow the usual convention in writing *Deaf* with a capital "D" to mean people who use a sign language and identify with the Deaf community, as opposed to *deaf* which is an audiological description of a person with a hearing loss whether they use a sign language or not.

Further reading

Jordan Fenlon and Erin Wilkinson's (2015) chapter "Sign Languages in the World" provides a really accessible description of sign languages internationally and the types of communities in which they exist, with plenty of examples. They explain how and why some sign languages are closely related and others are very distinct from each other. The chapter also provides historical information about Deaf education and how this has impacted the development of sign languages and discusses multilingualism (using two or more languages) in Deaf communities.

David Crystal's (2005) book *How language works* includes a clear description of the structure and some unique characteristics of signed languages compared to spoken languages. He also introduces fingerspelling and talks about differences between sign languages and other types of manual communication systems. This is a good place to start for people who are new to linguistics.

Bencie Woll, Rachel Sutton-Spence and Frances Elton's (2010) chapter "Multilingualism: The Global Approach to Sign Languages" is a fascinating description of many sign languages around the world including very interesting details about their development, who uses them and how they relate historically to other sign languages.

For readers who want much more information on the linguistics of sign languages, *Australian Sign Language: An introduction to sign language linguistics* by Trevor Johnston and Adam Schembri (2007) is a great book to look at. Although most of the chapters focus on Auslan, the first chapter includes an overview of the history of sign languages, and it also dispels some common sign language myths.

References

Brown, Roger. (1978). Why are signed languages easier to learn than spoken languages? Part two. *Bulletin of the American Academy of Arts and Sciences*, 32(3), 25–44.

Crystal, David. (2005). *How language works*. London: Penguin Books.

Fenlon, Jordan and Erin Wilkinson. (2015). Sign languages in the world. In Adam Schembri and Ceil Lucas (eds.), *Sociolinguistics and Deaf communities*, 5–28. Cambridge: Cambridge University Press.

Johnston, Trevor and Adam Schembri. (2007). *Australian Sign Language: An introduction to sign language linguistics*. New York: Cambridge University Press.

Kemp, Mike. (1998). Why is learning American Sign Language a challenge? *American Annals of the Deaf*, 143(3), 255–259.

Ortega, Gerardo and Gary Morgan. (2015). Phonological development in hearing learners of a sign language: The influence of phonological parameters, sign complexity, and iconicity. *Language Learning*, 65(3), 660–688.

Quinto-Pozos, David. (2011). Teaching American Sign Language to hearing adult learners. *Annual Review of Applied Linguistics*, 31, 137–158.

Rosen, Russell S. (2008). American Sign Language as a foreign language in U.S. high schools: State of the art. *The Modern Language Journal*, 92(i), 10–38.

Stokoe, William C. (1960 [1978]). Sign language structure: An outline of the visual communication systems of the American deaf. *Studies in linguistics, Occasional papers, No. 8*, Dept. of Anthropology and Linguistics, University at Buffalo (2d ed.). Silver Spring: Linstok.

Woll, Bencie, Rachel Sutton-Spence and Frances Elton. (2010). Multilingualism: The global approach to sign languages. In Ceil Lucas (ed.), *The sociolinguistics of sign languages*, 8–32. Cambridge: Cambridge University Press.

10 Can you forget your native language?

Monika S. Schmid

Introduction: is native language loss an affectation?

On 31 May 2014, US soldier Bowe Bergdahl was released after having been held as a captive of the Taliban in Afghanistan for five years. President Barack Obama announced the release at a press conference at which Bergdahl's father also spoke. One of the things he mentioned was that his son was having "trouble speaking English".[1]

The response by the Twitterati did not disappoint. "What? He forgot he was American, maybe!" fulminated a user with the poetic handle @ForGodAndCountryInSC, while others insisted that Bergdahl must be "playing to his audience" (@ROCKWITHBECK) and that this was a clear "sign of a traitor" (@OYAHHH). The Nevada Tea Party was convinced that the public had been fed an "obvious lie by father saying son was having trouble w/English" and Sarah Palin let off a storm of tweets querying why a "true American hero", such as her running mate in their unsuccessful 2012 bid for the US presidency, John McCain, had survived more than five years as a prisoner of war with his English intact, and wittily recommended several times that Bergdahl should use the online software Rosetta Stone to re-learn English.

There are several common themes to these remarks. First, none of the commentators appears interested in what the "trouble" referred to by Bergdahl's father actually consisted of. Was it word-finding difficulties? Resorting to words of another language (code-switching)? A foreign accent? All of these are well-documented phenomena routinely experienced by language users who exclusively or predominantly use a language other than their native one in their daily lives. The process of language development characterized by these phenomena is referred to as "language attrition" (e.g. Schmid and Köpke, 2017). The assumption in most of the discussions and contributions above, by contrast, was that "trouble speaking English" must mean a wholesale inability to produce or comprehend any English whatsoever. For a mature native speaker such as Bergdahl, such a scenario is indeed not very likely, while less sweeping indications of language attrition are only to be expected and could very well fall under the umbrella of "having trouble" with the language. The second widely and axiomatically shared view was that the father's general claim was ludicrous: one does not forget one's native language, and certainly not after as short a period as five years (and especially if that language happens to be American English).

These sentiments are common. While it is relatively rare for language attriters to be accused of treason by their compatriots, the assumption that any linguistic manifestations of a relatively infrequent use of the native language must simply be an affectation is ubiquitous. One of the less likeable characters in Hilary Mantel's historical novel *Wolf Hall* is the ill-fated Anne Boleyn, who was raised in a French-speaking environment from childhood and returned to England around age 20. "Now she speaks her native tongue with a slight, unplaceable accent, strewing her sentences with French words when she pretends she can't think of the English", is how Mantel puts it (Mantel 2009, p. 27),[2] with the emphasis clearly on the word *pretend*.

There are myriad examples from public debate and individual experience illustrating that the idea that language attrition must be an affectation is very common. For example, an article by Tobias Jones in the newspaper *The Guardian* on "The Joys and Benefits of Bilingualism", published on January 20, 2018,[3] attracted over 500 comments, among them one which said:

> I live in Brittany. My wife does not speak any English apart from "I love you" and "Shut up!" I find it very difficult when I have to speak English as it is very very rare. I too tend to drop in French words when I do speak English.

The response from another reader to this introspective analysis of a personal experience of language attrition was concise (and almost comically representative of the worldview of the archetypical monolingual speaker of English): "Should have taught her then. The second part I don't believe." Multiple other readers responded to this comment, saying that they found the statement perfectly believable, as they had either experienced similar things themselves or seen them in a relative, friend or partner.

About two months after Jones' article was published, *The Guardian* ran a piece which I wrote on the common linguistic phenomena experienced in first language attrition, such as word-finding difficulties, errors and hesitations.[4] This piece also received an extensive number of comments, including one equally concise sweeping dismissal: "This whole article is utter nonsense." Again, a number of other readers protested that what I had described perfectly aligned with either their own experience or that of someone close to them. This prompted the first commentator to elaborate:

> Ok. I live in the reverse. I never ever speak English. [...]
> I have 100% confidence in writing English. I have never lost that. Speaking English takes a short time of correction. [...]
> The author suggested that English or European citizens may encounter difficulties. I do not think so.
> I had a good friend who was fluent in English, French, German, Spanish and Italian. For a few minutes she got confused when changing countries because she thought in the previous language. The brain need a short time to switch.
> I think all day in French except when I come on the Guardian.

I find this little exchange interesting and am presenting it here at such length for three reasons. The first one is that it illustrates to what extent many people believe that they have an expert understanding of language, simply by being language users. Accounts by linguists, despite being based on a large amount of empirical evidence and expert theoretical insight, years of painstaking research and scientifically vetted publications, are often summarily dismissed on the basis of people's introspection or anecdotal counter-examples.

Secondly, even this short paragraph contains a multitude of examples that are epitomic of attrition, such as awkward word order ("I think all day in French" instead of "I think in French all day"), odd expressions ("Speaking English takes a short time of correction") and grammatical errors, such as the absence of subject-verb agreement ("The brain **need** a short time to switch" instead of "needs").

The third – and most surprising – reason why this statement is so interesting is that the reader who contributed it was *the very same person* who, two months previously, had provided the comment cited above about finding it "very difficult" to speak English and dropping in French words all the time!

As these and other examples[5] show, the field of language attrition research still has a long way to go in effectively disseminating research findings and raising awareness that language attrition is indeed a real and tangible phenomenon, experienced by thousands of people, which may not only cause them to experience feelings of guilt and shame, but also to be judged as liars or show-offs by others.

What types of language attrition are there?

The examples above cover various contexts of language attrition with potentially very distinct outcomes. In the first instance, situations of forgetting or erosion of the native language have to be distinguished based on how old a person is when access to the L1 becomes limited. The first context is that of a speaker who has little or no knowledge of other languages, or uses other languages in very limited contexts until adolescence or adulthood (for example when learning them as part of their formal education), and who is then transposed to another linguistic environment, for example because of marriage, work or education. Bowe Bergdahl and the *Guardian* reader who went to France as an adult and got married there exemplify this context. Anne Boleyn, on the other hand, is an example of a child who was raised speaking several languages, one of them the language of her parents and family (English) and another the language of her environment and education (French). Research to date suggests that, in the former case, changes are likely to be comparatively subtle and will not lead to massive language loss, while younger speakers are indeed capable of losing a language entirely, even if it had developed to completely age-appropriate levels prior to around age ten (e.g. Bylund 2019).

Childhood attrition and language forgetting

Anyone who has ever witnessed the joyful process of a child making their way into one or several languages may find it hard to believe that the development, knowledge and proficiency which come so naturally and effortlessly may be vulnerable to erosion. To give another literary example, the author and artist Judith Kerr wrote about her experience as the child of a family of German-Jewish refugees in her three-volume fictionalized autobiography, *When Hitler stole Pink Rabbit* (Kerr, 1971 [2002], *Bombs on Aunt Dainty* (Kerr, 1975 [2017]) and *A small person far away* (Kerr, 1978 [2002]). In the final volume, the central character Anna (Kerr's alter ego) – now grown up – has a conversation with a friend about having forgotten most of her childhood German. This is overheard by the friend's six-year-old boy, who is incredulous at the thought and asserts very forcefully that something like that would never happen to him. His father tries to explain that the reason why Anna had forgotten her German was because she had moved to a place where no-one had spoken it, and that she had learned English instead. Still the child insists that that would not matter, he could not imagine ever forgetting all his English words – no matter how many new ones he might learn in another language (Kerr 1978 [2002], p. 29).

There is a strong ring of authenticity to the view expressed here, its semi-fictional nature notwithstanding. At any age, the language or languages we use are linked very intimately with the core of who we are, and the little boy's essential Englishness would seem robust and natural to him as well as to his parents. A similar sense is expressed by *Guardian* writer Ellie Mae O'Hagan:[6]

> If someone had told me 10 years ago that I would one day start forgetting how to speak Welsh, I would have been incredulous. Growing up, the Welsh language was such a central part of my life and identity that forgetting it would have seemed as likely as my arm spontaneously falling off. And yet here I am, 10 years later, shamefully putting Welsh words into Google Translate to make sure I've got them right.

O'Hagan concludes that "language has an intimacy and power that shapes a person existentially". Because, for her, learning Welsh was bound up so intimately with learning to speak in the first place, and with becoming a proper person and an individual, "losing Welsh, then, is like losing a whole person". Many similar accounts exist, describing the shock, guilt and shame experienced by people who find that they have unexpectedly lost the language they spoke as children, alongside very strong reactions from others who blame them for so delinquently and thoughtlessly having squandered away a precious part of their heritage and their identity.[7]

A great deal of research has been conducted on multilingual acquisition in childhood. We know that children have the ability and potential to develop not just one but several languages. The long-standing myth that multilingual acquisition means that each language will somehow be less perfect than if it had been acquired on its own has also been thoroughly debunked. However, research has also clearly shown that simply being exposed to more than one language does not guarantee that the child will indeed learn each of them completely. The factors that enter into the mix of heritage language development are complex, and while most children will eventually attain native or near-native proficiency in the language spoken in the wider society in which they live (the "environmental language", e.g. English in the US), in particular if that is also the language of formal education, the proficiency they will have in the language of their ancestry can vary hugely. An investigation of around 2,000 bilingual families in Belgium (De Houwer 2007) revealed that about a quarter of the children ended up with proficiency only in the language of the environment (French or Dutch), and researchers to date often struggle to come up with models capable of predicting proficiency based on factors such as input and output – how often the child hears or speaks the language in question (e.g. Montrul 2016; Pascual y Cabo and Rothman 2012; Unsworth 2016).

One of the reasons why it is so difficult to attain a comprehensive understanding of how well speakers will ultimately command a language to which they were exposed as children may be that models seldom consider that children may not only learn language but also forget things they had already learned. Heritage language learners often develop perfectly age-appropriately in their home language until around age five or six. This age is an important milestone for two reasons: firstly, it is the age at which children are usually capable of using all of the grammatical features of their native language (such as grammatical case, embedded sentences, the different past tenses etc.) in the same way that adult native speakers do. Secondly, it is the age at which, in many countries, they begin their formal education, which typically means an increase in exposure to the language of the environment, including incipient literacy. Very often, children begin to rebel against home language policies around that time (in particular if they have older siblings with whom they can speak the environmental language in the home) and that is when parents begin to struggle to maintain home language policies.

All available research suggests, however, that simply being able to use the home language age-appropriately at this age is not enough: a consolidation period is needed in order to render the knowledge of the language stable, and that period typically lasts until around the onset of puberty. Findings from studies investigating international adoptees suggest that, even if a child was a monolingual speaker of their birth language up until as old as eight to ten years, but then is transposed to a different linguistic environment, the birth language may be entirely replaced by the new language, leading to a catastrophic breakdown in, first, production and, subsequently, comprehension, to the point at which there is no recollection left at all (e.g. Ventureyra, Pallier and Yoo 2004; Pallier 2007; Bylund 2019). Any advantage in attempting to re-learn the language is minimal in comparison to novel learners with no previous experience with it (e.g. Park 2015; Pierce, Genesee and Klein 2019; Oh, Au, Jun and Lee 2019).

Returning to Anne Boleyn and her less-than-flattering portrayal in Mantel's *Wolf Hall*, we should conclude that – far from deserving to be branded as an inveterate show-off – having spent most of her childhood away from England and her family and having been raised and educated at the French-speaking Burgundian court, she was actually doing very well to be a fluent English speaker with a slight accent and occasional word-finding difficulties!

Language attrition among adults

What, then, about speakers for whom the move away from their country and language of birth occurs at a later age, after puberty? The case of Bowe Bergdahl shows that attitudes towards native language loss are even more negative for such speakers. In cases where trauma may also play a role, such as prisoners of war like Bergdahl or refugees, it is very likely that psychological mechanisms such as suppression are contributing to language loss. My own investigation of the attrition of the native language among German-Jewish refugees (Schmid 2002, 2004) demonstrates that it was the speakers who had been exposed to the most dramatic experiences of persecution and violence prior to leaving Germany who showed the strongest signs of language attrition.

This study – which investigates 35 speakers, all of whom had left Germany when they were older than 11 years and had lived in an English-speaking environment for more than five decades – finds a great deal of variability as to the overall levels of proficiency, with some people clearly struggling with the language while others appeared fluent, at ease and native-like. I asked 13 native speakers of German to rate each participant on a nativeness-scale from 1 to 3, and the scores received in this mini-experiment ran from 1.0 (everyone agreed the person was a native speaker) to 2.85 (11 out of 13 people rated the speaker as unambiguously non-native, with only two intermediate ratings). Similarly wide ranges were found with respect to the accuracy of many grammatical features (such as gender, case marking or word order). None of the background variables, such as age at emigration, amount of use in various contexts or educational level were able to account for these differences and explain why one speaker had lost their German to a higher degree than another. The only explanatory factor which did play a role was the level of persecution and trauma each speaker had experienced.

Given the historical context of this study, one can hardly imagine a setting that would be more conducive to the complete loss of the native language: German Jews were explicitly and brutally excluded from the country and people to which they had been born and which they had considered their own. They were humiliated, brutalized and, in many cases, close family members and friends of theirs were murdered. They were told that their "blood" made them belong to a different, inferior race, and they were stripped of all of their rights. In one of the more heart-breaking stories I encountered in the course of my investigation, one of the survivors told the interviewer how, as a young girl, she had asked her uncle (who was a doctor) to draw a drop of blood from her finger and show her under the microscope just how it was different from "Aryan blood" and thereby "inferior".

For many of these survivors, the response was a (more or less deliberate) erasing of all traces of "German-ness" from their identity, and of all traces of the language from their lives – one of them wrote to me "America is my country, and English is my language" (see Schmid 2011: 97). Many stated that they had not used any German at all for decades. Given the natural limits of the human lifespan, these survivors therefore had the best possible opportunity to entirely forget their native language, along with the best possible motive for doing so. That notwithstanding, the study found that all participants were all still capable of speaking and understanding German – for some this was more effortful than for others, but all of them retained levels of proficiency that allowed them to communicate effectively. It seems, therefore, that when circumstances conspire to facilitate language attrition, speakers who leave their country of origin after around age 11 are capable of forgetting some of their native language, but that even in the most drastic cases of trauma and decades of non-exposure, they will not forget all of it.

What kind of "forgetting"?

The question which this chapter addresses is "Can you forget your native language?" As such, the question is problematic, since it does not specify what "forgetting" actually means. This lack of specificity was at the root of the Bergdahl controversy: his father had merely stated that Bergdahl was experiencing "trouble speaking English" – which, as pointed out above, was widely interpreted to mean that he could no longer speak nor understand it at all.

The psychological concept of *forgetting*, however, is complex and multifaceted and subsumes a number of very distinct processes which can impact on memory access and retrieval. A very useful and detailed outline of theories of memory and their relevance for language attrition research is presented by Ecke (2004). Among these are three aspects that are particularly relevant to native language attrition: *decay*, *repression/suppression* and *interference*.

The notion of *decay* (as Ecke notes, probably the oldest of all approaches to forgetting) underpins the common assumption that language attrition is "a kind of forgetting" (Ammerlaan 1996: 1). According to this theory, when information is not used, the trace it has left in the brain gradually dissipates so that the information "evaporates". This notion is linked with the common assumption that attrition should occur only in "extreme situations of reduced L1 use" over very long periods of time (Costa and Sebastián-Gallés 2014: 399).

The second mechanism is *repression/suppression*, "an (at least initially) intentional mechanism in which the individual refuses recalling/using a memory structure" (Ecke 2004: 324). In psychology, this strategy has most often been discussed in the context of traumatic experiences, and it goes a long way towards explaining the experiences of the German-Jewish Holocaust survivors discussed above. It may also be an explanatory factor in the experiences of prisoners of war, such as Bergdahl, in cases where their captors may actively have employed strategies such as torture to prevent them from speaking their language. In settings where the use of the community language by children incurred more or less draconian punishments – a practice sadly not uncommon during large parts of the 20th century, for example in Welsh-speaking, Native American or Australian Aboriginal communities – similar mechanisms will have facilitated the complete loss of these languages.

However, even in the absence of such negative experiences, repression/ suppression can involve the withdrawal of attention from highly active memory structures in order to allow the retrieval of other, less active structures (Ecke 2004: 324). This is something that everyone who has ever tried to learn a foreign language is familiar with: preventing words and structures from the native language, and perhaps even more so from another foreign language learned earlier, to creep in and encroach on speaking the new language is something that takes a great deal of conscious effort. This process of suppression goes hand in hand with *interference* where competing bits of information stored in memory can inhibit or block recall of each other. We are all familiar with the phenomenon that we cannot remember a particular word, because another one that may sound similar or have a similar meaning gets in the way and we cannot move past it.

One theory of native language attrition which is built on these mechanisms of forgetting – *decay* on the one hand and *suppression* and *interference* on the other – is the Activation Threshold Hypothesis (ATH), first formulated by Michel Paradis (1993, 2007). This theory proceeds from the fact that, in order to retrieve any information stored in our memory, we need a certain level of effort or neural stimulation (energy travelling through the brain). How many neural impulses are necessary depends on how accessible the item is for activation, and this in turn is a function of the frequency and recency of activation events. A word, grammatical structure or piece of information which a person has used often or recently needs less effort to activate than something that has been used only rarely, or not for a long time. This is the process linked to the notion of *information decay*. As Paradis points out, "[c]oncert pianists and professional tennis players cannot skip practice with impunity" (Paradis 2007: 125) – in other words, no matter how skilled and highly practiced you are at a particular activity, you need to keep on using the skill in order to keep it from decaying.

The problem with this assumption, however, is that it may not translate as easily to language use as one might think. If a pianist stops playing the piano and takes up the guitar instead, the abstract underlying musical skill may still receive stimulation, but the concrete and specific muscle movements involved are not drawn upon, and the neural processes necessary to carry them out may indeed decay rather quickly. But it is impossible for (healthy) human beings to stop using language – even if they were put in isolation or stranded on a desert island, they would still go on thinking, talking to themselves or to imaginary interlocutors.

When it comes to bilinguals and migrants, the situation becomes even more complex. The Holocaust survivors mentioned above may have stopped using German, but they switched to using another language. Since the multilingual's linguistic subsystems (such as the sound system, the lexical system or the grammatical system) do not exist in isolation from each other, but are connected at multiple levels across all languages that reside in the same brain (e.g. Paradis 2007; Schmid and Köpke, 2017), any kind of use of any language means that all other languages will receive a certain amount of stimulation. All languages are fundamentally so similar to each other that using any one of them means that every other language stored in the brain continues to receive at least some level of stimulation, and can thus not entirely be switched off. Even two very distant languages, for example Japanese and Finnish, are far more similar to each other than playing the piano versus playing the guitar, or tennis versus football.

This brings us to the second relevant memory mechanism, namely that of *suppression* or *interference*. As Paradis points out, how much energy is needed to activate a memory trace is not only dependent on how accessible this particular piece of information is (due to how often and how recently it has previously been used), but also on the accessibility of its competitors, which are also stored in memory. Such competitors can consist, for example, of similar-sounding items, translation equivalents or similar grammatical constructions. If I want to retrieve the Spanish word for 'apple' (*manzana*) from my memory, I have to ensure that I do not say the German *Apfel* or French *pomme* by mistake. So my mental efforts and neural impulses do not only go towards activating the desired word, but also towards *inhibiting* any undesired competitors. This is why learning to speak a new and unfamiliar language is so effortful – but it is also why language attrition occurs in the first place: any item that had to be inhibited becomes that much more difficult to activate again later on – having said *manzana* means that saying *pomme* or *Apfel* will subsequently cost more energy. This process is known as *retrieval-induced forgetting* (e.g. Levy, McVeigh, Marful and Anderson 2007).

Everything we know about native language attrition among post-puberty migrants suggests that this is not usually a case of decay or "evaporation" of information – the common-sense meaning of "forgetting". All available evidence indicates that the linguistic knowledge is underlyingly intact, or largely intact, in memory, and that the problems which attriters may encounter are mainly or entirely linked with accessing it. The second language is clamouring so loudly to be activated that it is hard for the speaker to reach past it, and this causes the hesitations, word-finding difficulties and (sometimes involuntary) code-switches that are so common in language attrition.

Conclusion

The conclusion from the previous section may come as a surprise, given that the process that this chapter has described is called "language attrition". As has often been pointed out, the term "attrition" carries not only a generally negative implication but also a sense of definitive and permanent erosion. Given that such permanent erosion or complete loss of certain grammatical structures (among other things) simply do not seem to occur in native speakers, the question arises whether "language attrition" is still an appropriate term for describing the much more superficial and temporary phenomena found in how bilinguals use their native language.

The label "attrition" is an old one, going back to some of the work of the great linguist Einar Haugen, who described in detail the changes that he had found among the Norwegian of immigrants of the first and subsequent generations in the United States. As early as 1938, he wrote: "It is by slow, incessant attrition that each foreigner has been turned into an American, idea by idea, and word by word." (Haugen 1938: 1). Many linguists felt that the term was an appropriate one, and much research has been conducted, particularly over the past four decades, leading to attrition studies emerging as a distinct and distinctive subfield of investigations on bilingualism.

While most of this work does indeed use the term "attrition" as a label for the linguistic symptoms of language interaction that were found, there are no studies which have returned outcomes that could legitimately be described as actual underlying and permanent erosion of linguistic knowledge. Arguably, therefore, the findings that have emerged from the cumulative research efforts of the field have re-shaped and re-defined the scope of the phenomenon that is referred to as "language attrition".

On the one hand, the use of the label "attrition" has provided the field with coherence and stability; on the other, it does indubitably have potentially misleading and inaccurate implications. This has recently led Allen (2017) to argue:

> "It is high time that we as a field decide on a more accurate and more positive term for language differences across speakers that does not put emphasis on the apparent deficiency of bilingualism but rather highlights the increasingly evident reality that there is no one monolingual norm or clearly definable situation of 'complete acquisition'".

Time will tell if the field will heed her call to action.

Notes

1. https://washingtonpost.com/world/national-security/obama-statement-on-sgt-b owe-bergdahl/2014/05/31/1cf3ebc2-e8e1-11e3-a86b-362fd5443d19_story.htm l?noredirect=on&utm_term=.f7cfd4334476, retrieved 17/07/2019, used courtesy of Guardian News & Media Ltd under the Open Licence agreement.
2. Reprinted by permission of HarperCollins Publishers Ltd. © Hilary Mantel 2009.
3. https://theguardian.com/commentisfree/2018/jan/21/the-joys-and-benefits-of-bilingualism, retrieved 12/07/2019, used by permission of Guardian News & Media Ltd.
4. https://theguardian.com/commentisfree/2018/apr/03/first-language-voice-mother-tongue-attrition-brexit, retrieved 12/07/2019, used courtesy of Guardian News & Media Ltd.
5. A non-exhaustive collection can be found at this link: https://languageattrition.org/stories-and-responses/
6. *Losing my Welsh: what it feels like to forget a language*, https://theguardian.com/education/2015/jan/21/welsh-language-part-me-slipping-away, retrieved 14/07/2019, used courtesy of Guardian News & Media Ltd.
7. A collection of such accounts can be found at this link: https://languageattrition.org/blogs/

Further reading

For a comprehensive introduction to language attrition and how to study it, see Schmid (2011). A wealth of materials about language attrition as well as research instruments is available on https://languageattrition.org.

References

Allen, Shanley E. (2017). Comparison as a fruitful way forward. *Linguistic Approaches to Bilingualism*, 7(6), 668–672. DOI:10.1075/lab.00001

Ammerlaan, Ton. (1996). *'You get a bit wobbly...': Exploring bilingual lexical retrieval processes in the context of first language attrition*. PhD dissertation. University of Nijmegen.

Bylund, Emanuel. (2019). Age effects in first language attrition. In Monika S. Schmid and Barbara Köpke (eds.), *The Oxford handbook of language attrition*, 277–287. Oxford: Oxford University Press.

Cabo, Diego Pascual Y and Jason Rothman. (2012). The (il)logical problem of heritage speaker bilingualism and incomplete acquisition. *Applied Linguistics*, 33(4), 450–455. DOI:10.1093/applin/ams037

Costa, Albert and Nuria Sebastian-Galles. (2014). How does the bilingual experience sculpt the brain? *Nature Reviews Neuroscience*, 15(5), 336–345. DOI:10.1038/nrn3709

De Houwer, Annick. (2007). Parental language input patterns and children's bilingual use. *Applied Psycholinguistics*, 28(3), 411–424. DOI:10.1017/S0142716407070221

Ecke, Peter. (2004). Language attrition and theories of forgetting: A cross-disciplinary review. *International Journal of Bilingualism*, 8(3), 321354. DOI:1 0.1177/13670069040080030901
Haugen, Einar. (1938/reprinted 1972). Language and immigration. In A. S. Dil (ed.), *The ecology of language: Essays by Einar Haugen*, 1–36. Stanford: Stanford University Press.
Kerr, Judith. (1971[2002]). *When Hitler stole pink rabbit*. London: Collins.
Kerr, Judith. (1975 [2017]). *Bombs on aunt dainty*. London: Collins.
Kerr, Judith. (1978 [2002]). *A small person far away*. London: Collins.
Levy, Benjamin J., Nathan D. McVeigh, Alejandra Marful and Michael C. Anderson. (2007). Inhibiting your native language: The role of retrieval-induced forgetting during second-language acquisition. *Psychological Science*, 18(1), 29–34. DOI:10.1111/j.1467-9280.2007.01844.x
Mantel, Hilary. (2009). *Wolf hall*. London: Fourth Estate.
Montrul, Silvina M. (2016). *The acquisition of heritage languages*. Cambridge: Cambridge University Press.
Oh, Janet S., Terry Kit-fong Au, Sun-Ah Jun and Richard M. Lee. (2019). Childhood language memory in adult heritage language (re)learners. In Monika S. Schmid and Barbara Köpke (eds.), *The Oxford handbook of language attrition*, 481–492. Oxford: Oxford University Press.
Pallier, Christophe. (2007). Critical periods in language acquisition and language attrition. In Barbara Köpke, Monika S. Schmid, Merel Keijzer and Susan Dostert (eds.), *Language attrition: Theoretical perspectives*, 155–168. Philadelphia and Amsterdam: Benjamins.
Paradis, Michel. (1993). Linguistic, psycholinguistic, and neurolinguistic aspects of "interference" in bilingual speakers: The activation threshold hypothesis. *International Journal of Psycholinguistics*, 9(2), 133–145.
Paradis, Michel. (2007). L1 attrition features predicted by a neurolinguistic theory of bilingualism. In Barbara Köpke, Monika S. Schmid, Merel Keijzer and Susan Dostert (eds.), *Language attrition: Theoretical perspectives*, 121–134. Philadelphia and Amsterdam: Benjamins.
Park, Hyeaon-Sook. (2015). Korean adoptees in Sweden: Have they lost their first language completely? *Applied Psycholinguistics*, 36(4), 773–797. DOI:10.1017/S0142716413000507
Pierce, Lara J., Fred Genesee and Denise Klein. (2019). Language loss and language learning in internationally adopted children: Evidence from behaviour and the brain. In Monika S. Schmid and Barbara Köpke (eds.), *The Oxford handbook of language attrition*, 470–480. Oxford: Oxford University Press.
Schmid, Monika S. (2002). *First language attrition, use and maintenance: The case of German Jews in Anglophone countries*. Amsterdam and Philadelphia: Benjamins.
Schmid, Monika S. (2004). First language attrition: The methodology revised. *International Journal of Bilingualism*, 8(3), 239–255. DOI:10.1177/13670069 040080030501
Schmid, Monika S. (2011). *Language attrition*. Cambridge University Press.

Schmid, Monika S. and Barbara Köpke. (2017). The relevance of first language attrition to theories of bilingual development. *Linguistic Approaches to Bilingualism*, 7(6), 637–667. DOI:10.1075/lab.17058.sch

Unsworth, Sharon. (2016). Quantity and quality of language input in bilingual language development. In Elena Nicoladis and Simona Montanari (eds.), *Bilingualism across the lifespan: Factors moderating language proficiency*, 136–196. Berlin: Mouton de Gruyter.

Ventureyra, Valérie, A. Christophe Pallier and Hi-Yon Yoo. (2004). The loss of first language phonetic perception in adopted Koreans. *Journal of Neurolinguistics*, 17(1), 79–91. DOI:10.1016/S0911-6044(03)00053-8

11 Can people really disguise themselves when writing or speaking?

Corinne A. Seals and Natalie Schilling

Introduction

An anonymous bomb threat is phoned into a workplace; a criminal instructs a victim to comply with his violent demands under cover of night; an unsigned ransom note is found at the scene of an abduction; a young girl is found poisoned next to what appears to be a suicide note. These are all cases involving communications of questioned origin, and these are all cases calling for forensic linguistics. Among other matters, forensic linguistics involves the scientific analysis of language evidence. Anonymous voices and writings can be analysed for language features indicative of speaker characteristics (age, region, native language, etc.), or they can be compared against language samples of known origin (voices or writings of suspects and other parties associated with a crime) for purposes of speaker or author identification. There are many challenges in speaker and author identification, including the topic of this chapter: the possibility of disguise. How commonplace is language disguise in criminal cases? How good are people at disguising their voices or writings, or faking the linguistic usages of others? What effects does disguise have on correct identification, and how can linguistic science be of value in identifying disguise and otherwise solving language crimes?

Voice and accent disguise

A curious case

In 1981, 13-year-old Mary Doe, born and raised mostly in New York State, goes missing from her central California home. The disappearance goes unreported for more than 20 years, when her siblings finally report the case to the police. The police suspect homicide, and the girl's stepfather is interviewed and comes close to confessing. A short while later, a woman is stopped by the police in Phoenix, Arizona, for a traffic violation and claims to be the long-lost girl. She says she had run away from home and spent her 20 missing years mostly in California and Arizona. The police suspect that the adult "Mary Doe" is a fake. She can't answer the detectives' questions about her early life, disappearance or later whereabouts, and there's another big problem – her accent. To the detectives, it sounds like a strong Southern US accent, almost a stereotype – or a disguise. Is "Mary Doe" not who she says she is? Is she disguising her real accent in order to sound Southern, or perhaps mask a different regional identity? And if she's putting on "Southern", why, when she's purporting to be a non-Southerner?

Voice and accent disguise: speaker strategies, listener effects

Do people disguise or put on accents when committing a crime? If so, what do they do: what language features do they use and not use when attempting dialect disguise? And how good are they at it? Are they accurate? Are they effective in getting listeners to hear the intended language variety, or at least covering up a real one? Aside from accent, do criminals disguise their voices in other ways? And how does attempted voice or accent disguise affect people's ability to recognize speakers, whether expert linguists called in to assist in cases or non-experts who may hear the voice of a suspect during a crime and subsequently be called upon to provide so-called "earwitness testimony"?

There are a number of types of crimes and criminal circumstances in which it might be in a perpetrator's interest to try to disguise their voice or accent – for example, anonymous threatening phone calls, violent crimes committed in the dark, or crimes committed with the perpetrator's face obscured by a mask or other facial covering or with the victim blindfolded. And of course, in cases in which an individual assumes a fake identity for nefarious purposes, as may be the case with "Mary Doe". Statistics from police investigators and forensic linguists indicate that indeed voice disguise is commonplace: German authorities estimate that 15–20% of federal crimes in their country involve voice disguise (Künzel 1987); forensic linguists in England who specialise in voice analysis estimate that one in 40 cases involves disguise (Clark and Foulkes 2007); still other figures indicate rates of voice disguise in criminal cases as high as 52% (Masthoff 1996). And when voice disguise is used, it can cause problems for speaker identification, as studies show considerable decrease in listener accuracy in identifying anonymous voices when disguise is used. Common methods for voice disguise range from electronic manipulation to holding a pencil in the teeth to pinching one's nostrils. Perhaps the simplest and most effective method is whispering, since this technique removes nearly all information on pitch (intonation), and pitch often plays a key role in distinguishing one voice from another. In fact, one foundational study showed that correct

Disguise in writing and speaking? 153

identification of voices fell from 95% to 30% when speakers whispered (Pollack, Pickett and Sumby 1954). And these were the voices of people the listeners knew – not the strangers whose voices earwitnesses are often called upon to recognize in criminal cases.

Dialect or accent disguise seems to be less common than other types of voice disguise, perhaps because a disguise like whispering is much easier than attempting to put on an accent other than one's own, or to cover up features of one's own native language variety.[1] While some people are good at imitating others' accents and dialects, even trained professionals fall short: we are all familiar with actors, even famous ones, who do a terrible job at imitating non-native dialects. And non-experts are even worse. For example, one research project showed that native speakers of American English who attempted to fake Spanish-accented English used only a small subset of features of authentic second-language Spanish English in their disguises and in addition performed quite inconsistently across test sentences (Gunn 2014). Similarly, study participants attempting to imitate native regional US dialects like Southern White US English and African American English do not perform well either, relying on only a handful of usually stereotypical pronunciation features, failing to use features consistently, and, even more importantly for forensic linguistic purposes, neglecting to effect authentic patterns of variability (e.g. Preston 1993).

While non-linguists often assume that if someone has a dialect feature, they will use it without fail, decades of linguistic research on dialect variation has shown that all dialects are characterised not simply by regular patterns but also by regularly patterned *variability*. And the variability is often quite subtle. For example, one very well-known accent feature of Southeastern US dialects is the pronunciation of the 'i' vowel in words like *ride* and *right* as more of an 'ah' sound, as in something like *rahd* for *ride*. However, this pronunciation does not hold for all Southerners in all 'i' words but is different in Southern White and Southern African American dialects. For speakers of White Southern dialects like Appalachian English, the patterning is quite widespread and applies to nearly all words with 'i'. However, among African Americans, the pattern is more restricted; words like *ride* are pronounced as *rahd*, but *right* remains *right*. Linguists know about these subtle patterns, but as a rule, non-linguists do not. Thus, if a criminal were to attempt to fake an African American accent, they would likely get it wrong – and a linguist would be able to tell.

Voice and accent identification issues even without disguise

We have seen that voice disguise like whispering reduces listeners' ability to identify voices and that non-linguists may not recognize subtle inaccuracies in accent disguise. Unfortunately, difficulties in voice identification extend beyond cases of disguise. Non-experts are often called upon to identify voices; however, research shows that in general they are not very good at it. Part of the problem is often with the earwitness identification procedure. In parallel with better-known eyewitness identification procedures, earwitness identification procedures can be considered to be suggestive – that is, unfairly biased to point towards one particular suspect – if they are not composed of a properly constituted voice line-up. Linguist experts have determined this should consist of a sufficient number of voices in addition to that of the suspect, played via audio only (with no accompanying visuals or in-person confrontations), matched as closely as possible to the suspect's voice (for example, in terms of pitch, speech rate, dialect, etc.) and with each participant reading (not speaking) a passage of innocuous text having nothing to do with crime. In addition, a host of other factors can impact accuracy, as indicated in studies ranging from foundational works such as McGehee (1937) to ongoing work in the late 20th and early 21st centuries (e.g. Hollein 2002; Künzel 1994; Rose 2002). Among these are degree of familiarity with the voice of the perpetrator; amount of exposure to the voice of the perpetrator, during the crime and during the voice identification procedure; amount of time between the original exposure and the voice identification; familiarity with the language or dialect in question; and degree of witness attention to the voice during the crime (Solan and Tiersma 2005: 117–48).

Practically speaking, it can be quite difficult to construct and administer a properly constituted voice identification procedure. In the US legal system, voice identifications obtained via suggestive procedures can still be considered to be reliable, and hence admissible as evidence, under certain circumstances. Unfortunately, just what these circumstances should be is not always known or heeded, and miscarriages of justice can result. Consider for example, the case of People versus Eric Frimpong (People v. Frimpong 2010).

A case of suggestive and prejudicial voice identification (without disguise)

Frimpong was a soccer player from Ghana recruited by the University of California-Santa Barbara (UCSB) who led his team to their first national championship. His sports career was cut short when he was accused of rape in 2007. He was found guilty and sentenced to six years in prison. He served out his term and was deported to his native country in 2013. Several efforts at appeal were made, but none were successful. The quest for an appeal continues to this day, since attorneys and others associated with his case have pointed to a number of procedural issues in the investigation and trial, including problems with a voice identification procedure, evidence from which was admitted into trial in the case against Frimpong.

The crime took place in the dark, between 12:15 and 1:15 am. About eight hours later, the alleged victim, who claims to have heard the alleged perpetrator's voice but not to have seen him, was asked to participate in a voice identification task. This consisted of her listening to a short audio segment, characterized by the detectives administering the task as "a five second clip", from one of Frimpong's interviews with the police. There were no other voice excerpts or indeed any other suspects identified by the police. The alleged victim stated that Frimpong's voice was indeed that of the perpetrator and that he had an "island" or "Caribbean" accent. Clearly, this procedure is far from a properly constituted voice identification task, since it consisted of an extremely short sample of only one voice, that of the suspect, who was speaking about the crime in question; and so the voice identification task can be deemed to be suggestive.

But can it be considered to be reliable nonetheless? The court judged it to be so, but the circumstances surrounding the crime and identification task all point towards "no". The witness was admittedly very drunk during the commission of the crime, and so her level of attention to voice and other matters was low. (As a point of note, we absolutely do not suggest that the victim should be taken any less seriously. Rather, a forensic linguist's job is to analyse factors that can scientifically affect language evidence, therein ensuring due process is followed.) She was also unfamiliar with and had little exposure to Frimpong's voice, having just met him on the night of the alleged rape. In addition, her exposure to the voice of the alleged rapist was low; she claimed he said very little to her during the attack and that she could not remember what he said, due to her drunkenness. Further, while there are some accent similarities between Caribbean and West African varieties of English, the witness misidentified the location of origin of Frimpong's accent by about 7,800 kilometres, further demonstrating her lack of familiarity with Frimpong's voice. (In addition, Frimpong was far from the only student at UCSB at the time with a West African or Caribbean English accent.)

In sum, then, the voice identification procedure in this case was extremely suggestive and highly prejudicial, due to the flawed nature of the voice identification procedure and the highly problematic nature of the circumstances surrounding the crime and voice in question. Unfortunately, it took a forensic linguist (the second author of this chapter), called in long after the trial had taken place, to provide an expert opinion that the voice identification should not have been admitted as evidence; meanwhile, the earwitness evidence was used as part of the case against Frimpong, and his conviction was obtained without due process under the law.

Compounding the difficulties, including with disguise

The first author of this chapter served as an expert forensic linguist in a New Zealand case that also illustrates the unreliability of earwitness identification due to factors such as short exposure to voice during the commission of a crime and time delay between the crime and the identification. This case involved a number of other confounding factors: the presence of a weapon (and thus decreased attention to voice), the typicality of the voice of the perpetrator, and the effects of the witness's prior experiences and exposure to subsequent information related to the criminal event. And all of this is even further confounded by disguise – in this case, not necessarily purposeful voice disguise but the obscuring effects of a facial disguise. In November 2015, a rural New Zealand pub was robbed at gunpoint. The perpetrator was wearing a ski mask and full body covering. A suspect was taken into custody. In statements taken the day of the event and two months after the event, two bartenders named the defendant as the perpetrator. One stated that they recognized the voice as that of a regular bar patron who was frequently intoxicated. The other bartender noted that the perpetrator had a "deep husky voice", that their last contact with the defendant had been a week and a half prior to the crime, and that in addition to interactions in the bar, the bartender had a "teacher-student" relationship with the defendant.

At first glance, it seems that at least some factors are favourable for accurate identification: the two bartenders' claimed familiarity with the voice, their confidence in their identification, their observations of particular voice qualities and their agreement with one another. However, expert linguist examination revealed a number of concerns: the utterances were short (with little agreement among witnesses as to number and content of utterances); there was considerable delay between the bartenders' initial statements and their follow-up statements, and the voice qualities mentioned by the bartenders rendered identification more rather than less difficult (many male voices are deep and husky; voice quality is very different among intoxicated versus sober individuals). Furthermore, the bartenders reported discussing the event while waiting for the police and agreeing that it was the defendant, behaviour which research shows could lead to the construction of joint perceptions and even memories that could be different from those originally experienced by each individual. Finally, emerging research shows that face-concealing garments such as the ski mask worn by the perpetrator, have a degrading effect on the distinguishability of different speech features by non-experts and even experts utilizing state-of-the-art acoustic phonetic analysis (analysis of the wave forms of speech) in addition to auditory analysis (Fecher and Watt 2011, 2012).

Disguise in writing and speaking? 157

There is yet a further complication that arises in the cases discussed here, one with far-reaching implications for both voice and author identification in forensic contexts, including in cases of disguise: individual voices are not static but highly variable, across different situations and even during the course of a single interaction or text. For example, as in the pub case, a person's voice may be quite different while intoxicated versus sober. In addition, one bartender reported that the perpetrator's voice changed during the course of the robbery, as he became increasingly angry. Beyond voice, the interactional style of a teacher-student or bartender-patron encounter is very different from that of a robber-victim situation, and we can expect these differences to negatively impact identification accuracy as well.

Authorship attribution and deception in written text

Who wrote the letter?

In 2000, Michael Wallace of New York suddenly died of a heart attack and was survived by his wife Stacey and daughter Ashley. Three years later, Stacey married David Castor. However, suspicions started to arise when Stacey Castor called the Sheriff's Department in 2005 to report her husband David Castor as unresponsive and locked in the bedroom. When police arrived, they found David Castor dead. An autopsy showed antifreeze in his system, leading to an initial cause of death as suspected suicide. Yet, the story took a nefarious turn when the Sheriff's Department then found a container of antifreeze in the Castor home, as well as Stacey Castor's prints on the glass of sports drink mixed with antifreeze, from which David drank. Following police suspicions, a posthumous toxicology screening was done on Stacey Castor's first husband, Michael Wallace, and results showed that he too died of antifreeze poisoning. With attention now turning to Stacey Castor, in 2007, investigators questioned Stacey's daughter, Ashley Wallace, about her mother. Upset, Ashley called Stacey to inform her. The next day, Ashley was found in her bedroom unconscious and with a typed suicide note next to her claiming responsibility for Michael's and David's murders. Ashley survived and was questioned in the hospital by police about the suicide note, which she adamantly insisted she had never seen before. Did Ashley write the note? Did someone falsify the note and type Ashley's name at the bottom? How can an author be determined when a document is typed?

Similar to voice and accent disguise, it is not uncommon to find people attempting to disguise their writing styles when committing a crime. How do people attempt to disguise their writing? How successful are these attempts? What does forensic linguistics offer to the unmasking of unknown or suspect writers?

Authorship attribution – K Docs and Q Docs

Like speech, an individual also has a range of writing styles. There is variation across a writer's styles, depending on who their audience is, what they are writing about and what they are trying to accomplish. This stylistic or genre variation can pose quite a challenge for forensic linguists. However, there are also features of a person's writing that frequently transfer across styles and that make up an individual's idiolect (features that make an individual's language usage unique – see Bauer, Chapter 3 in this volume). So how do we analyse writing so that we can find consistent patterns in an individual's writing while still accounting for natural variation across styles and situations?

In forensic linguistics, the answer has come in the form of conducting authorship analyses through the comparison of patterns of language variation between anonymous criminal documents and documents of known authorship, including those from suspects (e.g. McMenamin 2002, 2010; Olsson 2009; Olsson and Luchjenbroers 2013). When an author of a document is known, that document is called a "K Doc". When an author of a document is unknown or questioned, that document is called a "Q Doc". Care must be taken to ensure that the K Docs and Q Docs are as similar in style and genre to one another as possible, though exact equivalence is rare. For example, it is not likely that a suspect will have written threatening letters or fake suicide notes to which they have signed their name, in addition to anonymous criminal communications. Various linguistic elements have been used in comparing K Docs and Q Docs for purposes of authorship attribution, including individual vocabulary items, unusual spellings and elements of word formation and sentence structure. These author comparison techniques have often been used to assist in forensic linguistics cases internationally (e.g. McMenamin 2002; Olsson 2009).

What does this K Doc and Q Doc analysis look like? As shown in the simplified table below, every possible instance of a specified linguistic feature (known as a "token") is included in a comparative analysis. For example, the table below would be used for comparing unique spellings found across documents. While one instance could indicate a simple typo or misspelling, a repeated use is more likely to indicate a systematic feature of that person's writing. The table below, for instance, would suggest that the same author of the K Docs is responsible for the Q Doc. A note of caution, however – an analyst would need many exemplars to prove their case; a single instance of similar (or different) language usage is never enough (Table 11.1).

It is this type of lexical comparison that led to a break in the case of the previously mentioned Castor note. When forensic linguist James R. Fitzgerald started working with the note, there were a few word choices and

Table 11.1 A sample Q-Doc, K-Doc analysis

	Q Doc	K Doc 1	K Doc 2	K Doc 3
down	2 (22.2%)	2 (20%)	1 (12.5%)	3 (27.3%)
donw	7 (77.8%)	8 (80%)	7 (87.5%)	8 (72.7%)
Total	9 (100%)	10 (100%)	8 (100%)	11 (100%)
just	3 (42.9%)	5 (50%)	6 (60%)	4 (44.4%)
gust	4 (57.1%)	5 (50%)	4 (40%)	5 (55.6%)
Total	7 (100%)	10 (100%)	10 (100%)	9 (100%)

phrases that stood out to him. One such instance was the use of '*it did it*' for '*I did it*' in the alleged suicide letter. While that could have been a typo, after careful scrutiny, Fitzgerald found the same usage in letters of known authorship that Stacey Castor had written to a friend. In addition, Fitzgerald noted another odd usage in the "suicide" letter: *antifree* instead of *antifreeze*. In a fascinating development bringing together speaker comparison and authorship attribution, a detective in the case testified that Stacey Castor had used the word *antifree* in one of her verbal interviews with the police. These linguistic clues along with additional forensic linguistic evidence played a major role in Stacey Castor's conviction of one count of second degree murder, one count of second degree attempted murder and one count of offering a false instrument in the first degree, resulting in a 2009 sentence of 51 years to life in prison (Stacey Castor died in prison in 2016).

Meeting the challenge of sophisticated deception

Sometimes, however, writers can be very good at impersonating another person's spelling, word choices, grammatical structures and other elements of writing style. For instance, in 2017, the first author of this chapter worked on a case involving a suspected falsified note. The challenge was to determine whether the variation found across the K Docs and Q Doc was natural language variation or something more.

In this case, the police were concerned that a young girl in primary school was being sexually abused by her step-father following verbal reports she made to a trusted adult. However, shortly after police began investigating, the girl's mother gave them a note that appeared to have been written by the girl saying that she had made it all up. The police, however, were unconvinced about the validity of the note, even though the handwriting looked very much like the girl's, because there was something about it that struck the police as "sounding different". When individuals comment on writing "sounding different", it is likely that they are describing writing style. Again, this includes word choice, sentence structure and matters such as spelling, punctuation and other features of formatting.

The police approached the linguistic expert, and she requested known pieces of writing from the girl. A comparative analysis was then conducted using three K Docs and the Q Doc. An initial comparative analysis of lexical items (such as described above) led to two major challenges. The first challenge was that there were almost no comparative tokens that occurred in both the Q Doc and the K Docs. Secondly, there were almost no comparative tokens across the K Docs themselves. Therefore, it was not possible to conduct a reliable comparative analysis based on word choice and use. So what happens now? Does this mean that the note was in fact written by the girl? Does this mean that forensic linguistics is unable to help?

In fact, this means that a more sophisticated forensic linguistic analysis is needed. Instead of looking at individual words, it is necessary to look to full sentence structures (syntax). Syntactic research has shown time and again that the development of syntactic complexity is a naturally occurring process with a predictable developmental timeline. More specifically, syntactic complexity increases each year while individuals are in school, and an individual's development of overall writing skills are directly connected to their ability to form complex sentence structures (Chall 1983; Gummersall and Strong 1999; Mokhtari and Thompson 2006; McNamara, Crossley and McCarthy 2010). Because of the large amount of research we have in linguistics related to syntactic complexity and individual language development in education, findings have established the expected range of "normal" syntactic complexity for students as they progress through years of schooling (e.g. Hunt 1977, 1998; Chall 1983; Scott and Stokes 1995; McNamara, Crossley and McCarthy 2010). This is important to remember as the potential authors of the Q Doc in this case included a child in primary school as well as an adult, that is, individuals at different stages in their syntactic complexity levels.

Analysing subconscious structures in writing

An analysis of syntactic complexity is another fascinating technical skill available in a forensic linguist's toolkit. It can be particularly useful in challenging forensic linguistic cases, as it considers elements of language that are usually below the level of consciousness for most individuals. Complex syntactic structures are part of the grammar of language that we acquire as our language develops to become more advanced. Because of this, people are not usually aware of their own or others' use or non-use of complex sentence structures in writing. However, they are just as much a marker of an individual's style as are individual lexical items. Measures of syntactic complexity include the average length of a sentence, how many phrases exist within a grammatical clause and the average length of grammatical clauses within sentences, in addition to other features of sentence structure.

While some degree of variation between writing samples is normal, the Q Doc in this case showed much higher numbers for measures of syntactic complexity than the K Docs. This indicates that the sentences in the Q Doc were likely composed by someone with access to much higher syntactic complexity than held by the child who wrote the K Docs (e.g. Hunt 1998). More specifically, the K Docs matched the writing of someone with the syntactic sophistication normally found in primary school, while the Q Doc matched the writing of someone with the syntactic sophistication normally found in secondary school or higher (e.g. Hunt 1998).

This linguistic analysis of syntactic complexity suggested that the Q Doc (the handwritten note) was likely not originally composed by the young girl. Therefore, while the young girl at the heart of the case might have written out the version of the note that was handed to police, it is highly unlikely that she was responsible for authoring its actual sentences. Based on this forensic linguistic evidence, the police decided to reopen the case, including now an investigation into potential coercion.

A note of caution: linguistic evidence versus DNA evidence

The cases above illustrate the value of forensic linguistic analysis in cases involving spoken and written language of unknown criminals, compared against language data from suspects and related parties, as well as the linguistic characteristics of larger population groups (for example, speakers from the US South). We have also seen that a number of challenges are involved, including variation within individuals across situations and styles, and of course disguise. It is also crucially important that we understand challenges pertaining to the nature of language data versus other types of forensic evidence. Linguistic evidence in the form of verbal or written communications can be extremely valuable in helping to identify persons involved in crimes, but it is *not* DNA evidence. Voice and writing samples are just that – samples, not the entirety of an individual's linguistic behaviours – and linguistic usages are behaviours, not innate characteristics like DNA sequences. They are formed by circumstances, habits, preferences and choices, not by biology, and they are changeable, not immutable – sometimes without speaker awareness (as for example, with changes in voice quality due to aging) but sometimes also purposely, by speakers, including in cases of deliberate disguise.

Concluding remarks

We have seen in this chapter how forensic linguistics can be used in cases involving speaker identification, including pointing out to attorneys and triers of fact the limits of non-expert identification in cases involving the obscuring effects of disguise and even involving no disguise at all. In the New Zealand pub case, the forensic linguist's expert testimony regarding the genuine unreliability of the bartenders' seemingly reliable identification of a voice obscured by a ski mask helped bring about an appeal overturning the defendant's guilt. Attempts at appeal in the Frimpong case, with no overt disguise involved, have not yet been successful, but at least the forensic linguist's expert report helped increase attorneys' and others' awareness of the factors involved in reliable versus unreliable and prejudicial voice identifications, so that further miscarriages of justice can potentially be avoided.

Returning to the "Mary Doe" case with which we began the chapter, the case has not been solved to this day, and no one knows quite where the adult "Mary Doe" really came from or who she is. However, linguists who worked on the case, including the second author of this chapter, are confident in their opinion that if "Mary Doe" is for some reason pretending to be a non-Southerner by affecting a "Southern" accent, she is going about it quite strangely. She uses some features of Southern US English that are typically too subtle for non-linguists to notice, let alone fake, for example, a pronunciation feature in which 'ih' vowels are pronounced as something like 'ee-uh', so that a word like *sit* sounds like *see it*. At the same time, though, "Mary Doe" does *not* use the single best-known feature of Southern American English, 'ah' for 'i' in words like *tide* and *time*. She is also remarkably consistent in her use of Southern-like features throughout two hour-long interviews with the police in which she struggles to provide consistent factual details. In short, "Mary Doe" seems to be disguising some things, but accent is not one of them. If she were, expert linguists would most likely be able to call her out, even if non-experts remain relatively poor at detecting disguise, or even recognizing undisguised voices.

Additionally, the Castor case and child's written note case showed examples of how linguists can uncover written disguise, in cases involving both more and less subtle attempts at deception. In the Castor case, Stacy Castor attempted to disguise her authorship of her daughter's "suicide" note by typing it, using next to no punctuation (perhaps in an effort to mimic young people's writing) and typing her daughter's name at the bottom. However, unique features in the mother's idiolect, especially regarding certain lexical items (e.g. *antifree*) gave her away anyway. Furthermore, even in instances where writers seem to be more skilled at disguising themselves,

Disguise in writing and speaking? 163

less conscious aspects of style and structure can still give them away if the correct linguistic tools are used.

For example, in the case of possible child abuse, the child's written note looked to be a match to her known documents on the surface – in terms of handwriting and word choice. However, forensic linguistics is *not* handwriting analysis, and there were not enough lexical items shared across documents to be conclusive. Additionally, there was still the matter of the note not quite "sounding right". After the deployment of sophisticated analysis of syntactic complexity, clear and concrete evidence of linguistic deception was revealed. These more sophisticated analyses are becoming increasingly important, especially as difficulties continue to arise, such as the increasing frequency of typed documents (in social media posts, in texts), automatic spelling correction, and predictive phrase and sentence completion. It is even possible that as more individuals compose criminal and other nefarious communications behind the seeming anonymity of Internet and mobile phone communication, they may become more skilled in deception. However, it is unlikely that they will learn to affect or mask the myriad very subtle linguistic features that help form part of each individual's unique style or idiolect.

Luckily, advances in research, science and technology can also work in favour of speaker and authorship analysis. For instance, Professor Xiaofei Lu at Pennsylvania State University has created the automated Syntactic Complexity Analyzer (see Lu 2010, 2011). As with any other automated system, this tool has some limits (such as being most useful for English and needing texts of certain lengths), but it is nonetheless highly useful for forensic linguistics, and more automated tools are continuously in development. At the same time, linguistic experts can never be removed from the equation, including in cases involving potential disguise. Trained forensic linguists are typically readily able to detect dialect disguise and other types of linguistic deception; however, an automated system would need to be trained on databases of disguised versus undisguised speech and writing, and compiling such databases and ensuring that they remain current presents a tremendous challenge (Eriksson 2010).

So, can people really disguise themselves when writing or speaking? As this chapter has shown – yes and no. There are some aspects of spoken and written language that people can be quite good at manipulating, especially if these involve features of which people are more consciously aware, for example, particular word choices or punctuation usages (or lack thereof). However, language is not simple; it is a highly complex phenomenon. When people attempt to disguise themselves in writing or speech, they are rarely aware of the many layers of language, including vocabulary words, pronunciations, grammatical constructions and interactional patterns, or of subtle, subconscious patterns. Expert forensic linguists are, however, able to pull apart levels of language and analyse the patterns within. Furthermore, with technological advances, the forensic linguist's toolkit is expanding even further. People might be able to disguise themselves in some ways, but forensic linguistics can help clear lesser known pathways to identification.

Note

1 The term "accent" refers to the pronunciation features of a particular language variety like British English, American English or New Zealand English. "Dialect" refers to language features on all levels, including pronunciation, words and sentence constructions.

Further reading

For more information on a range of techniques in forensic linguistics, see Coulthard and Johnson (2010). For more real-life case illustrations of forensic linguistics at work, see Olsson (2012).

References

Chall, Jeanne S. (1983). *Stages of reading development*. New York: Harcourt Brace.

Clark, Jessica and Paul Foulkes. (2007). Identification of voices in electronically disguised speech. *International Journal of Speech, Language and the Law*, 14(2), 195–221. DOI:10.1558/ijsll.v14i2.195

Coulthard, Malcolm and Alison Johnson (eds.). (2010). *The Routledge handbook of forensic linguistics*. London: Routledge.

Eriksson, Anders. (2010). The disguised voice: Imitating accents or speech styles and impersonating individuals. In Carmen Llamas and Dominic Watt (eds.), *Language and identities*, 76–85. Edinburgh: Edinburgh University Press.

Fecher, Natalie and Dominic Watt. (2011). Speaking under cover: The effect of face-concealing garments on spectral properties of fricatives. In Wai-Sum Lee and Eric Zee (eds.), *Proceedings of the 17th international conference of phonetic sciences*, 663–666. Hong Kong: City University of Hong Kong.

Fecher, Natalie and Dominic Watt. (2012). Effects of forensically-realistic facial concealment on auditory-visual consonant recognition in quiet and noise conditions. In Slim Ouni, Frédéric Berthomier and Alexandra Jesse (eds.), *Proceedings from the 12th international conference on audio-visual speech processing*, 81–86. Annecy, France: Inria.

Gummersall, Dawn M. and Carol J. Strong. (1999). Assessment of complex sentence production in a narrative context. *Language, Speech, and Hearing Services in Schools*, 30(2), 152–164. DOI:10.1044/0161-1461.3002.152

Gunn, David. (2014). *Spanish accent imitation for voice disguise*. Unpublished master's research paper. Washington, DC: Georgetown University.

Hollein, Harry. (2002). *Forensic voice identification*. London: Academic Press.
Hunt, Kellogg W. (1977). Early blooming and late blooming syntactic structures. In Charles R. Cooper and Lee Odell (eds.), *Evaluating writing: Describing, measuring, and judging*, 91–104. Urbana: National Council of Teachers of English.
Hunt, Kellogg W. (1998). *Grammatical structures written at three grade levels*. Research Report no. 3. Urbana: National Council of Teachers of English.
Künzel, Hermann J. (1987). *Sprechererkennung: Grundzüge forensischer Sprachverarbeitung*. Heidelberg, Germany: Kriminalistik-Verlag.
Künzel, Hermann J. (1994). On the problem of speaker identification by victims and witnesses. *International Journal of Speech, Language and the Law*, 1(1), 45–57. DOI:10.1558/ijsll.v1i1.45
Lu, Xiaofei. (2010). Automatic analysis of syntactic complexity in second language writing. *International Journal of Corpus Linguistics*, 15(4), 474–496. DOI:10.1075/ijcl.15.4.02lu
Lu, Xiaofei. (2011). A corpus-based evaluation of syntactic complexity measures as indices of college-level ESL writers' language development. *TESOL Quarterly*, 45(1), 36–62. DOI:10.5054/tq.2011.240859
Masthoff, Herbert. (1996). A report on a voice disguise experiment. *Forensic Linguistics*, 3(1), 160–167. DOI:10.1558/ijsll.v3i1.160
McGehee, Frances. (1937). The reliability of the identification of the human voice. *The Journal of General Psychology*, 17(2), 249–271. DOI:10.1080/00221309.1937.9917999
McMenamin, Gerald R. (2002). *Forensic linguistics: Advances in forensic stylistics*. Boca Raton: CRC Press.
McMenamin, Gerald R. (2010). Forensic stylistics. In Malcolm Coulthard and Alison Johnson (eds.), *The Routledge handbook of forensic linguistics*, 199–217. London: Routledge.
McNamara, Danielle S., Scott A. Crossley and Philip M. McCarthy. (2010). Linguistic features of writing quality. *Written Communication*, 27(1), 57–86. DOI:10.1177/0741088309351547
Mokhtari, Kouider and H. Brian Thompson. (2006). How problems of reading fluency and comprehension are related to difficulties in syntactic awareness skills among fifth graders. *Reading Research and Instruction*, 46(1), 73–96. DOI:10.1080/19388070609558461
Olsson, John. (2009). *Wordcrime: Solving crime through forensic linguistics*. London: Continuum.
Olsson, John. (2012). *Wordcrime: Solving crime through forensic linguistics*. London: Continuum.
Olsson, John and June Luchjenbroers. (2013). *Forensic linguistics*. London: Bloomsbury.
People v. Frimpong, 2nd Crim. No. B206433. (2010).
Pollack, Irwin, James M. Pickett and William H. Sumby. (1954). On the identification of speakers by voice. *The Journal of the Acoustical Society of America*, 26(3), 403–406.

Preston, Dennis R. (1993). Talking black and talking white: A study in variety imitation. In Joan Houston Hall, Nick Doane and Richard Ringler (eds.), *English old and new: Studies in language and linguistics in honor of Frederic G. Cassidy*, 327–355. New York: Garland.

Rose, Phil. (2002). *Forensic speaker identification*. New York: Taylor and Francis.

Scott, Cheryl M. and Sharon L. Stokes. (1995). Measures of syntax in school-age children and adolescents. *Language, Speech, and Hearing Services in Schools*, 26(4), 309–319. DOI:10.1044/0161-1461.2604.309

Solan, Lawrence M. and Peter M. Tiersma. (2005). *Speaking of crime: The language of criminal justice*. Chicago: University of Chicago Press.

12 What is universal about intonation?

Paul Warren

Intonation is the modulation of voice pitch over stretches of speech, reflecting changes in the rate of vibration of the speaker's vocal folds. This rate of vocal fold vibration is the primary determinant of what listeners perceive as pitch and is also what is usually reported as the objective measure of pitch, in terms of the fundamental frequency (F0) of the speech signal. Other factors that influence the perception of intonation include the duration and amplitude (loudness) of the speech signal. In addition, because voice pitch varies considerably based on non-linguistic factors such as the sex, age and body size of the speaker, it is not the absolute pitch values that determine our perception of intonation, but their relative values within an utterance.

This chapter considers some frequently asked questions about intonation, such as whether all languages have it, how it differs from language to language, and whether there are any universal features or properties of intonation.

Is intonation the music of language?

It has been claimed that every human culture has music. Both music and the intonation of speech involve modulations of frequency. They also use the same peripheral auditory system (the cochlear) and speaking and singing use the same production system (the vocal tract). On this basis it could be argued that intonation is the music of speech and is just as universal as music. The implication of a close link between intonation and music seems to be supported by cases of patients with brain damage who show difficulty in processing the melodies of both (Patel, Peretz, Tramo and Labreque 1998).

However, closer inspection reveals differences. First, the melodies of speech are more continuous than those of music, which tends to use pitch values from a limited set of distinct tones. This creates discrete musical scales with specific intervals. Second, and importantly, pitch in music requires much more precision than in speech; even a 50% compression or expansion of pitch range does not result in unnatural sounding speech, but it will make a song sound "out of tune" (see Zatorre and Baum 2012, who include links to examples demonstrating these effects). Compared with the somewhat course-grained encoding of the pitch movements found in speech, musical pitch requires a precise encoding of intervals on the musical scale. It is therefore not surprising that further brain studies have shown separation of aspects of the processing of intonation and of musical melody. People with congenital amusia (tone-deafness) have for instance been shown to have no difficulty with interpreting the large changes in pitch patterns typical of speech, but they are not as accomplished when it comes to more fine-grained changes, in either speech or music (Ayotte, Peretz and Hyde 2002; Zatorre and Baum 2012).

Although musical ability appears not to be related to the processing of intonation, it is linked to listeners' perception of the distinct tones used to distinguish between words in some languages. That is, there is evidence both that speakers of so-called tone languages (described below) show enhanced sensitivity to musical tones and that musicians are better than non-musicians at interpreting the types of tone distinctions used in such languages. These patterns of behaviour and of breakdowns in abilities in the case of brain damage suggest that there are two processing systems involved in the processing of pitch modulation, one dealing with overall pitch contours (in both speech and music) and the other with more precise encoding of pitch, and that intonation is not simply the music of language.

Do all languages have intonation?

Typically, linguists distinguish three types of language based on how pitch is used: tone languages, pitch-accent languages and intonation languages. As suggested above, it is important to distinguish intonation and tone. The term *tone* is used ambiguously in the literature, but in the present context it refers to the use of a number of different pitch patterns to distinguish words which are otherwise identical in terms of their sounds. Languages that use pitch patterns in this way are tone languages. There are two main types of tones in such languages – level tones and contour tones. Yoruba (spoken in Nigeria) has three level tones, using differences in pitch height to distinguish words. Thus the same syllable /bi/ spoken with a high tone means 'give birth', with a mid tone means 'ask', and with a low tone means 'vomit'. Thai also has three level tones, but in addition it has two contour tones, one rising and one falling. Other tone languages have more complex systems of tones. In some languages, tone can also be used to make grammatical distinctions between words; Ngiti (spoken in Zaire) uses high, low, mid and rising tones to show

What is universal about intonation? 169

different verb tenses. Tone languages are widespread in East and Southeast Asia, in Sub-Saharan Africa and in Central America.

Pitch modulation marks individual words or syllables not only in tone languages but also in so-called pitch-accent languages. In these languages, some words have a syllable marked by a pitch accent, i.e. by higher or lower pitch than surrounding syllables and often involving some sort of pitch movement. These pitch accents, like tones in tone languages, are properties of the words themselves, that is, they are lexically determined. Unlike tone languages, which have a number of different tone types (high, low, mid, etc.) that distinguish words, pitch-accent languages typically have just one type of pitch accent or lexical tonal melody. Words in pitch-accent languages are then distinguished by whether they carry a pitch accent, and in some cases by which syllable it falls on. For instance, the Japanese sequence /ueru/ without a pitch accent means 'plant', but with a pitch accent on the /e/ it means 'starve'. This pitch accent is realized by a prominent high pitch on that vowel followed by a sharp pitch fall.

Intonation is the use of voice pitch typically over larger stretches of speech than individual words. It has a wide range of functions. For example, intonation patterns can be used to show whether a speaker has finished their turn or plans to carry on speaking, to mark the difference between a statement and a question, to indicate which parts of an utterance introduce new or contrasting information, or to express the speaker's mood or emotions. Given that utterances can consist of single words, intonation patterns can, like tone, be realized over single words. Importantly, however, the different patterns of intonation convey differences in the meanings or structures of the whole utterance, rather than serving to distinguish one word from another.

Tone, pitch accents and intonation clearly use the same mechanism, that is, the modulation of voice pitch. For this reason, it is sometimes assumed that because tone languages already employ this mechanism for lexical or grammatical distinctions, they cannot also use it for the kinds of intonational patterns found in other languages, and therefore that intonation cannot be universal. This is, however, not the case. Although the situation can be rather complicated (for instance, the tones of adjacent words can influence one another), intonation in tone languages can be thought of as providing bands of utterance-level pitch movements, within which more local pitch fluctuations realize lexical or grammatical tone distinctions. Changes in the shapes of the overall pitch bands can reflect similar distinctions to those made by pitch movements in non-tone languages. Notwithstanding this observation that tone languages (and pitch-accent languages) also have utterance-level intonation, non-tone languages are sometimes referred to as intonation languages, highlighting the fact that pitch modulation in such languages functions primarily at the utterance level rather than at the lexical level.

Confusingly, perhaps, intonation languages such as English also have pitch accents, which in such languages have utterance-level functions, as described below. First though, it is important to note that lexical distinctions can be indicated in intonation languages by different levels of stress, realized as differences in duration, amplitude and vowel quality. Polysyllabic words typically have at least a primary stress and often a secondary stress, as well as unstressed syllables (so ˌpolysyˈllabic has primary stress on the third syllable, shown by ˈ before the syllable, and secondary stress on the first, shown by ˌ). In a few cases, a difference in stress pattern can distinguish otherwise identical words (compare for instance *import* as a noun and as a verb). While these stress patterns are properties of words in English, pitch accents express aspects of meaning above the level of the individual words, that is, in terms of the meaning of the utterance. Importantly, pitch accents are typically associated with (i.e. co-occur with) lexically stressed syllables. Consequently, stress in utterance contexts is also associated with pitch differences, although these pitch differences tell us about meanings at the utterance level, not at the lexical level. One such function of pitch accents in intonation languages that will be discussed below is that they indicate the information value of words or phrases in the utterance.

In terms of any putative universals, the cross-linguistic situation described above suggests that languages utilize the modulation of pitch to convey meaning. As a universal, this is deliberately vague, because typologically we can identify differences in terms of whether this pitch modulation is used to distinguish meanings at the utterance level (as in English), or is additionally used to distinguish words, that is, has a lexical function through the use of contrasting tones in tonal languages like Yoruba or the presence or absence of pitch accents in pitch accent languages like Japanese.

There is of course another group of languages that we have not yet considered – sign languages. While it may seem bizarre to ask whether sign languages also have intonation, this becomes less odd if we think of intonation as not just the pitch modulation found in spoken languages, but also the visual cues that accompany sign languages and which have similar functions. For example, Israeli Sign Language has a raising of the eyebrows (the Brow Raise) that has functional similarities to a high tone in the intonational systems of spoken languages (about which we will learn more below). American Sign Language uses raised eyebrows for similar functions, but differs from Israeli Sign Language in how some other facial expressions and head movements are used (Dachkovsky, Healy and Sandler 2013).

Are there universal patterns in intonation?

It has been argued that describing the intonation of an individual language is a difficult task because intonation is at the same time both a universal property of language and a highly language-specific feature. Nevertheless, claims have been made for general cross-linguistic patterns in how intonation is used. These include claims for the function of intonation in breaking utterances into smaller units, for the marking of closure versus openness via different pitch patterns, and for the indication of information value and other aspects of meaning.

Breaking down

Intonation has a delimitative function. That is, it breaks longer utterances into smaller parts. Most usually, these smaller parts will end in lower pitch. This is not surprising given both that lower pitch is usually associated with statements (see below), and that utterances typically contain more statements than other sentence types. One early study found that 87% of utterances in conversations between adults are statements. The proportion was much lower in child-directed speech, at 30%, compared with 44% for questions (Newport, Gleitman and Gleitman 1977).

An issue of debate has been whether the final low pitch reflects a preferred linguistic pattern or is rather a consequence of a physiological constraint (Landahl 1980). The preferred linguistic pattern is referred to as *declination*, that is, a gradual lowering of pitch across an intonation unit. It has been argued that this declination is a universal base form for sentence intonation. The alternative explanation in terms of physiological constraints has to do with breathing, and the relevant unit is the stretch of speech between taking breaths, the breath group. At the beginning of the breath group the lungs are relatively full and the flow of air through the voice box is strong, resulting in relatively rapid vibration of the vocal folds. As the breath runs out towards the end of the breath group, airflow is markedly lower, resulting in a drop in vocal fold vibration.

Analyses of the intonation patterns of young children and of adults from different languages (e.g. Mandarin and English) indicate that the fall in pitch across an utterance is not gradual, as expected of a declination theory, but a rather more sudden final fall (Lieberman and Tseng 1980). This suggests that the universal principle behind the general pattern of lowering pitch values is based on physiological constraints to do with breathing (referred to as the "respiratory code" or "production code"). It is argued that the consequences of these constraints have been co-opted linguistically for a delimitative function, with higher pitch at the beginning of an intonation unit and a drop to low pitch at the end of the unit.

The patterns of intonation across an utterance also have a role to play in conversational management, since the appropriate signals can indicate to other participants that they can now take over the floor. Indeed a study of former British prime minister Margaret Thatcher argued that the reason she was interrupted in interviews more often than her political opponent Jim Callaghan was because she seemed to give end-of-turn signals (pitch lowering and lengthening of speech sounds) at points in her utterances where she had not in fact finished her turn (Beattie 1982).

Opening up

One generality that is often claimed for intonation is that the distinction between low and high pitch corresponds to two very general "meanings", namely closure versus openness (Cruttenden 1981). We have seen that voice pitch typically falls to a low pitch at the end of statements. This low pitch indicates completion. If the voice has not reached that low pitch, then there is a sense of incompleteness. This is exploited linguistically by making the intonation at the end of certain utterances rise to a high pitch. Cross-linguistically this is frequently interpreted as signalling that the speaker wishes to engage the listener in the conversation, in some way. The listener's participation could be either by speaking, for example in response to a question, or by providing nonverbal signals (head-nods, etc.) that they are following what is being said.

This pattern – low for closure, high for openness– correlates with the common use of falling pitch on statements and rising pitch on questions. This is especially clear if we contrast statements with echo or checking questions, that is, questions that have the same word order and grammatical structure as statements, such as *This book is on language?*. The statement will end in low pitch, the question in high pitch. This correlation of pitch height with utterance type makes sense, given the more general universal claim stated above, since questions clearly invite a response and so keep the conversation open, whereas statements do not always invite a response. Note though that questionhood need not always be expressed through rising intonation, since in many languages the type of sentence can be marked by changes in word order (such as inversion of subject and verb in English: *Is this book on language?*) or the use of special words or particles (such as so-called wh-words in English: *Which book is on language?*). Indeed, there is an inverse relationship between the likelihood of rising intonation and the presence of other means of marking questionhood.

Note also that rising intonation need not always indicate that there is a question. Since high pitch signals incompleteness, if part of an utterance ends in a rise it can indicate continuation, as in lists and at the end of adverbials such as *Before we leave, we must* …. In addition, final rising intonation on statements can serve to invite other participants to engage in the conversation. This is one explanation given for the phenomenon of uptalk in English and other languages, that is the final high rising intonation found on statements, and (stereo-)typically associated with younger and mainly female speakers (Warren 2016). Of course, since final rises are also strongly associated with questions, it is understandable that non-uptalkers perceive speakers who use uptalk as insecure, since to them such speakers seem to be continually questioning their own statements.

The association of high pitch with questions also finds support in perceptual studies involving listeners with different native languages from different language families (i.e. languages that are not closely related). Such listeners show similar response patterns, with native speakers of languages as diverse as Mandarin, Dutch and Hungarian agreeing that higher pitch peaks and larger pitch rises indicate questions (Gussenhoven and Chen 2000). However, not all languages show a strong relationship. For instance, studies of Bengali provide inconsistent results, with some researchers claiming that it does not have rising intonation on questions but others claiming that it does, at least for yes/no questions (Hayes and Lahiri 1991). And while syntactically unmarked questions from younger speakers of Basque have rising intonation, possibly under the influence of other languages with which such speakers have come into contact, those of older speakers have a flatter intonation, albeit in a higher pitch register than other sentence types (Elordieta and Hualde 2014). For these older speakers it is possible that the higher overall pitch range provides the relationship of high pitch with questions. However, some varieties of Spanish, both in regional Spain and in Central America, have falling rather than rising pitch on syntactically unmarked questions (Hualde and Prieto 2015). This suggests that the tendency towards high pitch for questions is just that, a tendency, rather than a universal property of languages.

What about tone languages? Do they also use rising intonation to mark questions, and how does this interact with the lexical use of tone? As with other language types, tone languages often have other ways of marking questions, using word-order changes, question words (equivalent to the English wh-words) and question particles. When such devices are not used, then questions without syntactic marking often do have rising intonation, although this is not always the case. Because of the use of tone at the lexical level, for example, Mandarin utterances that end in a falling tone will have a final fall, even when they are syntactically unmarked questions. However, it has been observed that such questions in Mandarin are realized with an expanded pitch range on the final syllable. Consequently, the peak of the pitch contour on the final falling tone is higher than it would be on the statement version of the utterance. This height difference may be sufficient to mark the utterance as a question. But as with the interpretation of the higher pitch register for questions produced by older Basque speakers, we need to be cautious about how hard we push the case for a universal principle that relates high pitch to questionhood (or at least to openness, to allow for uptalk). We risk arriving at a universalist approach that is effectively unfalsifiable if every time we find an example where there is no final rise we look elsewhere for evidence of high (or not low) pitch. As a case in point, consider the final rising-falling pattern on yes/no questions found in some Eastern European languages. The universalist claim would be that the rising-falling pattern includes a rising element and therefore fits the pattern of high pitch being used in questions. However, the fact that speakers of Western European languages hear this rising-falling pattern as that of an emphatic statement weakens the universalist argument, which would presumably expect contours to be interpreted similarly across languages.

The general relationship between pitch patterns and sentence type has been claimed to be an instance of sound symbolism, that is, where meaning reflects some property of the speech sounds. If this relationship has this kind of strong external motivation, it is argued, then it is also likely to be found across languages, that is, as a universal property of intonation. Sound symbolism is somewhat controversial in linguistics, where in contrast it has long been argued that the arbitrary nature of the link between sounds and meanings is a key characteristic that distinguishes human language from many other communication systems.

What, then, is being symbolized by high or rising pitch that leads to its use in questions? Or by low pitch that leads to its use in statements or to mark closure? One claim is that there is a "frequency code" lying behind the acoustic signals used in face-to-face encounters (Ohala 1994). In the broader natural world, aggression is signalled by low-pitched sounds and submissiveness by higher pitch, as for instance in a dog's threatening growl versus its submissive whine. An explanation given for the considerable cross-species similarity in such patterns is that they are part of a more general strategy of trying to make yourself appear larger when you are expressing aggression, but smaller when you are being submissive. While in the natural world size is predominantly conveyed by visual means (e.g. by extending wings, arching backs, raising hairs, fanning out tail feathers, etc.), it can also be indicated by deeper pitch, since there is an inverse correlation between body mass and pitch (indirectly, through the mass of vocal folds in mammals and of the syrinx in birds, which is proportional to body size). The extension of this to the distinction between statements and questions relates to information sharing and gathering. While a questioner needs the cooperation of the listener, and so is appealing to the listener for help,

What is universal about intonation? 175

someone making a statement is more self-reliant or assertive. These positions are reflected in high and low pitch respectively.

Marking information

The meaning of an utterance can in part be signalled by its overall tune, as we have seen above. In addition, voice pitch can be used to highlight particular words or phrases, or to bring them into focus. This highlighting relates to the informational status of elements of the utterance. For instance, some words or phrases refer to old information that has already been shared by the speaker and listeners, while others are new pieces of information that the speaker wishes to introduce to the conversation. New information is typically highlighted, for example in English by carrying a pitch accent, where the voice pitch takes on a marked level and possibly a pitch movement over a syllable, word or phrase. Languages do not rely solely on intonation to indicate information status, but may also use special focus markers and/or word order (e.g. bringing words to the front of an utterance to highlight them, such as in cleft constructions like *It was the last movement of the symphony that Mary particularly liked*, rather than *Mary particularly liked the last movement of the symphony*).

English utterances without any particular focus typically have a series of pitch accents associated with the main lexically stressed syllables, with the last of these conventionally more prominent than the others. This last accent is often referred to as the nuclear accent. In a simple statement, the pitch accents will be marked by higher pitch than surrounding syllables. If any word within the utterance is placed in focus, then a more prominent pitch accent will be placed on that word. Greater prominence involves an expansion of the pitch range, so that the pitch peak is higher than it would be in a neutral utterance. In addition, prominence is frequently heightened by "de-accenting" (i.e. not placing a pitch accent on) the other words in the utterance. As a result, there is a compression of the pitch range in the area outside of the focused element. This pattern of expansion of the pitch range of focused elements and the compression of the pitch range of unfocused elements is common cross-linguistically.

Perceptual studies have shown that listeners are sensitive to this distinction between new or focused information being accented and given or old information being unaccented. In an experiment investigating this, participants were presented with an arrangement of letters such as QPKC and were then asked to decide whether each of a series of utterances was an accurate description of that arrangement. Both *The K is on the right of the P* and *The K is on the left of the C* are accurate descriptions, but if participants heard both of these utterances in this order and *K* in the second utterance (which is old or given information) was accented, then they were slower to verify the accuracy of this second utterance, even though accenting the *K* makes it clearer and therefore should make processing easier. The reason is that having heard *K* in the first utterance, participants expect that, as given information, it will be deaccented (Terken and Nooteboom 1987).

In addition to the general notion of focus to introduce new information, languages also mark various types of contrastive focus. (Note that it can be argued that focus for new information is also contrastive, since it introduces a particular entity into the discourse and not some other entity that might alternatively have been introduced.) The speaker may bring a particular word into focus because they want to correct a previous erroneous belief, as with the focus on *rice* in the answer in this question-answer pair: Q: *Did you bring the pasta?* A: *No, I brought the rice*. Or they may want to contrast one word with another word in a parallel structure: *No-one likes the pasta, they're all eating the rice*. Or they may want to indicate their selection from explicit alternatives offered to them: Q: *Did you bring the pasta or the rice?* A: *I brought the rice*. In intonation languages, contrastive focus is most often marked by more extreme pitch marking than non-contrastive focus. For instance, a high pitch accent will be higher under contrastive focus, and potentially made more prominent by lower preceding and following pitch levels. It is a matter of some debate whether the presence of these lower adjacent pitch values means that the pitch accent should be categorized differently, for example as a rising pitch accent in English, contrasting with a simpler high pitch accent.

Pitch accents in intonation languages such as English can be thought of as on a scale that includes non-contrastive (new information) focus and contrastive focus as well as the absence of focus. The height of the pitch accent and/or the size of the pitch excursion appears gradient. This gradience is argued to reflect an "effort code" which is linked to the amount of energy expended, leading to both greater precision and a wider pitch range. The wider pitch range is interpreted as signalling, in this instance, a higher level of informational significance.

The cross-linguistic generality of the intonational marking of focus can be tested against tone languages. Since the pitch information marking lexical identity needs to be recoverable from the utterance, so that listeners know which word is being uttered, speakers of tone languages need to ensure that any focus-marking does not mask the lexical tones. While they seem to make less use of pitch marking for focus than intonation languages, tone languages have at least two intonation-based strategies (Hartmann 2007). One is to expand the pitch range of the focused element, as reported for intonation languages above. So in Mandarin a high tone will be higher and a low tone lower, and contour tones will cover a large range; in the unrelated African tone language Hausa there is "local high raising" where a high tone is realized with an exaggerated high pitch to indicate focus. The other strategy is to use intonation to change the way in which an utterance is broken up, allowing the focused item to be placed at the (left or right) edge of a constituent in order to highlight it. For example, speakers of the Bantu language Nkhotakota Chichewa place a boundary immediately after the focused element. This boundary is marked by tonal lowering of the final vowel as well as lengthening of the penultimate syllable.

Further studies of tone languages have suggested that the marking of contrastive focus, and therefore the presence of degrees of pitch marking reflecting the effort code, does not function in quite the same way as in intonation languages. In Hausa, for instance, there is a strong tendency to use changes in word order (e.g. fronting of the focused element) to indicate contrastive focus (Hartmann and Zimmermann 2007). When contrastive focus in tone languages does not include word order changes, then the pitch excursion is not noticeably greater than that found for non-contrastive focus.

Expressing emotion

A further function of intonation is to express emotion or the speaker's emotional involvement with or commitment to what they are saying (Bänziger and Scherer 2005; Chen, Gussenhoven and Rietveld 2004). Like focus marking, this is a gradient function. That is, stronger emotions tend to be associated with stronger marking. And like focus, this function is argued to reflect the effort code, with larger and more dramatic pitch excursions resulting from greater effort and being used to indicate higher levels of emphasis, surprise, helpfulness, etc. In addition, the link between pitch levels and emotion might reflect the physiological arousal associated with the emotion.

Attempts have been made to associate specific emotions with particular patterns of intonation. Although some early claims were made for such associations, these were based on isolated examples, and the generalizability of the claims was unclear. This is to a large extent because while the level of emotional arousal may be reflected in the size of a pitch excursion, the interpretation of the particular emotion being conveyed depends on other factors, including the utterance content and context, voice qualities and non-speech gestures, such as facial expressions.

Many of the studies exploring the relationship between emotion and intonation have concentrated on global parameters, such as average pitch or pitch range. Relatively few have considered the types of intonation contour that might be associated with different emotions, and even these have focused on general patterns, such as rising and falling contours. A meta-analysis (Bänziger and Scherer 2005) reveals how rare these studies are, as well as highlighting the ambiguity involved. This analysis indicated that rising contours could be matched with anger (six of just eight studies), fear (found in all six studies considering this emotion) or joy (seven out of seven studies), while falling contours were associated with sadness (eleven out of eleven studies) and tenderness (three out of four studies). The small number of studies to consider detailed aspects of intonation patterns includes claims that local perturbations in voice pitch might contribute to the distinction between the types of rising contours that show fear and joy.

It may seem intuitively reasonable to assume that there are universal aspects to how intonation reflects emotion, because of the physiological consequences of states of arousal and because of the link between effort and phenomena such as pitch range. However, there are too few systematic studies for claims of universality to be properly examined. Perhaps the safest claim is that while there may be some basis for the signalling of emotional meaning in line with universal biological codes (such as, the effort code and the frequency code), it is likely that we will find language specific aspects to how this is implemented.

Is intonation innate?

If there are aspects of intonation that are universal, then we would expect there to be evidence for them also being innate or at least long established in the human species. It has been claimed that the frequency code interpretations of low and high pitch are genetically rather than culturally determined. Such claims are at least in part based on the observation that aspects of the mapping of form to function which are motivated (e.g. by sound symbolism) are less likely to change dramatically over time or between languages. Similarities found in the use of intonation cross-linguistically can thus be contrasted with differences in the form-function relationships in other areas of language structure, differences which reflect the considerable transformations that are frequently found for more arbitrary and therefore less stable relationships (such as, the series of changes that resulted in English *cow* and French *boeuf*, originating from the same common ancestor, being such distinct words).

In addition, there are arguments from sexual dimorphism that support the innateness of the frequency code. That is, in humans as in other species, physical changes occur at puberty that distinguish males and females. For instance, the adult male human larynx (voice box) becomes some 50% larger in its front-back dimension and considerably lower in the vocal tract. These changes result in lower voice pitch and lower vocal resonances in the adult male, and have been claimed to relate to sexual selection. As in other species (and including visual changes such as beard growth in humans and the growth of a mane in lions), the male deviates from the "norm" on reaching puberty because he needs to compete for and win the attention of a female. The evolutionary payoff for such changes implies that the listener is also innately predisposed to be responsive.

Studies of child language acquisition have shown that very young infants can discriminate falling from rising pitch and statement intonation from question intonation in a range of language contexts, and that they do so before they have acquired the ability to distinguish individual speech sounds (Frota, Butler and Vigário 2014). Does this show that intonation is more instinctive and therefore more universal than other aspects of speech, perhaps because intonation is somehow "peripheral"? An alternative explanation is that the perceptual and motor skills required for modulation of pitch are just simpler than those required for consonants and vowels. This is supported by research showing that children learning tone languages learn to distinguish tones before they distinguish speech segments (see Demuth 1995). A further explanation is that children get a head start with some of the features of spoken language that are relevant to the analysis of intonation. That is, there is evidence that some linguistic distinctions become familiar to the baby in utero, before the child is born (Höhle 2009). Typically, because of the filtering effect of being inside the mother's body, these distinctions are prosodic, that is, the rhythmic and intonation patterns of the language.

What does intonation tell us?

A thought exercise that might help us think about possible intonational universals is to consider what we would be able to tell from listening to the intonation of an unknown language. Or, if knowing a language already brings some baggage (e.g. knowing about how our first language uses intonational distinctions), then we might consider what a pre-linguistic infant can tell (and learn) from listening to intonation.

The first thing we might notice is that tunes are associated with chunks. Such chunks are frequently marked by cessation of speaking, which is particularly true of the shorter utterances typical of child-directed speech. In longer stretches of speech, we would soon notice chunks made up of recurring internal intonational patterns, at a very coarse level. Such chunks are most likely to end in either low or high pitch, often with exaggerated highs and lows in child-directed speech.

Of course, language is a social tool. If we are observing speakers in interaction, we might notice patterns of turn-taking. From the nature of the turn-taking, we might conclude that speakers seem to be using certain features of intonation to signal that their turn has finished, and other features to invite other speakers to contribute. We might also notice that there are momentary exaggerations of intonational patterns which draw listeners' attention, and we might notice both from speakers' actions (including aspects of non-verbal communication) and from listeners' reactions that patterns of intonation convey moods and emotions, and that these too can be exaggerated.

There will be a lot that we cannot reliably tell from intonation alone, and our interpretations will inevitably become more finessed once we start to understand the text that goes with the intonation.

Further reading

Insightful discussion of language typology and universals in intonation can be found in Ladd (2001). Reviews of the intonation systems of a range of languages are given in Hirst and Di Cristo (1998) and in the two excellent volumes edited by Jun (2005, 2014). For more general overviews of intonation see Cruttenden (1997) and Ladd (2008).

The frequency code discussed in this chapter was proposed by Ohala (1994), and this code together with the effort code and respiratory code are discussed by Gussenhoven (2016).

For a recent review of research linking how the brain processes music and linguistic pitch, see Tillmann (2014).

References

Ayotte, Julie, Isabelle Peretz and Krista Hyde. (2002). Congenital amusia: A group study of adults afflicted with a music-specific disorder. *Brain*, 125(2), 238–251.

Bänziger, Tanja and Klaus R. Scherer. (2005). The role of intonation in emotional expressions. *Speech Communication*, 46(3–4), 252–267. DOI:10.1016/j.specom.2005.02.016

Beattie, Geoffrey. (1982). Turn-taking and interruption in political interviews: Margaret Thatcher and Jim Callaghan compared and contrasted. *Semiotica*, 39(1–2), 93–114. DOI:10.1515/semi.1982.39.1-2.93

Chen, Aoju, Carlos Gussenhoven and Toni Rietveld. (2004). Language-specificity in the perception of paralinguistic intonational meaning. *Language and Speech*, 47(4), 311–349. DOI:10.1177/00238309040470040101

Cruttenden, Alan. (1981). Falls and rises: Meanings and universals. *Journal of Linguistics*, 17(1), 77–91.

Cruttenden, Alan. (1997). *Intonation*. 2nd edition. Cambridge: Cambridge University Press.

Dachkovsky, Svetlana, Christina Healy and Wendy Sandler. (2013). Visual intonation in two sign languages. *Phonology*, 30(2), 211–252.

Demuth, Katherine. (1995). Problems in the acquisition of tonal systems. In John Archibald (ed.), *The acquisition of non-linear phonology*, 111–134. Hillsdale: Lawrence Erlbaum Associates.

Elordieta, Gorka and José Ignacio Hualde. (2014). Intonation in Basque. In Sun-Ah Jun (ed.), *Prosodic Typology II: The phonology of intonation and phrasing*, 406–463. Oxford: Oxford University Press.

Frota, Sonia, Joseph Butler and Marina Vigário. (2014). Infants' perception of intonation: Is it a statement or a question? *Infancy*, 19(2), 194–213. DOI:10.1111/infa.12037

Gussenhoven, Carlos. (2016). Foundations of intonational meaning: Anatomical and physiological factors. *Topics in Cognitive Science*, 8(2), 425–434. DOI:10.1111/tops.12197

Gussenhoven, Carlos and Aoju Chen. (2000). Universal and language-specific effects in the perception of question intonation. In *Proceedings of the international conference on spoken language processing*, 91–94. Beijing, China.

Hartmann, Katharina. (2007). Focus and tone. In Caroline Féry, Gisbert Fanselow and Manfred Krifka (eds.), *Interdisciplinary studies on information structure*, vol. 6, 221–235. Potsdam: Universitätsverlag.

Hartmann, Katharina and Malte Zimmermann. (2007). In place – Out of place? Focus in Hausa. In Kerstin Schwabe and Susanne Winkler (eds.), *On information structure, meaning and form: Generalizations across languages*, 365–406. Amsterdam: John Benjamins.

Hayes, B. and A. Lahiri. (1991). Bengali intonational phonology. *Natural Language and Linguistic Theory*, 9(1), 47–96.

Hirst, Daniel J. and Albert Di Cristo (eds.). (1998). *Intonation systems: A survey of twenty languages*. Cambridge: Cambridge University Press.

Höhle, Barbara. (2009). Bootstrapping mechanisms in first language acquisition. *Linguistics*, 47(2), 359–382.

Hualde, José Ignacio and Pilar Prieto. (2015). Intonational variation in Spanish: European and American varieties. In Sonia Frota and Pilar Prieto (eds.), *Intonation in romance*, 352–392. Oxord: Oxford University Press.

Jun, Sun-Ah (ed.). (2005). *Prosodic typology: The phonology of intonation and phrasing*. Oxford: Oxford University Press.

Jun, Sun-Ah (ed.). (2014). *Prosodic typology II: The phonology of intonation and phrasing*. Oxford: Oxford University Press.

Ladd, D. Robert. (2001). Intonational universals and intonational typology. In Martin Haspelmath, Ekkehard König, Wulf Oesterreicher and Wolfgang Raible (eds.), *Language typology and language universals: An international handbook*, 1380–1390. Berlin: Mouton de Gruyter.

Ladd, D. Robert. (2008). *Intonational phonology*. 2nd edition. Cambridge: Cambridge University Press.

Landahl, K.H. (1980). Language-universal aspects of intonation in children's first sentences. *The Journal of the Acoustical Society of America*, 67(S1), S63.

Lieberman, Philip and Chiu-yu Tseng. (1980). On the fall of the declination theory: Breath-group versus "declination" as the base form for intonation. *The Journal of the Acoustical Society of America*, 67(S1), S63.

Newport, E.L., H. Gleitman and L.R. Gleitman. (1977). Mother, I'd rather do it myself: Some effects and non-effects of maternal speech style. In C. E. Snow and C. A. Ferguson (eds.), *Talking to children*, 109–149. Cambridge: Cambridge University Press.

Ohala, John J. (1994). The frequency code underlies the sound-symbolic use of voice pitch. In Leanne Hinton, Johanna Nichols and John J. Ohala (eds.), *Sound symbolism*, 325–347. Cambridge: Cambridge University Press.

Patel, Aniruddh D., Isabelle Peretz, Mark Tramo and Raymonde Labreque. (1998). Processing prosodic and musical patterns: A neuropsychological investigation. *Brain and Language*, 61(1), 123–144.

Terken, J. and S.G. Nooteboom. (1987). Opposite effects of accentuation and deaccentuation on verification latencies for given and new information. *Language and Cognitive Processes*, 2(3–4), 145–163.

Tillmann, Barbara. (2014). Pitch processing in music and speech. *Acoustics Australia*, 42(2), 124–130.

Warren, Paul. (2016). *Uptalk: The phenomenon of rising intonation*. Cambridge: Cambridge University Press.

Zatorre, Robert J. and Shari R. Baum. (2012). Musical melody and speech intonation: Singing a different tune. *PLOS Biology*, 10(7), e1001372. DOI:10.1371/journal.pbio.1001372

Index

abuse: linguistic 51–3, 58; physical 159–61, 163
accent: foreign 137, 138, 155; nuclear 175; pitch 168–9, 170, 175–6, 178; regional 39, 44, 61, 151–3, 162, 164; stress 175–6
acoustics 92, 93, 100, 101, 115, 118, 156
ambiguity 1, 68, 168
American Sign Language 125, 170
anacoluthon 71
analogy 85–7
anatomy 98, 99, 100, 101, 115
arbitrariness 8, 43, 125, 174, 178
Australian Sign Language 135
authorship 157–9, 162–3
average 111–12, 116

baby sign 125
bacteria 4
Basque 41, 91, 173–4
bats 10, 13
Bengali 173
Bgiyambaa 74, 78
bilingualism 41, 54, 141, 146, 147; *see also* multilingualism
biology 9, 13, 14, 91, 96–101, 161, 178
blasphemy 48, 49
breath group 171
Burgess, Anthony 40

Callaghan, Jim 172
Cantonese 40–1
case: grammatical 87, 142, 143
child language 67, 140–2, 160–2, 179
chimpanzees 3, 13, 58, 97

Chinese *see* Cantonese; Mandarin
classifier 130
clause 6, 8, 71, 74–5, 161; main 75–7; relative 76–7, subordinate 75–7
cleft 175; double 71
click (sound) 98, 100
climate 93, 96, 101, 102
code-switching 137, 146
codification 44
community: linguistic 40–5, 52, 69, 145
complexity 10, 74, 86; syntactic 160–3
construction 40, 71, 72, 73, 126, 146, 163, 175
contrast 130, 176–7
corpus 50, 59, 62, 71–3
Croatian 40
culture 42, 59, 80, 91–2, 96, 99, 109, 119, 128, 131, 178; Deaf 128
culture shock 127–8, 134
Czech 40

Danish 38, 115
database 93–4, 163
decay: change as 80, 81; information 145–6
Decision Making 21–31
declination 171
descriptive versus prescriptive 69–70, 88–9
design feature 5, 7, 16, 93
dialect 36, 37, 40, 43, 61, 85, 88, 152–4, 164
discrimination 96, 143, 145
disguise 151–64
diversity: biological 91; linguistic 91–2, 95

Diyari 74, 78
DNA 161
duality of patterning 8, 11
Dutch 37, 173

earwitness 152–6
ecology 93–6, 101
education 1, 59, 67, 80, 140, 141, 143, 160
ejective (sounds) 93–4
email 20–31
emotion 169, 177–8
English: as a language 42, 45; as lingua franca 22–3; 'decay' of 80–1; 'forgotten' 138–9; grammar 6, 40, 70, 71, 74, 76, 87, 89; pronunciation 8, 44, 83–5, 115, 170–1, 173, 178; and related languages 38; standard 88; variation in 38; vocabulary 48–9, 56, 82–3, 89; *see also* English varieties
English varieties: African American 153; American codified 44; American comprehensibility 39; American dialects 40, 153; American grammar 71; American pronunciation 81, 100; Australian 44, 76–7; British 44; Canadian 71; Caribbean 155; Middle 85, 102; New Zealand 39, 44, 71, 156, 162; Old 85, 86, 87, 175; Scottish 39, 40; Tyneside 38–9; West African 115; Yorkshire 40
euphemism 50, 54, 55, 58
evolution 67, 77, 179; cultural 91–2
expletive 49, 50, 56, 57

false start 66, 71
fingerspelling 131–2
Finnish 76, 78, 146
fish 10, 13
forensic linguistics 151–66
formality 19, 21–3, 27–9, 32, 48
French: academy 81; dialects 37; etymology 178; from Latin 83, 92; national language 41; Old 83; source of English words 55, 82, 83; used in English 138–9, 146
Friesian 38
frogs 10, 14
fundamental frequency 167

Galton's problem 94
genetics 96–7, 99, 102, 178
genre 32, 66–7, 158
geography 91, 93–6, 100
German: attrition of 140, 143–4; in international communication 22; interference from 146; pronunciation 115; variation in 37
gesture 11, 124, 130, 133, 134, 177
Ghosh, Amitav 65
grammar 65–79, 87; books 44; in sign 134; *see also* cleft; descriptive versus prescriptive; morphology; noun; object; subject; verb
grammaticalization 92
Greek: Classical 86–7; Modern 22–6
Grimm, Jacob and Wilhelm 80

handshape 8, 128, 130
Hardy, Thomas 37
Hausa 177–8
here and now 10
Hindi 38, 41
Hindustani 41
Holocaust 96, 144, 146
Hungarian 173

iconicity 125, 131, 133, 134
identity 28, 30, 109–11, 112, 113–19, 141, 143
ideology 96–8, 118
idiolect 39, 40, 43, 102, 158, 162–3
idiom 6
informality *see* formality
insult 28, 51–2, 56
interference 144–6
intonation 116, 152, 167–82
Israeli Sign Language 170
Italian 38, 75–6, 78, 82, 92

Japanese 82, 115, 146, 169–70

K Doc and Q Doc 158–9

language 1–3, 4, 31; academy 81; acquisition 179; Acquisition Device 12; attrition of 137–49; change 77, 80–90, 84; contact 94; corrupt 44; decay 144; definition of 4–17, 36–46; diversity 95;

environmental 141; evolution 67, 99; family 91–2, 95–6, 102, 173; first 69, 137–49; global 19; heritage 141–2; learning 93, 126–32; local 19, 29, 30; minority 42; and music 167–8; mutual comprehensibility 38; national 41–2; number of 91; offensive 49; processing 84; racist 49; second 55, 68, 146, 153; spoken 60, 66–7; standard 44, 88; tone 94, 168–9, 173, 176–7; universal 92, 101, 124, 167–82; use 22, 31, 110; variation 110, 132–3, 153, 158; variety 36–7, 153; women's 114; and the workplace 18–35, 19; written 66–7; *see also* sign language
larynx 98–9, 178
Latin 58, 83, 87, 92; Vulgar 83
laziness 47, 48, 59, 61, 80
lingua franca 22
lipreading 133–4
lisp 83, 114–16
literacy 67, 142
loanword 82–3
location of signs 8, 128
Lofting, Hugh 4
loudness 167

Mandarin 40–1, 91, 171, 173, 176–7
Maori 44
Mari 41
medium 8, 67, 69
mice 10, 13–14
migration 143, 146
Minion 55
Montaigne, Michel de 37
morphology 8–9
multilingualism 18, 31, 41, 53, 135, 140–1; *see also* bilingualism
mutual comprehensibility 37–9

Neanderthals 99
negotiation 18, 19, 21–2, 28, 31
Neogrammarians 83
new information 175–6
New Zealand Sign Language 125–7, 128–9
Ngiti 168
Nkhotakota Chichewa 177
Norwegian 37, 38, 41

noun 7, 70, 133, 170
noun phrase 7, 73–4

object 6, 7, 70, 87
old information 175
onomatopoeia 125

pheromone 10, 13
phoneme 8, 94
phonetics 39, 92, 93, 99, 100–1, 115, 156
phonology 7–8, 11, 82, 92, 93, 99, 100; *see also* phoneme
phylogeny 92, 95
pitch 116–18, 152, 167–8, 171–2
Polish 37, 49, 87
politeness 19, 21, 51, 76
polygraph 54–5
Portuguese 38
pragmatics 14
prescriptive *see* descriptive and prescriptive
prestige 44, 68, 83, 88; covert 88–9
puberty 142, 146, 178–9
punctuation 160–3

question 71, 169, 171–3, 179

Received Pronunciation 44
recursion 7
repetition 39, 54, 66
repression/suppression 144–5
rhotacism 86
ritual slanging 52
Romanian 92
Russian 36–8, 74, 78

Šafárik, Jozef 36
Serbian 40
sign language 8, 11, 43, 123–36, 170
slang 48, 61, 128–9
Slovak 36–7, 40
social media 124, 137, 163
socio-economic status 59
songbirds 10, 12
sound symbolism 174, 178; *see also* onomatopoeia
Spanish 91; academy 81; comprehensibility 38; from Latin 83, pronunciation 83, 153, 173; source of English words 82; vocabulary 146

speech production 84, 89
spelling 2, 39, 41, 131, 158, 160
statement 77, 169, 171–5, 178
statistics 93, 94, 112, 152
stereotype 110–19, 153, 173
stress (anxiety) 56–7
subject 6, 70–1, 74, 75, 139, 172
Survey of English Usage 72
swearing 47–64; social 51, 57
Swedish 37, 38, 76, 78
Swift, Jonathan 80
syntax 6, 8, 11, 82, 160, 173; development of 160–1; *see also* grammar

taboo 48, 49, 57–9
Thai 168
Thatcher, Margaret 172
tone 41, 94, 168–9, 170, 173, 176; deafness 168; language 94, 174–7, 179
Turkish 6

Ukrainian 37–8
ultrasound 10, 13
umlaut 85, 86

uptalk 173
Urdu 38, 41

variation 3, 28, 39, 70, 93, 97, 98–100, 110, 115, 116, 132–3, 153, 158, 159
verb 6, 7, 70, 73, 74, 86–7, 139, 169, 170
Verner's law 86
vervet monkeys 14–5
violence 58–9, 143; *see also* abuse
voice identification 154–5
vowel 85–7, 99–100, 102, 162, 170

Walpiri 41
Welsh 141
West Greenlandic 9
whales 12
whisper 152–3
Wilde, Oscar 114
word 5, 6, 8, 9, 43, 47–61, 74, 76, 158, 160, 168–70, 173, 175, 177
word-stress 170
workplace sociolinguistics 18–20

Yiddish 40–1
Yoruba 41, 168, 170

For Product Safety Concerns and Information please contact our EU
representative GPSR@taylorandfrancis.com
Taylor & Francis Verlag GmbH, Kaufingerstraße 24, 80331 München, Germany

www.ingramcontent.com/pod-product-compliance
Lightning Source LLC
Chambersburg PA
CBHW051644230426
43669CB00013B/2439